C

# CORONATION QUAY

AMAZON BOOKS
Editor Antonio Olinto
CORONATION QUAY

# CORONATION QUAY

JOSUÉ MONTELLO

*Translated by Myriam Henderson*

**REX COLLINGS • LONDON • 1975**
In association with *SEL EDITORA: RIO DE JANEIRO*

First published in Portuguese by Martins Editoria,
São Paulo, Brazil in 1971.
This edition published by Rex Collings Ltd
69 Marylebone High Street, London W1

ISBN  0860  36  0075

Typeset by Malvern Typesetting Services Ltd and
Printed in Great Britain by Biddles Limited, Guildford Surrey

# FOREWORD

This novel, *Coronation Quay*, is part of a new series called *Amazon Books*. The purpose of the series is to publish Brazilian books, preferably recent, in an English translation, aiming to show aspects of contemporary literature in the largest country of Latin America. It must be said, before anything else, that Portuguese is the language spoken in Brazil. Portuguese and not Spanish as in almost the rest of Latin America, with the exception of Haiti, one Guiana and some islands that have been French colonies. So, deleting this French participation, we can divide Latin America into two parts: the Spanish speaking one, and the Portuguese speaking one. The first comprises eighteen countries with a total population of 170 million. The second is Brazil alone with 110 million inhabitants.

On the literary side, the Brazilian contribution, written in Portuguese — or in what could be called 'Brazilian Portuguese' — is sometimes in quantity almost the same as the Spanish contribution. For example in one year in the sixties the Spanish speaking countries in Latin America printed around three hundred new works of fiction, while in Brazil alone in the same period, two hundred and eighty new novels and collections of short-stories were published.

Portuguese literature became known in the XVI Century, that is, during the same period when English and Spanish literature were at their zenith. The great epic poet of Portugal, Luiz de Camões (1525-80), published his major work, *The Lusiads*, in 1572. it is worth comparing the dates of Camões with those of Cervantes (1554-1616) and of Shakespeare (1564-1616). It was the period immediately after the Discoveries, and these three literatures followed the general movement upwards and outwards in Europe, a movement whose initial push had been given by the Portuguese Prince Henry the Navigator (1394-1460). The Portuguese first landed on what is now the South American continent in 1500, and from then on until 1822, they were the conquerors and the colonizers of what is today Brazil.

Brazilian literature was, in the first three centuries, a part of Portuguese literature, but even then it could display the novelty of the tropics, by showing tropical fruits and flowers, local customs and habits, in a style of adventure natural to a country still being shaped.

The first known novel published in Brazil, *The Fisherman's Daughter*, by Teixeira e Souza, printed in 1843, was followed, in 1845 by two novels written by the author who is still today one of the bestsellers in Brazil: Joaquim Manuel de Macedo. Novels would become very popular in Brazil from then on, and ten years later José de Alencar (1829-1877) would give a nationalistic twist to the *gendre* by publishing *O Guarany*. This novel has a main character who is an indigenous man, a Brazilian Indian, although still romanticized in an European way, it tried to depict an important aspect of the country's reality. From 1855 till 1910 the Brazilian novel became widely diversified, and two authors can be mentioned as having achieved a high degree of excellence in the field: Machado de Assis (1839-1908) and Lima Barreto (1881-1922)—it is worth noting, as an example of the Brazilian racial formation, that they were both mulattos, one less, the other more.

Brazil had a literary and aesthetic revolution, of lasting influence. It was the Week of Modern Art held in São Paulo in 1922, exactly the year of Lima Barreto's death. The Week was fertile in manifestoes, *mots -d'ordre*, aesthetic programmes, almost all of them nationalistic in purpose. The Week produced notable poems, it changed the direction of Brazilian literature and produced one great novel of the Brazilian twenties: *Macunaíma* by Mario de Andrade. It also influenced a new wave of novels in Brazil beginning with *A Bagaceira* by José Americo. The great decade of Brazilian novels was the thirties, equivalent to what the twenties had been in the United

States. During the twenties, in the North of the Continent, a diversified group of very good novelists published their first book. Among them were John dos Passos, Scott Fitzgerald, Ernest Hemingway, William Faulkner and John Steinbeck. In Brazil, between 1930 and the beginning of World War II, among many others, the first novels of Jorge Amado, Rachel de Queiroz, Graciliano Ramos, José Lins do Rego, Erico Verissimo, Jorge de Lima, Octavio de Faria, Lucio Cardoso, M. Rebelo, Dalcidio Jurandir, were published.

To this group is also linked Josué Montello whose novel *Coronation Quay* opens the *Amazon Books* series. Being a country of continental dimensions (3,288,000 square miles), Brazil has had novelists writing about almost every one of its regions, and the work of each has shown local realities that, put together, may make a full portrait of the country. Josué Montello comes from Maranhão, a State of the North of Brazil, bordering the Amazon and part of the region of the big rivers. Maranhão has always been a kind of cultural capital of the country. Its capital, the city of São Luiz (founded by French invaders in 1612), has been known as 'the Brazilian Athens'. Josué Montello's literary life, however, as has happened to many of his countrymen, has more roots in the city of Rio de Janeiro than in Maranhão. His first novel, published in 1940, was the novel of a narrator who could master with a firm hand his happenings and his people. Each of his new novels showed that his firmness was becoming stronger. By writing *Coronation Quay*, Josué Montello went back to his Maranhão, with its seas and its fishermen, its traditions and its changing face. His style is harsh and his people hard. They are men and women with the roughness, almost asperity, of people used to live and eat and make love in the face of the tropical Atlantic. The final structure of the novel has an extraordinary strength.

It is good that *Amazon Books* start with a novel like this. The name and prestige of Josué Montello in contemporary Brazilian literature, the importance of his work — not only as a novelist, but also as a literary critic, an essayist, a biographer and a journalist — in today's Brazil, make his book an ideal one to begin a series aiming to show the English reader anywhere in

the world, important works of Twentieth Century Brazilian
literature.

ANTONIO OLINTO
*London, September 1975*

# PREFACE TO THE
# ENGLISH EDITION

Among the illustrious dead who lie in Westminster Abbey rests
Thomas, tenth Earl of Dundonald, better known as Admiral
Lord Cochrane (1775–1860), British naval hero who bore
also, as his tomb attests, the title of Marquis of Maranhão in
the Empire of Brazil.

A Northern State, bordering the region of the Amazon,
Maranhão, both politically and strategically, was one of the
most important States during Colonial times. Cochrane was
one of the leaders who helped the country to achieve its
independence in 1823, for which he was rewarded by a
Marquisate by the grateful Emperor, Dom Pedro I.

This is a story about Maranhão and its coastal seas that
Cochrane knew so well, and its capital, São Luis, which he
visited several times. It is not concerned with the Maranhão of
the Marquis' day; it is about a Maranhão caught half-way
between progress and a deep-rooted medieval mentality,
whose physical aspect is slowly changing, and where can still
be found, in the villages and small towns, men and women
whose primitive emotions have been moulded by over four
hundred years of tradition and prejudice.

It is essential that non-Brazilian readers should understand
that the action of this story takes place between two poles: São
Luis, the sixteenth-century city rapidly being modernized,
Capital of the State, and a little coastal town where life has
gone on with very little change since its foundation, lying a day
and a half's sail from São Luis, where the paramount moral
authority is the parish priest, unhesitatingly accepted by the
population as the interpreter of the will of God.

I was born and brought up in São Luis, and have often seen
the triangular, earth-coloured sails of the boats which
navigate the seas off Maranhão, linking its capital to the towns

and villages along the coast, I have seen the fishing *igarités*, making for home each evening at sunset.

In this novel I have attempted to portray one of these anonymous boatmen, wedded to the sea by family tradition, and made myself the spokesman of his feelings, perhaps the more intense for being less articulate than those of a more sophisticated type of man.

The telling of stories is an art which has been admirably practised by English writers whose works I have known from youth, among them Sterne, Fielding and Thackeray. It has been said that all fiction consists of variations of Don Quixote and Angus Wilson, in his biography of Dickens, mentions the debt that every novelist owes that great Victorian story-teller. For my part, I acknowledge the debt.

JOSUÉ MONTELLO

# INTRODUCTION

It was in São Luis that I first met Severino the boatman, who is the most important person in this story. He was sitting on the parapet of Coronation Quay, his corn straw cigarette at the corner of his mouth, looking out silently over the sea.

He must have been nearing sixty, a lean, dried-up man with lines scored deep in his tanned face, fiery hair beginning to fade and whiten, his Adam's apple prominent in the long neck, a worn cotton shirt hanging outside his trousers, and crude sandals on his tough feet.

This was about twenty years ago, in the dry season, towards evening, beneath the breath of the trade winds.

I had walked down the steps of Palace Hill while the sun, still high, beat dazzling on the tiled house-fronts, and groups of boatmen rested on the steps in the shade of the old trees that grew there. Before me, the sea lay boundless and blue, dotted with boats and canoes showing up clear against the horizon, each with its coloured sail. I stopped at the bottom of the hill next to the Bulwark Wall, looking for the man who, down by the quay, next to the big Treasury building, had a stand where he sold hand-printed, home-bound little books of stories, folk-tales, told in primitive rhymes.

I could not see him anywhere; so crossing the street, I asked the woman who sold *manuê* tarts* and corn-starch puddings near the bandstand on Palace Ramp.

'He was here just now, with Severino the skipper,' she said, pointing to the paved edge of the quay. 'It's the first thing Severino does whenever he comes here, he always goes looking for the books.'

* Manuê Tart: A sweet made from maize and coconut, eaten in the Northeast of Brazil.

'Who's Severino?' I asked idly, more for the sake of hearing her talk than because I really wanted to know.

She raised her eyebrows and lowered her head, looking sideways at me with a smile.

'You're joking, sir! I can't believe that you've never heard of the most famous boatman in Maranhão, a greater seaman even than Jeronimo or Januario!'

But no, I had not heard; no, I knew nothing about him; she cut me short by stretching out a fat arm and pointing to a spot far down the quay.

'If you go along there you'll see him sitting on the wall opposite his boat, the 'Fair Weather'.'

Gradually it had become a habit of mine to stroll down Palace Ramp in the cool of the afternoon, and then turn left, towards the Long Beach or right, in the direction of Coronation Quay, drawn by my curiosity to hear the talk of the boatmen and fishermen, who alone knew the true stories of the wild sea that breaks on the coast of Maranhão.

I liked to sit on the deck of one of the boats anchored next to the quay, at the lazy hour of the ebb tide, when the waves, drawing back, leave the piles uncovered, and sandbanks rise up through the low water like bare brown breasts. I would listen to tales of shipwreck, storms, and the sudden staggering blows of raging gales springing up without warning, of waves rearing up like giants before the prow of the boat; tales of the miraculous intercession of Our Lady of Deliverance, invoked by sailors in the moment of danger, of ghost ships sighted in the dark of Friday midnights, and of Our Lady who shows the safe way home to sailors lost on the broad sea.

It was from Lucas, one of the younger skippers, that I first heard the story of the phantom King Dom Sebastian of Portugal, who haunts a certain beach along that coast. I can see him still, as twilight falls, looking at me quietly with his small deep-set eyes, leaning against the hull of the boat, clasp knife open in his right hand as he chops at the thick piece of chewing tobacco he is holding in his left hand. As he speaks in a peaceful voice, without gestures, almost sleepily, I can see burning beneath the moon, the lights of a galleon floating on the dark sea. From the deck, a mounted man leaps his horse onto the sand and gallops along the beach, the silver and gold of his armour glinting in the white moonlight. He rides the length of the beach and gallops back to the ship, for he must be aboard before the sky grows pale with dawn.

This story haunted me so that I finally wrote it down, using the old traditional ballad metre,

> Rider of the midnight
> Sailor of the dark
> God forbid we meet you
> Beneath the bright moon's spark.
> Woe to the seafarer
> Who should sight your sail,
> For his race is run,
> And his day is done
> And he'll soon lie cold and pale.

And it is on Palace Ramp that Turibio taught me the special prayer to Saint Barbara and Saint Jerome that will turn the roughest sea smooth as silk, and that other prayer, very old and powerful, that brings the fish to the net, past counting, thanks to the intercession of Saint Anthony.

Sometimes, when night had fallen, I would hear, far off, the notes of a guitar, a sound which drew me away from the quay and into the backroom of a bar, down by the Little Port or on Caju Beach, where I would stay as the night wore on, listening to the old Iberian folk songs, about the Enchanted Moorish Princess, and the good ship Catarineta, songs that were brought to Maranhão long ago by the Portuguese caravels, and handed down faithfully by sea-going men to their sons, fishermen and boatmen like their fathers.

And then there was the chronicle of each day's loves, challenges, rivalries, hates, revenge and forgiveness — all these things were so many reasons why I left the terrace of the Central Hotel, cool in the shadow of the old Sé Church, to go down every afternoon to the Long Beach or Coronation Quay, walking without haste, and seeming to gather, as I passed, something of the poetry stored in the souls of the people.

On the other hand, the walk itself is worth the trouble. I would often spend hours in either of the semi-circular bastions where, once on a time, the two watch-towers of Saint Philip's Fort used to stand, leaning on the parapet with the sea breeze, damp and salty, blowing in my face, while my eyes wandered over the waters, trying to see, within the rifts of mist, the dim shapes of the city of Alcantara, now lost forever.

It is the loveliest sight at sunset, when the fishing canoes come back to port from the high seas.

Lingering by the bandstand, I asked the fat woman, whose face was creased and dimpled by her laugh, if the *manuê* tart displayed on her tray was as good as it looked.

'It's as good as the tart Our Lord serves in Heaven on feast days,' she replied, and her round cheeks were stretched even further by a broad smile.

With my mouth still full of sweetness, I agreed that her puddings were truly worthy of the Tables of Paradise, and then crossed over to the pavement in front and turned right, following the parapet of the quay.

The taste of the tart awoke nostalgia, memories of my childhood, and I looked about me at the scenes of my birthplace, glowing in the slanting light of late after-noon—there was the Memory Rock by Saint Damian's Fort, the avenue which led uphill to the big square, the old houses with their verandahs open to the sea which lined the sloping streets.

I walked on, looking alternately at the sea and at the town until I found I had reached the place where the quay widens between two stone ramps that run down to the water's edge. Then I noticed for the first time the inscribed stone that was let into the sea wall:

'The building of this quay was begun on the 14th of September of the year 1841, on which day this Province celebrated the Coronation of the Lord Dom Pedro the Second, Constitutional Emperor and Perpetual Defender of Brazil.'

When I looked up from reading I saw a man sitting on the wall between the ramps watching me; and I knew at once that it was Severino. Our eyes met for a moment, then he turned his head away indifferently and went on sitting there, facing the sea, his back slightly bent, his hands on his knees and his legs dangling on the wall. I still remember what that first swift look showed me, the green eyes, the frowning brows, a long grave, tense face, an air of sadness.

Leaning on the wall beside him I would have liked to get him to talk — our common interest in the book-seller would have been a good excuse — when he suddenly leapt from the parapet to the deck of a boat anchored below. It was an acrobat's jump, smooth, elegant, landing precisely on the tips of his toes, his body gathered up and his legs easily taking the strain.

Unaware that I was watching, he moved about his boat with the grace and agility of a dancer, loosening the jib sheets, raising the anchor, running back to fix the rudder, hoisting the mainsail, until the boat, riding the incoming tide beneath its sails, slipped over the waves and moved forward serenely, like a great bird about to take wing, heading toward the open sea. It would soon be halfway between Bomfim Point and Sand Point, the triangular brown sail outlined against the light blue horizon and Severino standing upright in the poop; on it sailed, meeting the first rough buffets of the open sea, and then, apparently unmoving, disappeared within the last glow of daylight.

After this first encounter, I only met Severino twice more, still on Coronation Quay; once in 1960, and the other time two or three years later, but did not speak to him. I only watched him pass, erect and weather-beaten, unshaven; I met him the first time, coming down the Ramp, with bent head. On the second occasion he was walking along the Quay, head held high. Strange how these three encounters live so vividly in my memory, as if time, taking so much else, left these behind. Strange, too, that never having spoken to Severino, he seems always to be there, living and breathing, in all the stories I was told about him, at the quay side, in that twilit hour when the light dims and something rises in our hearts asking for the relief of words.

This was how, little by little, I came to know of the tragedy and strength of the man, his crime and his greatness. Time, like a wheel, spun on and on, but Severino lived in imagination and memory, a figure of rude grandeur, as solid and whole as stone, waiting for the moment when, for lack of marble or granite, I must try to put down on paper all that I knew, saw or sensed about him, filling in the gaps and uncovering what lies hidden, as story-tellers have done since the beginning.

# *CHAPTER I*

Before reaching the top of the slope Severino, panting, had to stop and try to draw into his thin chest the breeze blowing off the sea; but still he could not breathe, but stood motionless, his right hand spread open on his breast, tense and frowning, until slowly the air came back into his lungs.

He had to stop once more, still panting, opposite the church at the very top, to look down at the houses in the square beneath, searching for the overhanging eaves of the building where Doctor Estefanio had his consulting room, now that he was back from São Luis.

'That's the one, with the green windows and a brass plate by the door,' he thought as he started to walk again.

The afternoon sun shone down fiercely on him, glittering in the sifting sand of the roadway and dancing in sparkling motes of dust that blew in the wind; there were no trees to give him shade. Severino remembered the sleepless night, his head thrown back against the hammock while his feet touched the straw mat which covered the floor, in the room where the small oil lamp cast a faint light. When he lay in the hammock, there seemed to be a suffocating weight on his chest; sitting upright he was able to breath without the stifling sensation of tightness in the chest which tormented him during his uneasy sleep.

'Go and see the doctor, you stubborn man,' said Antonia from the room next door, as she got up to prepare his herb tea. 'He'll soon get you breathing properly again.'

He drew on his cigarette and coughed, a confirmed smoker's cough.

'If doctors could heal, they'd live forever.'

He had thought, at first, that the trouble came from a lingering cold he had caught on his last voyage. The cold had

1

gone and its harsh cough, but the stifling feeling continued, better on some days, worse on others, so that there were times when he thought he would choke to death. Also, he had fits of giddiness, so that he had to close his darkened eyes and cling to the furniture or the walls while the room spun around him.

'I feel the house heaving and plunging, as if I were at sea,' he told Antonia, during one of these attacks of vertigo.

The old woman hesitated, then tried to reassure him as he stood there, livid and fighting for air.

'It's habit, Severino. After so many years, your body thinks it's still sailing the sea, even though you're back on land. Don't worry; it'll pass.'

However it did not pass but happened more and more frequently, the cold sweats, the pain in the breast, the struggle for breath. And the fits grew more severe, leaving him dazed and exhausted. During the day, while he worked on his boat in the boatshed, Severino felt better. It was at night, when the damp sea air seeped in through the cracks of the doors and the spaces between the roof-tiles, that he grew worse, breathing became torture, he could not sleep nor even lie down, but had to sit up, sucking in air through his open mouth.

During the long years in jail he had picked up the habit of reading so as to escape from his surroundings, and now he usually had by him some old almanack, worn and greasy with much handling, and when the fit eased a little, he would read over again the stories of voyages and shipwrecks, consult the tables of tides, check on the phases of the moon, wonder at the lives of the saints. Almost always he ended by falling asleep where he sat, the magazine on his lap and the flame of the oil lamp still high.

Antonia used to say to him, 'You're lucky, when you can't sleep you can look at a book until you drowse off! I can't read, so therefore I must lie in my hammock praying and rocking to and fro, to and fro, until the Lord in his mercy closes my eyelids, gently, out of pity . . . '

Lately, however, it was not out of sleeplessness that Antonia clung to the glass beads of her rosary. She was afraid for Severino, afraid of those terrible struggles for air, and fearing the worst, tirelessly asked Heaven's protection for the old man.

'What'll become of me if I lose him, alone in the world with only Pedro, who's just a boy? Oh, dear Lord, hear my prayer, don't let me live on alone, bewildered in my wits, not knowing where to turn, I'm old, I've suffered so much, have mercy on me.'

When Aunt Noca, the *rezadeira**, came back from Alcantara, Antonia brought the old woman to say her charms over Severino, in case his illness came from having been ill-wished by some enemy.

Thin and tall, Aunt Noca always carried in her big leather bag a pack of cards and a sprig of rue; she had said charms over Severino seven times running, calling on Saint Cyprian's help at the same time.

But the painful struggle for breath returned, worse than ever, and Aunt Noca went out on the verandah and laid the cards out on the table. Silently, a deep crease showing vertically between her brows, she considered them:

'It wasn't ill-wishing; it's an illness, a real illness, very bad. He ought to see the doctor right away.'

Severino, hand on breast and still panting, said dourly,

'Don't speak of doctors to me. Do you think that at my age, seventy-six years, you hear, I'm going to let the doctor strip me naked and feel me all over, and then take my money as well? No, ma'am; I've lasted until now without ever needing a doctor and I can die without one, thank you!'

Privately he considered it a humiliation which he was not prepared to accept. He, Severino, tough as weathered wood. ask for a doctor's help!'

But Antonia gave him no peace.

'Go to the doctor,' she would cry, whenever he grew pale and fought for air, 'If you won't do it for your own sake, do it for mine and your grandson's. What harm can it do? Don't be so stubborn!'

Severino let a week go by. This illness, which had come upon him by stealth, might go away suddenly, too. Since he still had strength and spirit enough to sail the open sea, steady

* Rezadeira: A white witch, who uses herbs and charms for healing.

at his boat's rudder, surely he would get well. He would. Patience was what he needed. A time was sure to come when, of a sudden, he would feel ill no more. It had happened before, with those stabbing pains in the back he had suffered from, for more than a month, before he caught that damned cold.

'God only takes from this world those who have nothing left to do. And my job isn't finished,' thought the old man as he rolled a fresh cigarette, holding the thin corn-straw covering in his open palm.

But in the morning, when it was time to go to his boat, he felt, with anguish, that his hour must have come. Suddenly his heart shrank in his breast, as if clenched within two long-clawed merciless hands. He stopped by the window, dizzy and unable to breathe, leaning his head against the shutter, eyes closed, sweat running icy down his pale face. It was as if everything inside him, from the waist up, was being torn out.

'It's happened,' he said to himself. Desperate for air, he threw his head up like a man drowning, struggled with the opening of the shutter and threw it wide. His grandson Pedro looked at him appalled.

'It'll pass, Grandfather, it'll pass,' the boy said, surprised by shock and feeling the old man's pain in his own breast.

Luckily, only the wind drove a cloud of dust along the long sandy street, empty in the morning sunshine. The rough-haired dog, dozing on the pavement opposite, at the sound of the opening window raised his muzzle, pointed his ears, and barked at nothing.

'Drink, Grandfather, drink and you'll feel better.'

And finally Severino, although still giddy and wet with sweat, could tell his grandson, standing anxiously in front of him with a glass of water, trying to help and not knowing how, 'It's passing', Pedro. 'I'll be all right.'

With his hand still pressing on his breast, breathing short and fast, he sank into a chair and waited for his strength to return, while Antonia, carrying the cup of herb tea in her trembling old hands, blundered through the door.

'For God's sake,' quavered the old woman, handing the cup

4

unsteadily, 'For God's sake, Severino, go and see the doctor today!'

As he stood and looked down on the eaves of the doctor's house, it was the memory of the look in Pedro's eyes that led Severino across the square which lay bare and lonely beneath the blazing sun.

As he passed in front of the worn stone steps of the church he saw fat Abdala the Syrian coming out of the central door of the church, mopping his jowls with a discoloured handkerchief. The huge man was in his shirtsleeves, baggy trousers held up by his braces, unshaven and disheveled.

Before Severino had time to greet him, the Syrian spoke, wiping his sweaty throat in its unbuttoned collar with the grubby handkerchief.

'Severino, when will you be taking your boat out?'

'Tuesday of next week, at the latest.'

'I may have to ask you for a favour, Skipper,' said Abdala as he came down the steps. 'A great favour, Severino — a priceless favour. I've just been speaking to Father Dourado. I know that you're the person to help me.'

Intrigued, Severino stopped at the edge of the pavement, but the other man continued on his way with short mincing steps, murmuring as he went. 'A family matter, Severino. These never-ending family matters! Oh, don't ask me about it — nobody knows the troubles I've had!'

Severino watched him go, his big bulk swaying in the sun, his shoulders drooping, twisting the wet handkerchief in his left hand, the flabby body quivering within the loose trousers. Then he turned away and followed the narrow pavement which led to the doctor's surgery. In front of the door he looked back and saw Abdala gesturing in the distance; Severino smiled, shrugged, and straightened his shoulders once more.

Looking through the open door of the waiting room, he saw a row of people sitting on a wooden bench and waiting their turn to see the doctor. Should he also sit there and wait for his turn? Severino paused on the stone doorstep, tried to clean his sandals on the iron scraper, patted his hind pocket feeling for his cigarettes and matches, while sensing all those waiting

5

eyes, now turned in his direction, weighing him up. A thin elderly man who was sitting at the end of the bench by the door made room for him, and said in a high-pitched voice that somehow suited his bony frame:

'Come and sit by me, Severino, it'll be a pleasure to have you as a neighbour while we wait.'

Before answering, Severino gave his sandals an extra scrape, eyes cast down, flushed, and feeling his face grow hot. He lit the cigarette that was already between his lips, drew on it deeply, and only then looked at the thin man whose hand still patted the empty space beside him.

'Thank you, Major. I haven't come for my health; I'm leaving for São Luis soon, and came to ask if there's anything the doctor would like me to bring back from there.'

# CHAPTER II

If Severino had had his way Celita would not have come in a hat — a striking hat of red straw, with a wide brim encircled by a gold ribbon, which fell over the edge of the brim and hung in two long streamers over her shoulder. But she had gazed at herself in the living-room mirror, enchanted; and it was true that her smiling eyes and round face, framed in thick black hair, with a beauty spot at the corner of the mouth, looked even prettier, set off by the big red hat.

Severino, in the blue suit he had worn for the civil marriage in São Luis, his feet cramped by tight elastic-sided boots, sat stiffly in an armchair, watching her as she stood before the mirror.

'We haven't even got electricity in this town yet — I think you'll be the first woman ever to wear a hat here' he said complacently — Celita smoothed the hair above her ears.

'Someone's got to be the first.'

'I can imagine what'll happen when you walk into the church,' Severino continued, his voice warm with pride, 'They'll be twisting their necks round, to look at you before you're through the door even, their eyes like saucers. Lord! There'll be more talk about you and your hat than there ever was about the comet!'

It was not only the hat — it was the long-sleeved dress of white satin clinging to her shapely body, the gold brooch on her breast, the bright bead necklace from which hung an Italian cameo, the three gold bracelets on her left wrist, the aquamarine ring.

There had been a shower of rain earlier in the morning. Puddles of water still lay here and there in the unpaved streets by the beach, sparkling in the hot midmorning sun.

Celita looked at her reflexion one last time, then glanced out of the window at the corner of the sky, where clouds were gathering. Running to the bedroom, she came back carrying with studied grace a smart umbrella with a mother-of-pearl handle, and took Severino's arm with such an air of elegance that he stood with parted lips, lost in admiration of his wife's beauty and charm.

'Come, darling, it's time to go.'

Some days earlier there had been an argument in the sacristy, about the marriage, between Severino and Father Dourado.

'How can you want her to be married in a veil and bridal wreath,' asked the priest after an uncomfortable interval of silence. 'You've just told me yourself that your fiancée was a — woman of loose life! A veil and wreath! Certainly not! If you wish her to be married according to the laws of our Holy Mother Church, here in our parish church, and by me, she must come in an ordinary dress.'

Severino, unconvinced, scratched the back of his neck. He repeated his argument, 'She's pure again, Father, I swear. Do you think I'd give her my name and all, have everything written down by the Judge, if I wasn't certain that her past was

7

buried forever? Never! I'd put my hand in the fire for her now. She worked in a house, it's true, but that was her family's fault. They made her do it. She's a different girl now, as pure as any virgin.'

The priest was inflexible.

'But she is not a virgin, Severino. Or is she?'

'No, she isn't.'

'Then how can you expect me to consent to her wearing a veil and wreath? No,no, ask me for anything else, but a veil and wreath, no, never!'

Severino stood up and walked toward the narrow door opposite the high altar, nervously twisting his hat in his tense hands.

'But,Father Dourado, you married Miguel Lemos' eldest daughter, wearing a veil and wreath in this very church, and her baby was born two months later!'

'That's true,' said Father Dourado, looking him in the eye, 'Quite true. I married the girl as you say, but I didn't know she had already—if I had known, I wouldn't have done it. And anyway, Severino, one mistake is no excuse for making another.'

He raised his hand and said firmly, ending the argument:

'Bring the young woman here Sunday morning, at ten o'clock, and I'll marry you. But no veil, no wreath.'

When he got home, Severino was taken aback to find that Celita, instead of being upset by the priest's refusal, took the news cheerfully.

'Well, if he doesn't want me in a veil and wreath, that's all right. We'll manage, you'll see. I'll wear a hat—the big straw hat you gave me, remember?'

And now she was beside him, pleased with herself and her hat, skipping over the puddles as they walked arm-in-arm to church. It all seemed a dream to Severino. Was it really he who walked there, in a blue suit and tight boots, his bride on his arm? Yes, indeed it was. People were in the right of it, when they said that marriages were made in Heaven; how else could he explain his marriage to Celita?

Obscurely moved, he said to her, as they reached the slope

8

which led up to Church Square,

'Celita, don't you feel as if you were dreaming?'

'Dreaming? Why?' she asked, as she opened the umbrella to protect her clothes from the rain-drops falling from the branches above them, 'If it were a dream, it wouldn't be any fun.'

'Well, for me it's like a dream; I feel like pinching myself to make sure I'm awake.'

They walked up, the sandy surface creaking underfoot, trying to keep clear of the wet grass that pushed up from the soil.

Severino remembered that day in São Luis, at the top of the steps which led from the quay down to the water, he could see himself waiting there, just before daybreak, although he should have left for home at moonrise the night before. But he had been tired and sleepy after an exhausting day's work, and lying down in his hammock for a moment's rest, had awoken when the incoming tide swept the dock with crests of foam. He leapt ashore, went up the steps and sat on the parapet to wait for the first light of morning. And it was there, a little later, that Celita had appeared, wearing a scarlet dress, a dying flower in her hair, one foot bare while she clutched the shoe in her hand, and laughing, laughing as if she had lost her wits.

'Tell me, are there no trams on this street?' she asked, leaning against the lamp-post, held in the shaft of light, and then slipping down to the ground and beginning to laugh again, 'Hold me up, I'm falling!'

Severino took her up in his arms, went down the steps and jumped aboard the boat, still holding her. He settled her in the hammock and watched while the morning light slowly brightened on her sleeping face. Before she was awake, he hoisted his canvas and sailed out to sea, going round by Sand Point to anchor beyond the ruins of the Fort, where the land drew back to form a cove where the sea swung drowsily to and fro. There, in that peace, he waited for her to awaken, fascinated by the perfect body, the charming face, the softness of the small feet, the warmth of the brown skin heightened by the beauty spot at the corner of her mouth. And what eyes!

They seemed to draw all the morning brightness into their depths and shine with changing lights beneath the arched eyebrows.

She was looking at him now from beneath her slanting lids, a look at once pensive and mischievous, head bent, her body ready to shake with laughter once more.

It was nearly evening when Severino sailed back to Coronation Quay with Celita sitting beside him in the stern. The wind played in her long hair and heightened the glow in her cheeks and looking at that ripe beauty, he realized that he had become a different man, and that his whole life was changed. How could he go back to Antonia and her faded prettiness waiting for him in the depths of the hammock, after having loved Celita beneath the open sky, in the swaying boat? He was obsessed by the body that had fused with his during the long embraces rocked by the sea. He wished they could sail back to the cove beyond Sand Point, and lie together on the straw mat once more, beneath the dark arch of night. Severino had never seen such breasts, high, firm, with small hard nipples; he had cupped them in his hands, faint with pleasure, feeling their throb and quiver. And no other woman had a waist like hers, so gently curved, and the small neat navel, the full hips, the faint line of a scar above the mound of Venus, the joined thighs, heavy but graceful, flowing in long curves to the knees, all that smooth-skinned nakedness a pale rose-flushed brown, without a flaw anywhere, the tiny soft hairs that stirred beneath his caressing fingers. And the meeting of their two bodies in the moment of love, lost in the same pleasure, locked in a double ecstasy, relaxed in mutual languor, her face wet with tears of fulfilment.

The boat anchored by the quay and Severino turned to Celita.

'You're never going to belong to another man,' he said.

She raised her head, half surprised, half amused.

'How can you stop me? I'm not your wife.'

He took her hands in his, remembering what she had told him, the troubles and miseries she had known.

'You're going to be my wife. All that's over.'

Her eyes were wide with amazement.

'Your real wife? With a marriage certificate?'

'Yes, with a marriage certificate.'

'Married by a judge? By a priest?'

'Judge and priest both.'

Her eyebrows rose, her lips quivered, then she said:

'Oh no, you're joking. One shouldn't joke about these things.'

'I mean it,' said Severino, and his taut features grew stern. 'You're not going back to that house.'

Celita still did not believe him; she laughed and said:

'And who's going to fetch my things and pay what I owe?'

'I'll do it.'

'You?' She said, and laughed again. 'I've never heard anything funnier! Married! Me? Old Joana will think it's a trick of some sort — she'll throw you out, darling. Better be careful; we'll go together.'

'You're never going near that place again,' he said between his teeth. 'I'll go, pay what's owing and bring back your things.'

'Then promise me something,' she said meekly, 'Please tell everyone there that we're going to be married by the judge and by the priest. Be sure to do it. I want to show them all! And then tell me what they say — I wish I could see their faces when they hear the news, the old woman's specially!'

She leaned against Severino, lay her head on his shoulder and began to laugh louder than ever, her clenched fists tight against her stomach.

'God, they'll be so jealous! What a shock it'll be! Me, married, properly married by a judge and a priest!'

When he told her later that she would no longer live in São Luis, but in a little fishing village a long way off, she was quiet for a while, looking into the distance. Then she said: 'Once I'm married I must go wherever my husband wants me to.'

When they reached to top of the slope Severino saw that the church was full of people who had come to Sunday Mass; for a minute he felt like turning back; then he went forward again, thankful that Celita, instead of crossing the open square, had chosen to walk along the pavement in front of the houses. Presently she closed the umbrella and took his arm again, more posed and graceful than before. Feeling her hand on his arm, Severino strode forward setting down each foot firmly, throwing out his chest and looking straight ahead, so that he could see, as they came to the open space before the church, that people drew back to let Celita pass, holding her head high as if to show off the new hat.

# CHAPTER III

The room had been newly whitewashed, the doctor's desk stood against the wall at one end, three armchairs placed near it, there was a glass-fronted bookcase full of books and magazines; along one wall a weighing machine stood next to the patient's couch. Coming out of the dark corridor, Severino was dazzled by the light from the windows; it was as if he had passed suddenly from dusk into bright sunlight.

His hat tucked beneath his arm, he hesitated at the door of the room, twisting his hands together uneasily. Finally he took two steps forward and standing in the middle of the room glanced round, looking for the doctor.

A deep voice coming from the next room startled the old man, who turned in the direction of the voice.

'Make yourself at home, Severino.'

He took another step forward and hesitated, turning his hat round and round in his hands. From where he stood, peering through the open door, he could see the stout figure of Dr Estefanio, his back turned, leaning over the small china basin and washing his hands. Severino felt a trickle of sweat cold on his forehead; he wiped it away with the back of his hand, and went on fidgeting with his hat, trying to straighten the crown, while drawing a long cautious breath.

More than once, while he was sitting on the hard bench in the passage, he had felt like getting up and leaving. What was he going to say to the doctor? He couldn't say he'd come about his health because he hadn't paid the fee. If he wanted to see Dr Estefanio professionally, he should have put his money down and waited his turn, like the others. On the other hand, if he spoke to the doctor without mentioning his health, he would feel like a fool.

'I'm an idiot,' he grumbled to himself, 'And the best I can do is to get out of here while I can.'

But the memory of what had happened that morning, the terror in his grandson's eyes, kept the old man in his seat. And, anyway, it was too late to leave now. The Major had already entered the consulting room, he would surely tell the doctor that Severino was outside and wanted to speak to him. Just then the Major came back into the passage.

'Doctor Estefanio wants you to go in, Severino.'

Standing near the desk crushing his hat in his hands, Severino felt again the small obstinate trickle of sweat on his lined forehead. He had looked away from the door into the next room and pretended to be interested in the calendar picture; it really was pretty, a picturesque hut reflected in a lagoon, with a background of tall trees and bright blue sky.

Doctor Estefanio came into the room.

'So you're going to São Luis, Skipper?'

'Yes, Doctor. Tuesday night'll be clear, with plenty of moonlight, God willing, and I'm putting out to sea. I just stopped by to ask if there's anything you want from São Luis.'

'Thanks for the thought Severino, but I don't need anything at the moment. Perhaps by the end of the week I will; if I do, I'll send you a message, or pass by your house. Doctor Estefanio tightened the belt of the white overall which emphasized his bulk. 'Souza's daughter, Celeste, who was in here yesterday, is going with you, and so is Rufino. They both offered to do errands for me, but I prefer to rely on you.'

Severino turned away towards the door, but the doctor interrupted him.

'What's this? You're not leaving already? No, Skipper, just sit here, if you please. We must have a chat.'

Doctor Estefanio walked round the desk and sat in the high-backed chair; he picked up the pen which lay before him, then began tapping on the sheet of glass that covered the top of the desk, his small brown eyes on Severino's face. Sitting there, his high forehead, bald crown and grey whiskers showing up against the chair's dark background, he looked fatter than ever. A blue shadow darkened his close-shaven pendulous cheeks.

'So you still own the 'Fair Weather', Severino?'

'Yes, Doctor. The old boat's still pretty good.'

'Still under sail?'

'Still under sail. The wind's all she needs, and there's wind enough along the coasts of Maranhão, thank God. My father, my grandfather and my great-grandfather before them, always relied on the wind to take them to São Luis and bring them back; and the wind never failed them.'

Doctor Estefanio laid the pen down on the desk, leant his head against the chair and turned his eyes to Severino, 'How long is it since you've been going to sea, Skipper?'

'It'll be forty-one years next October — if you don't count the twenty-one years I spent in jail. Otherwise, it would have been sixty-three. Sixty-three years at sea.' The old man sighed.

The doctor rested his hands on the arms of the chair.

'Sixty-three years,' he said, 'and you've never had an illness in all that time?'

'Not one. I thank the Lord that, in all my life, I've only lain down to rest, never from sickness.'

The tough old hands smoothed the worn hat. 'Well, maybe I shouldn't say 'never'. I caught a bad cold a month ago, I had quite a fever and a nasty cough. I got rid of it at last, but it's left me with an ache in my chest and a tight feeling — sometimes I can't breathe. Antonia nags me about coming to see you, Doctor, but somehow I always forget. If you hadn't mentioned illness, I wouldn't have remembered.'

14

Doctor Estefanio leaned forward, resting his arms on the desk top.

'Why don't you let me have a look at you now?'

'It'll make you late for the others. There're a lot of people waiting outside who got here before me.'

'Is there anyone out there who's older than you?'

'No, sir, I don't think so.'

'Then don't worry; I always see the older patients first.'

'I could come back another day,' Severino said weakly, shifting uneasily on his chair. But Doctor Estefanio was already on his feet. 'Not at all, I'll have a look at you right now. Take off your shirt, please, and sit down on the couch.'

Leaving his hat on the chair, Severino went up to the couch. The white-capped Negro nurse came into the room carrying a towel. Ill at ease, the old man asked, 'Must I really take my shirt off?'

The doctor nodded, and Severino began slowly to undo his shirt-buttons, while the nurse stood attentively at his side. Finally he sat down on the side of the couch, while the doctor stood before him holding what looked like a small hammer. He felt a sharp tap first on one knee, then on the other, and kicked out instinctively; his embarrassment gave way to amusement as he thought, 'I wouldn't have believed that a *hammer* could be part of a doctor's equipment!'

For nearly an hour he was turned and prodded this way and that, feeling sometimes indignant and sometimes amused. They made him lie on his back, on his side, and on his belly, and finally he was told to go up and down the three steps of a little ladder the nurse brought into the room. Then it was over and he put his shirt on again slowly, while the nurse left the room; he noticed that Doctor Estefanio was stroking his chin and frowning, while he looked away from Severino.

He waited while the doctor went next door to wash his hands, sitting in the same chair he had sat in before, holding his hat in his thin hands. The doctor came back and Severino, looking anxiously at him, spoke before he was through the door.

'Well, Doctor, what do you think?'

15

The doctor walked slowly up to the desk and sat down in his chair. The pen beat a tattoo on the glass top. He countered Severino's question with another:

'Isn't there anyone that could take your place and sail the 'Fair Weather' to São Luis?'

'What's the matter, Doctor? Why can't I go?'

'I'll be frank with you, Skipper. There's something wrong with your heart, my friend, and it's pretty serious. That's only natural at your age, that heart of yours has been working night and day for seventy-six years! Of course it's tired; now we've got to prevent it from stopping. You can't go to São Luis; I must tell you the truth, Severino, in the state you're in, it would be fatal. If you want to live a while longer you must do exactly what I tell you. No physical effort, be as quiet as you can, avoid stairs, don't go walking up or down hills. I'll give you some medicines to relieve your pain and breathlessness, but they won't cure them — they'll only make them less acute, specially the pain.'

Severino's hands lay nerveless on his knees, his hat forgotten, his mouth half open, his dark face drawn and pale. He felt as if he was sinking, endlessly, through deep black waters, never to rise again. Then he took a long breath.

'Doctor, are you sure? Couldn't you be mistaken?'

Doctor Estefanio was writing a prescription; he folded the sheet of paper and went on holding it, while he looked straight at Severino.

'No, Severino, I haven't made a mistake. I'm sorry to have to tell you this, but you have a very bad heart condition. It's my duty to let you know, so that you'll take care of yourself and not do anything you shouldn't. If you take your boat out yourself, you may die before making port. And I'd be responsible, wouldn't I? No, Severino; you've got to take it easy, follow a strict diet, avoid worry, and rest as much as you can. Take this medicine with your meals, and the other when you go to bed, or whenever you feel pain and difficulty in breathing.'

Severino sat forward on his chair, eyes wide with anguish.

'When can I go to sea again?'

16

'Not for six months,' Doctor Estefanio said deliberately.

'Six months! Six months shut up between four walls! As if I were serving my sentence all over again!'

The doctor looked at him with compassion, and nodded.

'Six months at least, Skipper.'

Severino was silent; the muscles along his jaw stood out, and he looked at the fat hairy hand holding out the folded sheet of paper. Slowly he stood up, took the prescription from the outstretched hand and put it in his pocket, then bent down and picked up his hat from the floor where it had fallen. The room seemed to rock about him, like the cabin of a storm-tossed ship, and he held on to the back of the chair, dizzy and sick. When his sight cleared, he turned away and went heavily toward the door. Outside, Church Square lay in the glare of the afternoon sun. With dragging feet he went past the church and down the steps of the broad terrace that stretched before it. He walked with bent shoulders and hanging head, two thoughts going round and round in his mind. What would happen to Pedro without someone to look after him? What would become of Antonia, old and weary, and knowing nothing of the mysteries of the sea?

As he went by the tall stone cross that stood in the middle of the square, Severino suddenly raised his head and threw back his shoulders.

Somehow, deep within him, he found what he so desperately needed; and strength rose up again, sure and stubborn, to brace his muscles and steady his nerves.

He thought of the ridiculous little hammer tapping his knees, the three silly steps he had been made to climb up and down at least twenty times, the wires strapped on his wrists and legs, the fat doctor with his puffy eyelids and hairy hands.

'The fool! The great fool!' He exclaimed. 'Tapping people's knees with a hammer! How can he tell who's going to live and who's going to die? Rubbish!'

And pulling the doctor's prescription out of his pocket he crumpled it in rage and threw it away, as far as he could, as he went quickly down the hill.

17

# CHAPTER IV

He knew the way so well that he scarcely bothered to look at the maze of narrow streets, alleys and short cuts through which his rolling seaman's stride took him, eyes on the ground, as if looking for something, the inevitable cigarette at the corner of his mouth, to the steady rhythm of his sandalled feet.

Reaching the long, sandy road along which untidy shacks stood at intervals, their fenced yards shaded by the spreading branches of tall trees, Severino pulled his hat further over his brows to protect his eyes from the slanting light. He passed the narrow bridge of planks that spanned an arm of the river, and instead of continuing in the direction of the beach that swept in convolutions away to his right, he turned off into a path that led to the shack where Lucas Faisca lived, a spindly *cajazeira* tree in front of the door and jasmine running wild over the fence.

He seemed to move with his old vigour, his steps resolute, a vertical groove bitten deep between his eyebrows. He had a taciturn, withdrawn look, the same look with which he had walked away from the prison where he had served the long years of his sentence. The afternoon heat beat up around him, flushing the hollow cheeks and lending them the tinge of health.

His sandals brushing through the sand woke a brindled dog that slept curled up in the bare roots of the tree. The dog pricked up its ears and stood, ready to leap at the intruder and then, cowed by Severino's attitude, backed into the doorway, barking, its tail between its legs, its small eyes fixed on the old man.

'Get out!' cried Severino, as he walked toward the door. The dog's hackles rose again, but Severino aimed a kick at it, calling out Lucas Faisca's name.

18

'Come in,' a voice said weakly from the neighbouring room, as he stood at the bedroom door, and coming from the bright daylight, Severino, at first, could barely see the drowsy face peering through the hammock fringe, with its high cheekbones and yellow skin, a thin beard covering the chin.

'What's wrong, Faisca?'

The small head moved up against the taut hammock while the body shifted restlessly. Lucas moaned again.

'I'm very sick, Severino. It's the same old fever I had in jail, remember I nearly died? Malaria, that's what it is. I'm worse than ever, can't even stand, I've been like this for a week. When the fever hits me, I get so cold my teeth chatter. It's like the cold of death already; yesterday, I thought the end had come. And the light hurts my eyes.'

'Severino stood near the hammock, his hat pushed back, narrowing his eyes as he tried to see through the darkness.

'Nonsense, Faisca,' he said sternly, holding the man's eyes with his own. 'You've got to pull yourself together while it's still time. Otherwise, the sickness'll take hold. A man only dies when he gives up. And you're giving up, I can see. Well, you can't do it. I need you.'

It was not the sick and shivering man that Severino was seeing as he spoke, but the other Lucas Faisca, his old cellmate, agile as a wildcat, handy with a knife, guilty of six killings, not to mention the eight or nine other deaths which he said didn't count as he was only carrying out orders.

'I'm not to blame for those,' he would say seriously, 'they were jobs I was told to do, and I did them, that's all.'

Before they became cellmates Severino had already heard of him and knew his reputation for cold-blooded cruelty. When Lucas came to join him he was surprised to find the famous killer was just a little man, soft spoken, sparsely bearded, a knife-slash across his left cheek and a medal of Saint George hanging on his scrawny breast.

As time went by he grew fond of the little man who seemed so different from the murderous figure about whom so many legends had grown up. There seemed to be no connection between Lucas the inhuman killer and this quiet man whose serene patience had finally tamed a wild *sabiá*\* which now came at his whistle to peck at the grains on the palm of the hand outstretched between the bars of the window.

And yet, this same skinny little creature had handled the 'Fair Weather''s mainsheet alone, in front of Severino's astonished eyes. And at sea, during a storm which seemed to be tearing the world apart, while lightning blazed lividly in the sky, he fought the straining canvas as no other man could have done, clinging to the mast like a monkey, darting about the deck, incredibly swift, matching his movements to the fury of the waves and the boat's crazy motion, struggling with the jib and the mainsail, screaming obscenities, cursing the devil, defying the raging winds and sea.

'This isn't like you, Faisca,' said Severino, drawing closer to the hammock. 'You can't just lie there, as if you'd fallen into a ditch and couldn't bother to get out.'

Faisca's voice came thinly, between long-drawn-out sighs.

'You're wrong, Severino. I *want* to get up, but my strength's gone. I could lie here all day and sleep, like a woman who's just given birth. You don't know the struggle it is, just to keep my eyes open. They feel so heavy; as heavy as lead. And I get weaker every day; I can't eat, food sticks in my throat. Poor Chica, she's done everything she can think of, she even cooked me a piece of pigeon's breast in milk, but I couldn't get it down. This morning I was just able to swallow three spoonfulls of *canja*,\* but Chica had to make it very thin—just a watery broth. I can't bear the smell of food, it makes me feel sick.'

Severino spoke up encouragingly.

'Listen, Faisca, if you forget about the illness, it'll go away. That's what I've done, and it's worked. Now listen; I'm not going to die unless I'm *willing*, you hear? I swear to God, death isn't ever going to creep up behind me and take me by surprise. I'll chose my own time, Faisca, and go when I feel like going, not a minute before. God gave me my life,' and his mouth grew hard, 'God gave me my life and I won't give it up before I'm ready! Not until I'm ready,' he repeated.

\* Sabiá: A bird of the thrush family.
\* Canja: A thick nutritious soup made from chicken, rice and vegetables.

Deep in the hammock Lucas Faisca moaned, changed his position, and huddled together, shuddering with cold.

'That's easy to say, Severino. But things look different from here, lying helpless in this hammock, my teeth chattering. Even Christ Our Lord, who was God's own Son, had to let death take him after all.'

Severino was taken aback by the unexpected answer. He stood looking down at the wizened face that was half hidden by the fringe of the hammock. Severino cleared his throat and felt in his hip pocket for his cigarettes.

'It's just a way of talking. But you can be sure that I'm not going to die until I think it's time to go.'

Behind the hammock, a streak of sunlight showed where the closed shutter met the window frame.

Hands clasped behind his back, Severino walked to the window and back, moved again to the window and then came up to the hammock's side, brows knitted and jaw set.

'Well, Faisca! After everything I've said to you, won't you try? Make an effort?'

'I only wish I could! But my legs won't keep steady, my arms are weak as water, I feel so sick and giddy.'

'Well, it wouldn't have to be today; or even tomorrow.'

'You want me to sail with you?' asked Faisca, in surprise, raising his head and opening his eyes wide.

'Yes,' the old man replied.

Lucas Faisca gave a dry chuckle and let his head sink back against the hammock, 'Stop joking, Severino. It'll take me a month to get well — if I get well. A whole month, at least. I'll thank God on bended knees if I'm up again in a month's time.'

Severino let his arms drop by his side.

'All right,' he said, as if speaking to himself, in a strange tone of excitement. 'I'll go alone.'

'Alone? All the way to São Luis?'

'When I was a young man, I sailed everywhere by myself. Now I'm seventy-six, I'm going to prove that I can still do it.'

Lucas Faisca riased his heavy eyelids once more.

'You're out of your mind, Skipper. All the way to São Luis, with a full boatload, all by yourself?'

21

'And eleven passengers,' added the old man decisively. 'I can't stand to sit about the house doing nothing all day long. It's a month since I was last at sea. I should have gone last week, then I decided to wait a few days; now, I've put it off till next week. I'm not going to wait any longer. If I spend another week idling at home, I'm going to end up like you, thinking I haven't got a chance. No, I won't do it! I'm strong enough to sail my boat all right. I'm going to São Luis and coming back. I give you my word that I'm going and coming back.'

# CHAPTER V

When Severino told Antonia that he was going to be married, she smiled, hung her head, and her copper-brown pupils melted with tenderness. Then, looking at him sidelong, she asked,

'When is it to be?'

'Next week.'

Severino put his hands down side by side on the edge of the table on top of the cloth. The light coming from the oil lamp gave a ruddy warmth to his face.

It was only at the end of his journey, as the boat sailed round the promontory that stretched out to sea like a long finger of earth and he came in sight of the town lying in the last light of sunset, that he suddenly became conscious of what he must tell Antonia that same evening. During a night and a day, all the way from São Luis, he was lost in memories of Celita, now settled with all decency in a respectable boarding house. The sight of the wharf with its ramp leading up to the shed where he kept his boat reminded him suddenly of the woman he had lived with for so long, who was surely waiting for him, the table laid and his meal ready, occasionally looking for the 'Fair Weather' to show up on the horizon. His disquiet grew when he saw her, a rose in her hair, wearing a new dress, her freshly washed feet in braided sandals, sitting on the step of the front door in the dusk starred here and there by the first fireflies of evening.

'Next week?' she said in surprise, holding on to the corner of the table, while a queer cold feeling seemed to creep up her legs.

'Yes, next week.' Severino repeated.

Moths hovered round the lamp, the damp breeze blew off the sea into the verandah, and the remains of their supper, a glass dish of jackfruit sweet and an old tin plate on which was a piece of São Bento cheese, were still on the table.

After a moment's silence, Antonia said, with a wide smile of happiness, 'I'll just sit down for a minute.'

Her shaddow was thrown on the wall behind her, showing her bust and her head in profile, her hair drawn smoothly back, the long neck, the gently sloping shoulders.

She rested her elbow on the table and turned toward Severino who looked at her darkly, his joined hands resting on the table edge.

Far away, a dog's howling mingled with the cadence of the waves breaking on the beach.

'Why next week,' she asked, breathing deeply because of the lump in her throat, her lips suddenly dry, fighting to keep back the rising tears. 'We've waited so long, we can surely wait a little longer. Next week's so sudden—I wasn't expecting—I won't know what to do.'

There was another silence; then she raised her wet lashes, blinking, and looked at Severino's set face. She said quickly,

'You've made up your mind already, well, you're the boss, forget what I said. We'll get married next week.'

His brows drew together, his Adam's apple moved convulsively in the opening of his collar.

'That's so,' he said evasively, drawing back his hands as if about to rise.

But he continued to sit where he was, and his eyes hardened.

'The thing is, it's not you I'm going to marry. It's a girl I met in São Luis on this last trip, and she's coming to live here with me, with everything properly done, marriage certificate and all.'

The night breeze grew damper, stirred the long drooping fronds of the ferns which hung in pots from the verandah roof, made the flame of the lamp shiver and wink, and filled the house with the penetrating scent of wet greenery.

At first Antonia felt stunned and confused as if she had been suddenly struck on the head. She sat, her arms hanging nerveless, her lips apart, her eyes closed beneath motionless lids. Her heart beat so hard that she thought it would burst inside her thin heaving breast, the lower part of her body violently contracted in a spasm of anguish. She felt neither hate nor rage, however, only fear, a black overwhelming panic that made her say,

'What are you going to do about me?'

Severino could scarcely hear her voice, it was so thin and weak.

'I'm not sending you away,' he answered, his dark fingers smoothing first one eyebrow then the other.

'You'll stay here.' He made his decision, coughed a little and cleared his throat.

Antonia said nothing, neither yes or no. She dropped her eyes breathing quickly, her face grew pale, her blank pupils shone feverishly. Finally she stood up and, dragging her feet along the bare boards of the floor, moved toward the kitchen. Suddenly she tore the flower from her hair and threw it out of the door into the yard.

Later that night, while Severino sat with head lowered at the table on the verandah, writing down the expenses and profits of his journey in an old black copybook by the wavering light of the lamp Antonia hung her hammock in the spare room and moved her things in there.

'You don't have to do that tonight,' he said awkwardly, seeing her go by carrying first her clothes, then the picture of Saint Lucy, the cushion with her bobbins and a half-finished

24

piece of lace on it, an old tin trunk with flowers painted on its lid.

But she continued to go back and forth, back and forth, until she had finally brought away her Sunday shoes, her umbrella and the long pipe of *taquari* she was accustomed to smoke, and shut herself, dumb and ravaged with grief, into the room.

All her life sleep had come to her swiftly once her eyes were closed, but on this night she lay awake until morning, hearing the groan and sigh of the hammock strings and the metallic click of its supporting hooks as she swung ceaselessly from side to side the long night through.

What was she like, the woman who had cast such a spell on Severino? As she lay drawing on her pipe, Antonia tried to blame it all on the haphazard unfairness of life. It would have been a comfort to think of herself as ill-used; but she had to admit that it wasn't so. The truth of it was that Severino had given her a home, food, clothes, affection, when he took her from her father's house (who used to beat her), and she had given him nothing, not even a child from the seed he left within her on all those nights when he came back from sea.

'It's my fault, I'm the one that's to blame.'

So it was Antonia herself who made the house ready for the other's coming, the woman who was taking her place. She put an embroidered bedspread on the double bed, a crocheted doily on the table where they ate, she cleaned the knives and forks until they shone, polished the furniture, made two desserts and set them out in their glass dishes on the sideboard and cooked the sucking pig, the chicken with giblet sauce, and the crisp brown rice mixed with slices of different sorts of sausages that no one else knew so well how to prepare. From time to time she stopped her bustling and stood, arms folded across her breast, her heart full, staring at nothing. Then she would pull herself together, and get back to work, with heavy sighs.

It was near the end of the afternoon and everything was ready when she heard Severino's deep voice coming from the kitchen. Her hands went cold, her heart beat wildly, she felt her throat grow tight. For a moment she thought of locking herself in the little back room and staying there — but finally she stopped where she was, defeated, humiliated, praying to Saint Louis, Saint George, and the suffering souls in Purgatory to give her strength to bear her trial.

'It's my fate to suffer. Patience! Patience!' She said to herself.

Minutes later, she was struck speechless at the sight of Celita coming into the verandah heralded by an overpowering waft of scent; Antonia stood bewildered at her beauty, as Celita walked in showing off her dress, and her shoes with the pointed toes, a tortoiseshell comb in her hair, gold rings in her ears, a golden chain round her neck, gold bracelets tinkling on her wrist, rings on her fingers, her face made up, a small dark mole by her mouth, looking just like one of the beautiful girls that appear on illustrated calendars.

After her first amazement Antonia was conscious only of the abiding pain that was with her day and night, the pain of feeling like an exile in the house which had been hers. She had come to it a girl, plump-bodied, with firm young breasts, fresh of skin and bright of eye, and now she was ageing; already in her thirties, careless about changing her dress and combing her hair in the afternoon, finding no pleasure in feast days or parties, given to brooding, chin on hand, whenever Severino was late coming back from São Luis. During those long hours of waiting she would console herself by thinking that everything about her was hers, was home. And at night, when he was back once more and she gave herself to him, she would be suddenly twenty again, as if, in the wide creaking bed or the hollow of the hammock, time ran backward as her body rejoiced in the love spent on it.

All this she had lost, lost forever, and the blame was her's alone.

'If I'd had a child this wouldn't have happened,' she thought with repressed bitterness.

Slyly she began to watch Celita from beneath lowered lids, and although the girl's presence became familiar, the pain grew worse, the small nagging pain that unceasingly

26

devoured her. She would compare her own country ways to the city-bred smartness of the girl from São Luis, and silently she agreed with Severino. Herself barefoot, or wearing shapeless old sandals and a faded dress, bare of trimmings, the first threads of white in the hair which fell to her shoulders, two deep lines running from the sides of her nostrils to the corners of her mouth; worn by work and worry; Antonia had to admit that there was no way of competing with Celita who, even without her fine dresses, her jewelry and make-up was beautiful, always beautiful. At night, in her room, she would gather the sheet about her ears so as to shut out the sounds from the bedroom where the other woman gave herself in love. Outside, the wind whistled in the rattling leaves of the coconut palms, and blew thinly beneath the doors and through the cracks of the shutters, its high-pitched keening troubling her wits and reminding her of Celita, moaning with pleasure in the room next door. Beside herself, she would screw up the sheet and thrust it into her ears and cover her head with the hammock fringes; sometimes, in dreams, she would lie naked in Severino's arms once more.

As for Celita, she had only one thing to do from morning to night, and that was to care for her looks. She would wake up late, when the sun was already high in the sky, spend an hour in her scented bath, perfume herself with cologne, manicure her nails, let time go by unheeding while she looked in the mirror, and wear a different dress each day. The Lord only knew how many she had, and of how many colours. Fine materials, that felt wonderfully soft, or thicker stuffs that could be gathered up in both hands without crumpling. Whatever the colour—and there was a deep purple, like the *quaresmeira** blossom—it always suited Celita. And she was always doing her hair in different ways, sometimes rippling loose over her shoulders, held in place by a comb high on her head; or tied at the nape of the neck by a large bow of silk ribbon; elaborately combed high above her brow, and held in place by a multitude of hairpins, or done low, in coils over her ears, making her face look rounder, but as lovely as ever.

* *Quaresmeira:* A tree that flowers during Lent (Quaresma), whose blossoms are a vivid purple.

27

Antonia, alone in her room in the swaying hammock, unable to sleep, would brood.

'Whatever she does or doesn't do, she's beautiful. Always beautiful.'

During the day, when she had finished adorning herself, Celita would sit in the rocking chair in the dining-room reading magazines or wander about the house, as soft-footed and sleek as a pet cat, enveloped in a cloud of perfume. She would walk as far as the sitting-room, then come back; Severino had probably forbidden her to look out of the window. She would walk up to it, as if she were going to lean on the sill, and then turn away and go toward the corridor.

When Severino was at sea, she would sit rocking and sighing, looking pensively out to sea, a magazine on her lap, dressed in all her finery.

On the days when Severino came back Antonia would look out from the kitchen window and watch Celita running down the slope of the yard like a mad thing, and then climb home again, clinging to her husband with an eagerness that seemed indecent.

'Just like an animal,' Antonia would say to herself in disgust. Then she would shut herself in her room, so as not to have to listen to them in the bedroom. But later, as she waited on them at table, she could see, by the reddish light of the oil lamp, both their faces lax with satisfied desire.

And yet she never felt hatred, only an envy which held no malice; an agonizing, aching wish to be in the other's place, to be once more the woman of the house, obedient to Severino's wishes. Perhaps that was why she could never bring herself to meet Celita's eyes or say a word to her.

There came an afternoon when Antonia, having tidied the kitchen, went into her room. She heard Celita's steps in the corridor and her fingers began flying over the lace maker's cushion beside her, moving the bobbins expertly, her eyes fixed on her work. Without looking up she saw Celita stop by the door, hesitate, and then come impetuously into the room. Antonia kept her eyes on the threads of the pattern while her fingers continued to move the bobbins.

'Why won't you speak to me?' said Celita, and the shadow of her body fell across the cushion. 'There're only the two of us in this house, and I do need someone to talk to! Whenever I ask you a question, you grumble something, shrug your shoulders, draw your mouth down or point at whatever it is, but you never *speak* to me! Why not?'

She came nearer, drew up a wooden stool which stood by the hammock at the end of the room and sat down beside the cushion which lay between them, her eyes on Antonia, her hands on her knees.

'Why not?' She said again. 'What have I done to you? I can't sit dumb the whole day, when Severino's at sea. I get tired of reading magazines, tired of walking about the house, tired of looking at the yard and the sea! I need someone to listen to me, someone to answer!'

Her excitement changed to plaintiveness, she drew the stool closer to Antonia and sat up straighter.

'Say something, speak to me, for the love of God!' She said imploringly.

It's easy to ask, thought Antonia, as she went on with her work. But to get the words to come — that was too difficult. Her head seemed empty, her tongue refused to move, she could think of nothing to say. She could no more speak than she could raise her head and look the other in the face, eye to eye, even though Celita went on begging, 'Don't you see I'll go crazy without someone to talk to? Won't you even look at me?'

And there was another afternoon when Celita came back into the room and sitting down on the stool crossed her legs and began to tell Antonia about herself, where she had been, what she had done, breaking into fits of wild laughter, as amused as a child by her own stories, while Antonia's bobbins flew faster than ever, and she sat in remote silence, her eyes never moving from the lace taking shape beneath her fingers.

# CHAPTER VI

The house and the boat seemed to complete each other, linked by the jutting planks which advanced into the sea forming a pier that the waves swept over at high tide, especially on nights when the moon was full.

Rooted in time as in the sandy soil, the house gave the impression of having been set down on top of the dune so as to overlook the whole of the bay spread out below, and it had been there for almost a century, its verandah open to the sea's horizon, with the dark old tiles of its roof and the ridgepole on which the *urubus*\* perched, spreading out their black wings to dry, after a shower of rain.

The boat was a different one, although it had the same lines and the name of the one Severino had inherited from his father, Rufino the Skipper. Rufino, forever sucking at his old pipe, had known the seas off those coasts better than any man; it was said of him that, as he lay dying, he had wept for grief that he was dying on dry land and not at sea. Someone had made up a song about him:

> 'The wind blew, the rain fell,
> Many a ship was cast away,
> But the men who sailed with Rufino
> Lived to sail another day.'

Rufino also had inherited a boat from his father, slightly bigger but not as fast as Severino's, likewise named the 'Fair Weather', which had belonged to Rufino's grandfather Pedro, a tall bony man with fiery hair, half pirate, half pioneer, who had built the house and the wooden pier and brought into the yard, bedding it down within a border of stones, the great anchor that had belonged to a Portuguese galleon.

As the years went by it seemed to Severino that he saw, emerging ever more clearly from the dark cave of time past,

\* *Urubu*: A scavenger bird, rather like a vulture, native to Brazil.

30

the tall slim figure of his father, Rufino. They were always the same visions, and it was as though his memory, unable to recapture other scenes, tried to make up for it by lending them a special vividness. There was a queer trick Severino had, when he wanted to summon up the image of his father handling the old 'Fair Weather's' sails beneath a stormy sky, of opening a cardboard box where he kept old documents. Then Rufino seemed to rise before him suddenly, pipe in mouth, conjured up by the yellowed folds of an old chart that had his name written across the bottom and, in Severino's imagination, his father would once more move about and gesture, shouting challenges at the wind, the rain and the sea.

Of his mother he had only a dim memory of seeing her come up the path in the yard, her heavy figure and sad face — the same sadness he had seen on her features as she lay in her coffin in the sitting-room, dressed in black, her blank face turned up to the ceiling.

As far as Severino was concerned, his family was a dynasty of males only, who all belonged to the sea, unconquerable, burned black by the sun, their boat's prow slicing through the waves. If it were possible for him to go back in time, he knew he would find others, skippers like his father, like his grandfather, like his great-grandfather, faithful to the sea until death, in an endless succession of undefeated seafarers.

So when Celita began to wake in the mornings, pale and sick, her shadowed eyes dreamy with a mysterious new beauty, he never doubted that she carried the son, so long desired, Antonia had never given him. He thought of nothing else. He watched over her fussily, and would not sleep with her while her pregnancy lasted. However, so as to make up for all the tiresome restrictions she had to bear, he let her sit by the window and look out into the street and along the curves of the road that stretched beyond it.

Never would he be able to forget his disappointment when Aunt Noca, with Mercedes in her arms, told him he had a daughter.

'A girl?' He said, astounded.

'A girl,' she assured him.

'No! It can't be!'

31

And holding the lighted stub of a candle in his hand as he bent over the wicker cradle he had brought from São Luis specially for his son, he looked and looked again, between the baby's tender thighs.

He blew out the candle, turned his back on the cradle and went past the big double bed in which Celita now lay asleep. Turning his eyes away from Antonia standing silently in the middle of the room, he went out of the house, into the dark. He took the path which led to the wooden pier and went down to the beach where the waves were breaking. Severino stood there a long time — he never knew how long — looking out over the bay where a glimmer of moonlight seemed to tremble on the long smooth swells. His eyes followed the dissolving silver patterns that played over the heaving waters, but his tormented mind held to one unchanging thought. There was no son. What would happen to the 'Fair Weather' when he grew old, when his strength finally left him? This was more than a stroke of bad luck, it was punishment — but punishment for what? What had he done? He screwed up his eyes, as if trying to see deeper into the night, but it was his own depths that he was searching, desperately trying to find the reason why he had been singled out for this. Against the faint milky light of the horizon, he could distinguish the silhouette of his boat at the end of the pier, and he felt wrung with pain and guilt. Every month, year after year, he had waited expectantly for his son. He had been harsh with Antonia, blaming her barren womb. And now, instead of the man-child he needed, he had a daughter. Why? he tried in anguish to understand.

But later, as he went up the slope from the beach, while the morning light spilled over the sea, his haggard face was calmer, almost hopeful. The house was plunged in silence as in sleep. On his way to the bedroom, glancing from the dark corridor toward the kitchen, he saw Antonia lighting the wood to heat the stove so as to make coffee. Aunt Noca sat waiting with her back to the window, a skinny old woman with a clay pipe in her mouth. Carefully he opened the bedroom door and slipped into the room, stepping softly so as to not waken Celita and the baby, lying quiet in the cradle. The small flame of

32

the nightlight quivered, streaks of bright daylight showed between the roof tiles. The room was still in disorder from the birth, he could see a tin jug, a basin of water, a blood-stained sheet lay crumpled up in a corner; on the marble-topped bed-table lay a pair of scissors, a bottle of surgical spirit, a roll of gauze; two towels hung over the back of a chair, and a candle still burned before the picture of the Virgin, who watched over women in childbed. He took hold of the chair, meaning to carry it to the bedside, then changed his mind, and sat down gently on the edge of the bed, propping himself up on his hands. Leaning over, he gazed down at Celita's tranquil face. His feeling for her had changed; she had been in labour for two days, and it had gone hard with her. A deep tenderness and compassion filled his heart and it seemed to him that his love for her was somehow refined and purified. As she awoke he took her moist hand in his and kissed her gently. Still holding her hand he said, looking at her with love,

'Next time you'll give me a son, won't you? Now that we've got a girl, we need a boy!'

She started up, tearing her hand away, eyes wide with fear.

'No! No! I've suffered enough! For God's sake, don't ask me that! I know I'll die if I have to go through this again!'

Severino's face darkened and then grew red with contained rage. He folded his hands around his right knee and stared at the bud of light that showed through the glass shade of the nightlight. Then he relaxed. Of course, he had spoken too soon. Time would take care of it. How could he expect her to want another child, with the memory of her pain still alive in her raw nerves? In a month or so, she would feel different. He took her hand again, and his frown slowly smoothed itself out.

During her pregnancy Celita had announced she would not suckle the child; she had no intention of spoiling the shape of her breasts. So Aunt Noca had brought Felicia, fat and moonfaced, with immense overflowing breasts, to act as wetnurse. She lived a little way down the street, and could come over whenever the baby was hungry.

Once Celita was up again, the 'Fair Weather' spread its sails and made for São Luis. Celita grew conscious of the loneliness of the house, which seemed so empty; she took the baby into the dining-room, where the sun poured in through the tall open windows. Sitting in the rocking chair, a pile of magazines on her lap and Mercedes lying beside her in an improvised bed, made from pillows laid on the palm-leaf matting which covered the floor, she said to Antonia who was changing the baby's wet napkin,

'I'm her mother, but I won't know how to care for her. You've got a gift for it, it seems; it's easy to see from the way you hold her, give her her bath. I can't even pick her up without feeling afraid she's going to break! *You'll* rear the child.'

Antonia, as usual, said not a word. The baby was crying; she would have to go and call Felicia, if the nurse didn't come soon. She kept an eye on the windows in case the evening breeze were to rattle the shutters, frightening the child. She continued to spend her days in silence, as if she had been dumb from birth, but a seed of happiness began to grow, deep within her, as she cared for Mercedes. While Celita sat in the rocking chair idly turning the pages of some cheap magazine, Antonia washed the baby's clothes, spread them out in the sun to dry, and ironed them, taking special pains with the tiny embroidered ruffles and bits of ribbon and lace. Celita had recovered her bloom, her breasts were fuller, she was once more wearing the bright dresses whose colours seemed to echo her laughter.

There was an evening when, as soon as Severino got back from São Luis, Celita asked Antonia to take the baby to sleep with her in her room,

'I've spoken to Severino and he agrees. I sleep like a log myself, and don't even wake up when she cries. She'll be better off sleeping with you.'

Antonia said nothing, but went to fetch the baby's cradle and put it in her room, out of the way of any drafts that might come from the window through which the wind blew gustily in bad weather. That night, when she had locked her door, she picked up Mercedes and settled with her in the hammock, holding her close to the warmth of her body and rocking to and fro while she sang a half-remembered lullaby, low-voiced.

Next morning Celita said to her:

'You're going to carry the baby to her christening. Aunt Noca has to be godmother, she brought her into the world; but Severino and I have talked it over, and you'll be a kind of godmother too, and carry her yourself.'

There was not a word from Antonia, but on the same afternoon she began to work at the lace that was to trim the christening robe. At night while Mercedes slept peacefully in her cradle, Antonia would sit before the cushion on which the lace was taking shape, the light of the single candle flickering on her long fingers as they moved the bobbins, whose steady click seemed to answer the chirping of the crickets in the yard. Evening after evening she sat at her lace, while the hours slipped by in quiet happiness.

As long as she lived, Antonia would remember the day of the christening, the warmth of Mercedes lying in her arms, plump, smooth and rosy, with her mother's lively eyes, the tiny perfect hands, the downy head in its cap of lace that matched the long filmy dress bordered at the sleeves and hem with rose-pink ribbon. What a shame that, although it was Sunday, there were so few people in church, no doubt because it was late, near sundown already; only two or three old women, all in black, and Fidelis the sacristan who was filling up the basin of holy water. Then Father Dourado came in, his stole over his shoulders, one finger between the pages of his breviary

For Antonia, the sweetest memory of all was not when the baby quivered and whimpered at the strangeness of water and salt, but the long leisurely walk to the church, with Mercedes in her arms, and the return home after the christening. She walked in front, wearing her freshly-ironed Sunday dress, with Aunt Noca beside her, tall and thin, with earrings dangling from her long ear-lobes. Behind them, Severino and Celita were arm-in-arm, he wearing his wedding suit and elastic-sided boots, and Celita in a skin-tight dress and high-heeled shoes, the tortoiseshell comb in her hair, gold rosettes in her ears, wearing far too much make-up for a woman respectably married.

35

Mercedes lay peacefully in Antonia's arms, shielded from the sun by Aunt Noca's umbrella. All the way to the church Antonia smiled at the people she recognized among the passers-by, secretly treasuring the approving looks that rested on the baby's chubby face. She felt as though the baby were truly hers, her very own child, and cherished it against her thin breast, once more at peace with the world and with life itself, although she kept her silence unbroken.

Back from the church, standing in the dining room, Antonia heard the sound of a horse galloping up the street outside. From where she stood she could see the street go tilting down toward the beach, half hidden by the clump of bamboo through which the late sunlight came in shafts. Vaguely worried, she looked in the direction of the noise, and a moment later a man rode into sight, sitting his sleek chestnut with an air, riding-crop in hand, wearing a checked cap, leggings and spurs. She recognized him at once; he was the new Public Prosecutor.* She had seen him in Market Square, a month ago, full-bodied, with luxuriant whiskers framing his plump face, walking with his wife, red-haired and as tall as her husband, who was expecting a baby. She had seen him again a fortnight later, riding back from the beach, alone. And the whole of last week, on alternate days, and always at the same time, he had ridden by the house. Antonia walked softly into the corridor and toward the sitting-room door; then she shrugged, and turned away. What good would it do her to spy on Celita? No; she was not cut out for spying. So she went into her room and closed the door softly, then went quietly over to the cradle where Mercedes lay.

The days passed; the 'Fair Weather' went to São Luis and returned half-a-dozen times, the rainy season drew slowly to an end. Then it was a clear cool day in July; the 'Fair Weather' swung gently with the tide at the end of the pier and the breeze played with the trailing fronds of the ferns on the verandah. Antonia saw Severino coming up from the beach with Celita in his arms. Dead. Her long silence ended in a shriek.

'Oh Christ, what happened?'

* Public Prosecutor: Corresponds to Council for the Crown in England, and District Attorney in the United States.

36

With eyes aching and swollen, Antonia undressed the dead girl whose clothes were dripping with sea-water, and prepared her for burial, pressing down the eyelids and crossing the cold hands on the motionless breast, and hanging a crucifix on the wall above the head while Celita lay on the big double bed, a candle burning on either side. In a corner of the room Severino sat weeping, his face hidden in his hands.

And yet—there was a grain of comfort in the horror. Suddenly, Antonia was once again the woman of the house, back in possession of her own spacious room with Mercedes sleeping beside her in her little curtained bed.

It was true that she missed Severino; but during the long years as a boatman's wife, she had grown accustomed to his absence. And twice a week, in the afternoon, she would visit him at the jail. To herself she admitted that although he was in prison, he was also hers once more.

When the housework was finished, she would rest in the rocking chair with Mercedes on her lap. Looking over the crests of the coconut palms growing in the yard she could see the 'Fair Weather' anchored at the end of the wooden pier; the tall bare mast, rolling from side to side to the rhythm of the waves, seemed to be sending lonely signals to its master. She had had several good offers for it, but, obedient to Severino, she had refused them and the boat stayed at the end of the pier, year after year, slowly rotting away in the wind, the spray and the salt air, becoming a place of refuge for stray gulls, and then a den for beggars until, one stormy night, the sea swallowed it up.

Twenty-three years after Celita's death Severino sailed his new boat up to the pier; it came from far away but bore the same name and had the same strong graceful lines as the old boat. One would have thought the sea, for once, had given up its dead and restored the 'Fair Weather', shining with fresh paint, with its old skipper at the helm. And yet there was a difference; a little man named Lucas Faisca handled the sails.

Once more, the boat and the house, linked by the narrow bridge of planks, formed a single entity. Once more Severino sailed out of the bay, on his way to São Luis.

# CHAPTER VII

Death came on a sudden to Felicia who had just finished trimming the old fancy dress she planned to wear for Carnival. The suddenness made it harder to bear, and her husband sat numbly in an armchair near the coffin, while the children wailed and the house gradually filled with shocked and weeping friends.

Felicia had gone down to the pier to try and persuade Mercedes to come back to the house. Mercedes, in those last days of pregnancy, spent all her time there, staring at the bay and searching with hungry eyes for any sign of her husband's returning boat. And then Felicia put a hand to her breast, cried out sharply, and fell.

The cruellest part of death, when it comes unexpectedly, is the feeling of having been deceived, cheated, that gives a keener edge to the survivors' grief, who must wake their dead confused and unprepared.

When Felicia collapsed, Mercedes, staring in amazement, thought that she had fainted. Bending down, she tried to lift her up, but the black woman's bulk was too much for her; even so, she managed to drag her half way up the pier. Kneeling on the narrow planks, she slapped the dead cheeks lightly, called her name over and over until, unnerved by the eyes gazing fixedly at the sun, she began to scream for help. Nobody came, so she ran up the pier to the sand, still screaming and on the verge of hysteria, until a couple of fishermen who had been mending their nets on the wet sand further down the beach, dropped their work and came toward her at a run. They closed Felicia's eyes and straightened her dress decently around her, while Mercedes ran up the slope to the yard calling for Antonia, while the evening breeze freshened behind her.

38

At the wake, as Mercedes sat in tears by the head of the corpse, she felt her pains begin again. Their first onset had come as she scrambled up into the yard, calling hoarsely for Antonia. And then, nothing. Now they were back, much sharper; she dried her eyes and beckoned to Antonia.

'The baby's coming. We'd better go home and call Aunt Noca.'

After a stifling day, dazzling and fiery with light and heat, the wind had shifted bringing heavy rain; lightning flashed in the sky and thunder rolled; a dog was barking somewhere down on the beach. Night had come early, and one by one, the wind blew out the lamps along the street.

They left Felicia's wake huddled together beneath the same umbrella; the lighted windows threw yellow squares on the pavement. Slowly they made their way home, toward the glow coming from the lamp that hung from the verandah roof. Severino never forgot to light it.

He was asleep when they reached the house. Mercedes, in the room next door, began to take off her clothes, walking back and forth and moaning, as her pains grew worse. Antonia woke him and told him to fetch Aunt Noca quickly. He got up still dazed with sleep, felt for his hat hanging on the wall, struggled into his shabby old coat, and went out into the rain, his sandalled feet slapping through the puddles.

Mercedes went into the big bedroom while Antonia poked the fire and put a pan of water on the trivet to boil, so as to have everything ready when Aunt Noca arrived. Mercedes came and went between the bedroom and the sitting-room, her hands on her belly, holding her breath and grinding her teeth as each pain reached its peak. Her eyes closed, slowing in her walk, she thought, God, how she missed Vicente. No, he had not died at sea, she would not accept that; he would be back sometime, any time — perhaps tonight. She could see him, young, gay, full of life, getting ready for his last journey; hauling up the sails, his trousers rolled up to his calves, a wide straw hat protecting his head from the sun. Gradually the mainsail became a small blue triangle against the pale horizon and then slowly sank from sight, as though extinguished by the fading sunset. How could she believe that a good boat, fresh from the builder's yard and bright with new paint, sailed by Vicente, of all people, bred to the sea from childhood, might have lost its way forever in the ocean mazes? All her life she had heard of her father coming and going in the 'Fair Weather', and this certainty of return, of survival, had become part of her and kept alive the stubborn hope of her husband's home-coming. Vicente had youth and strength, and knew the sea as intimately as Severino. As the days passed and he was overdue, and then more days went by, she finally asked Aunt Noca to come and bring her pack of cards. The old woman stood by the table frowning over the bright cardboard squares, her lower lip pushed out; eventually she raised her eyebrows and shrugged her skinny shoulders.

'A boatman can be given up for lost, and one fine day he comes home again. It's happened before and it'll happen again; Vicente isn't the first, and he won't be the last.'

'He'll be back, I'm sure he'll come back,' Mercedes said with conviction, folding her hands together .

That same afternoon, at the hour when the fishing boats began to come in, she went out to the end of the pier and settled down to wait for Vicente, her hands busy with yarn and crochet hook. From time to time she narrowed her eyes against the glitter of sunlight dancing on the waves; one by one she watched the homing sails. Then it grew dark and she walked slowly up to the house. After that she went back every day, at the same hour and to the same spot; when it rained, she watched the sea from the shelter of the verandah. Sometimes Antonia came to fetch her home, at other times it was Felicia. The child grew in her womb, and her confidence seemed to grow with it, everything was made ready for Vicente, the freshly-washed hammock with his slippers beside it, his favourite dessert already prepared, the baby's clothes for him to see and admire.

Antonia pushed the door open with her knee and came in, carrying a wooden stool and a tin basin. She put the stool down beside the bed, set the basin on top of it and told Mercedes to lie down.

'Try to get some rest, child, it won't do you any good to wear yourself out.'

'Aunt Noca told me to keep on walking as long as I could. And the pains seem to get worse when I lie down. I'd better wait a little.'

They were both silent for a while. The wind blew between the tiles of the roof and beneath the doors and the noise of the rain never stopped. Antonia went to the cupboard, took out the bottle of spirit and put it on the bed table. In silence she lit a candle and placed it before the picture of the Virgin.

'It'll soon be over, you'll see,' she said, blowing out the match.

Mercedes leaned with closed eyes against the wall, her hands pressed to her belly, waiting for the spasm of pain to pass. Then she took a deep breath, opened her eyes and went on walking to and fro, stopping now and then to stifle a groan and prop herself against the wall or the chest of drawers. She smiled at Antonia who never took her eyes off her, although she was busily preparing the room for the birth.

'Just think how wonderful it would be if Vicente came back tonight! I wouldn't care how bad the pain was, you'd never hear a whimper from me, if only he came back!'

'Come back in this weather?' Antonia said doubtfully.

'Oh, the weather! What's that to Vicente? He knows the bay by heart, just like Father. Something tells me *here*,' and she pressed her hand to her breast, 'that the door's going to open, and Vicente'll be standing there, please God!'

'Yes, it would be wonderful. Who knows, dear? God can make anything happen.' Antonia did her best to sound hopeful.

She watched Mercedes move away with her slow heavy step, and thought of Celita. From the back they were alike; the daughter had her mother's figure, narrow-waisted and round-hipped, the slope of the shoulders, the hair, the plump legs. But their faces were different, the colour of the eyes and the shape of the mouth. And in their ways they were as different as could be. As Antonia stood looking about the room, the memory of that other night came back to her

41

vividly, the night of Mercedes' birth. Antonia made the sign of the Cross and prayed silently for the peace of Celita's soul.

She had quietly put away everything which had belonged to the other woman, her dresses, her perfumes, the high-heeled shoes and silk scarves, the old magazines, the sewing basket and the sunshade, Celita's rings and necklaces, she had put them all away carefully, for Mercedes. And she had left hanging on the wall the photograph of Severino and Celita taken on their wedding day. Sometimes, she seemed to see Celita standing at the door of the room, laughing in that wild way of hers. And now looking toward the same door, she saw the dead woman's daughter there, her face drawn with suffering. Mercedes came toward the bed and paused.

'Lie down, child, lie down! Aunt Noca'll be here in a minute.'

The girl sat down on the bed.

'Poor Felicia,' she murmured. 'She'd promised to stay with me while the baby was born. How good she was, always thinking of others, never of herself, until the very end! And to think that she had to die almost in my arms!'

'Well, she's in Heaven now, and better off than we are,' Antonia reminded her, while she shook up pillows for Mercedes to rest her head. 'Some die, some are born, that's how life is.'

It was after midnight when Aunt Noca arrived, and the rain still fell in glistening sheets of water.

Mercedes was lying on the bed with bent knees, biting on a corner of the sheet to keep from screaming. The old woman washed her hands in the basin beside the bed.

'There, child, it'll soon be over, the stronger the pains, the quicker the birth. A little patience, and you'll be all right,' she said encouragingly.

Severino stayed in the dining room, listening to his daughter's moans. The cigarette between his lips had gone out without his noticing. He sat down in the rocking chair and got up again, restlessly, walked out into the verandah, came back into the room, careless of the clothes that clung soaking to his body. Livid streaks of lightning showed the rain pouring down

42

from the edge of the roof and the leaves of the coconut palms flapping crazily in the wind. Then the darkness would shut down again and he could see nothing. The night grew chilly and Mercedes' sharp cries, the wailing of the wind and the crashing of the rain, seemed to run together in his head.

Sometimes there would come a high-pitched scream and he would run to the bedroom door and wait there dazed, holding his breath and wringing his hands. Then he would go back to the chair and light another cigarette, trying to steady his nerves. From the beginning of his daughter's pregnancy he had been sure she would have a boy. A manchild. It had to be a manchild. And he would be named Pedro, after Severino's grandfather. But now that the time had come, he felt a gnawing fear — suppose it was a girl after all? He went back to the verandah, indifferent to the rain blowing in. There was a sudden high scream of agony: the child was born. He seized his cigarette by the lighted end, swore, and threw it away. He heard the cry of the new-born baby above the clamour of the wind and his grim face broke into a smile. As he went back to stand outside the bedroom, Antonia's voice came joyfully through the half open door.

'It's a boy!'

Alone in the dark corridor, Severino began to laugh. Relief, joy, thankfulness flooded him; he had not been defeated after all. Back in the dining room he got out a bottle of port wine, held it up against the light and poured himself a glass. Sitting at ease in the rocking chair he drank the wine slowly, drop by drop. The 'Fair Weather' would have a new helmsman of his own blood. He asked God to give him the strength and wisdom to bring the boy up .

The rain lashed the hanging ferns in the verandah outside while Severino finished the wine, rocking gently in the chair. Antonia's voice came abruptly, breaking into his dream.
Get the doctor, for God's sake.' she gasped, looking down at him with anguished eyes. 'Aunt Noca's done all she can but the bleeding won't stop! Get the doctor! Run —'

# CHAPTER VIII

Severino meant to take a look at his boat but as he reached the place where the pier began, he felt the pain he had come to know so well clawing at his breast and his sight grew dark as he stood dizzily holding his breath, his brows contracted, his hand pressed to his heart.

'Perhaps I shouldn't have thrown away that prescription,' he thought. 'After all, it couldn't have done any harm to try it.'

The pain seemed to grow less and the vertigo passed. He shrugged his bony shoulders.

'Well, it's too late now.'

As he walked down the wooden planks he felt on edge with annoyance, remembering the doctor, authority in a white overall sitting at an impressive desk, his small eyes commanding behind the thick lens of his glasses, fat fingers drumming on the desk surface.

'Fool, idiot! Telling me I've got to stay indoors doing nothing — does he think I'm a woman who's just given birth? Does he expect me to lie rotting away in my hammock? I'll show him what I'm made of!'

He had had enough of those long monotonous days ashore while Antonia anxiously watched his every move. He was certainly not the kind of man to spend his days like an invalid brooding in an armchair. There had been enough brooding — too much — during those sterile years in prison, and in those days there had still been something to look forward to, there were good years still ahead. Now — well, he had no intention of cowering between four walls waiting for death to catch up with him. Since he had to die, he preferred to die at sea. He was no Lucas Faisca, shivering in a hammock, his strength gone, crushed by illness. He would fight to the end.

'I'll go to São Luis and come back,' he said to himself with stubborn confidence.

It was late afternoon and the small triangular sails of the fishing *igarités*\* had turned back and were making for home. The surface of the waves broke into flashing crystal lights. Above the dancing waters a softer radiance melted from crimson to pale rose and deepened into violet, and gulls hovered, dark against the sky. Where sea met sky, a streak of purple slowly turned to ash, while the last fires of sunset blazed in the sky above it, as the sun sank down to quench its flames in the sea.

Severino looked on absently, while the light faded and the fishing boats came in on the evening tide. He thought of those endless days of waiting for Vicente's return; Vicente, who had disappeared beneath the boiling waters of the Alcantara Reef. He thought of Mercedes, pregnant with his grandson, sitting at the end of the pier, at sunset, day after day, surrounded as he was now by light and silence, watching the triangular sails of the returning *igarités*. Then night would fall, the first stars shone, fireflies drifted by, and the girl would walk slowly back along the pier and up the slope to the house.

She had been closer to Antonia than to her father. Antonia had brought her up without the help of anyone else, during the years of his imprisonment, when he saw his daughter only on those rare afternoons she came to visit him in jail. When he finally came home she was a woman already, engaged to Vicente. He had grown to love her; in a way, she brought Celita back to life. Her voice was just like her mother's, and there were times when he had to fight back tears as he heard her moving and talking in the quiet house. When she lay dead on the night of Pedro's birth, the old man had felt that his misery was the inevitable fruit of some strange personal doom from which there was no escape. It was only the thought of the new-born child, so utterly dependent on him, that kept him from sailing out blindly through the storm, to end it all in the sea out there.

To Severino. his whole life of trouble and sorrow had led to

\* Igarité: A one-man sailboat used by fishermen in Northeastern Brazil.

one miraculous achievement; the boy was his justification, his comfort and his crown. It was the thought of Pedro that now drew him towards home, the memory of his stricken face, that morning, anxiously holding out a glass of water while the old man gasped for breath and clutched at his heart. The boy's distress had somehow seemed to bring them closer, make them part of one another; and an immense tenderness filled him at the thought of his grandson. He wished he were standing at the 'Fair Weather's' helm, Pedro at his side; it was time to teach him the secrets of the 'Fair Weather's' moods, how to handle her sails and steer her through the great seas beyond the bay.

Far away where the curve of the beach came to an end at the foot of the crag, boys were playing football on the sand. Severino glanced at them through narrowed eyes; he did not think Pedro would be there. The boy never wanted company, preferring to invent his own games by himself, at home, to joining in the rough play of boys of his own age. By the time he was eight he could read as well as any grown-up, and his teacher was full of praise for his neat handwriting. Then, one day, during the holidays, the old man came on his grandson in the little room beside the kitchen, a heap of rags beside him, cutting out doll's dresses. Severino went at him, belt in hand.

'That's women's work! You're a man, do you hear? A man, like me!' The old man roared, blind with rage.

The belt rose and fell, rose and fell, until a thin stream of blood ran down Pedro's forehead, where the belt buckle had gashed the skin.

'A man! A man!' The old man shook with fury, and raised the belt again, but Antonia came running and sheltered the boy in the folds of her skirt, calling on the saints for help.

Three years later, on a day when Severino was at home, sitting in the rocking chair in the dining room, he saw Father Dourado standing in the door, stooping a little in his faded old cassock, a black skull-cap on his white hair; one hand held his breviary against his breast, the other clutched his stick; his face was red and moist with sweat from the blazing summer sun.

46

'Good morning, Skipper, I'm bringing you the best piece of news you've had all year. It's as good as a Christmas present — it *is* a Christmas present, sent to you by the Lord Himself,' said the old man, wiping his shapeless shoes on the mat before hobbling into the room.

Severino got up from his chair and stood waiting in the middle of the room. The priest put his breviary in his pocket and propped the stick against the wall; raising his head, he smiled at Severino.

'My friend, this is not just an old village priest you're looking at; it's not Father Dourado you're seeing, but one of God's angels, come to bring you good news. Yes, Skipper; good news. I know what I'm saying. Don't take me for a witless old priest who's only fit to mumble nonsense. Oh, no!' He opened the collar of his cassock.

'But first please get me a glass of water; I've come a long way in the heat.'

Severino went to fetch the earthenware jug that stood on the verandah's low wall; the shade and blowing breeze kept the water fresh and cool. He filled a clay beaker and brought it to the priest. Father Dourado sat down in the rocking chair, the hem of his long drawers showing between the cassock and the dingy socks. He rocked back and forth gently, puffing out his cheeks. When he had drunk, he smacked his lips and wiped them on the back of his hand, and then leaned back against the chair, his fingers folded in his lap, eyes smiling in their nest of wrinkles.

'Can't you guess what I've come to tell you? I daresay not. People never do. They never can see what's under their noses.'

His voice came slower, as if to emphasize the mystery of which he was the messenger. His smile showed the three yellow teeth remaining in the shrivelled gums. Then he fixed his eyes on Severino's.

'Haven't you noticed anything different, lately, about your grandson, Skipper? No? That just goes to show, people never see an inch before their noses. You may not have seen it, but I have, Severino, and that's what I've come to talk to you about. You can be proud of Pedro, my friend. You ought to lift your

47

hands to Heaven in thankfulness! You should go down on your knees and thank God, who looks down on our sins with loving mercy. Bow your head, dear friend, and beat your breast.'

Severino had taken the cigarette from his mouth and was looking at the priest from beneath his brows, intrigued.

'Your grandson's a good boy, an excellent boy. There're not many like him. And God has chosen him for the most glorious work there is on earth. Yes, Skipper! That's what I have to tell you.' The priest's voice grew stronger and he raised his head. 'He's one of God's chosen, Severino.'

He settled back in his chair, hands on his lap.

'It must have been around the end of August, beginning of September. I was in the sacristy preparing the banns to be read on Sunday (there's no one to help me to do these things now that Luisa's daughter has moved to São Luis, I can't trust that fool of a sacristan to do them properly), I was in my sacristy, preparing the banns, when I saw a boy kneeling before the main altar, lost in prayer. I watched him for a while, giving thanks to the Lord in my heart, and then I said to myself suddenly, 'Isn't that Severino's grandson Pedro?' And so it was. Yes indeed. It was Pedro, your grandson. I let a few minutes go by, then I got up and called him: 'Pedro!' He came to me, and knelt for my blessing. I asked for news of you and *Dona** Antonia, but I noticed that the boy never took his eyes off the big photograph of our late blessed Bishop, Dom Augusto, hanging over the chest of drawers where the vestments are kept. I let him look his full, and then I said to him, 'Pedro,' I said, 'Pedro, that old man was the one who led me to follow God's way. He is a saint. Truly a saint. I owe what I am to him, and to Our Lady.' Pedro took a step forward, as if he wanted to see it closer. Then he said to me, 'Father Dourado, what must one do to be a priest?' I dropped the pen and paper, I stood up, I asked him, 'My son, why do you want to know?' Pedro looked me in the eyes, just as you're doing now, serious, determined, and answered without blinking, 'I want to be a priest.'

* *Dona*: From the latin 'Domina', a form of address used to married or elderly women, and social superiors (female).

Severino stood with his lips apart, his arms by his sides. He threw his cigarette away, and said through stiff lips,

'Pedro said that?'

'In those very words, Severino. He knew what he wanted and said so, as clear as can be. I admit I was moved; I had to dry my eyes. I meant to come and speak to you, then and there, but then I thought I had better wait, let time confirm it. It might just be a boy's fancy, a spur-of-the-moment business, without the depth and strength of a real vocation. So I said to Pedro: 'Come and see me whenever you can; if I'm not here, you'll find me at home.' And he came, Severino. Gradually I got to know the boy, and now, just two days before Christmas, I've come to give you the best, the most wonderful news you'll have this year: Your grandson has a real vocation. He'll grow into a true, dedicated, priest. Who knows, he may even become a Bishop some day. Or a Cardinal! Why not a Cardinal? Our Lord Jesus Christ didn't chose his disciples among the big men of Galilee; He chose them among the fishermen. It's written in the Bible.'

Severino was deadly pale, his lips shook. There was a lump in his throat, and his jaws set like iron. Then his face grew red and swollen with rage, and he was able to speak once more.

'Father Dourado, the only reason I'm not kicking you out is because I know you didn't mean to insult me. And besides, I owe you many favours. So many, and I'm the first to admit it. But you've got to understand that I mean what I say: You're *never* to mention this to me again. Never. You hear me? Never. While I'm alive, my grandson'll not wear a skirt, not even a skirt like the one you're wearing. I'd rather see him dead.'

The priest looked at him in stupefaction, his mouth hanging open. Then he got hastily to his feet, upsetting his chair.

'Good day,' he managed to say, reaching angrily for his stick, 'Ask God's pardon for all the rubbish you've been talking. For my part, I forgive you, Severino!'

Severino stood in grim silence, his hard eyes watching the old priest make his way down the corridor. Later that day he called Antonia and forbade her to take Pedro to church again.

49

'Not even for Sunday Mass?' she said submissively.

'Not even Sunday Mass,' he shouted. 'And if I hear that he's set foot inside the church, against my orders, I'll beat him as he's never been beaten before.'

Pedro shot up during the next two years; he grew tall and thin, pimples broke out on his face beneath the red hair.

'He's taller than I am,' Severino said to himself in wonder, as he looked out over the bay and saw the first stars of evening coming out high above the masts of the homeward-bound *igarités*.

He got up from the bench and moved away from the helm, drawing the evening breeze into his lungs with a long deep breath, and jumping out of the boat, he noticed that the tide was already lapping at the planks of the pier. Darkness was falling as he went up the slope to his house. Drying his wet sandal-soles on the mat, he said to Antonia who was lighting the storm-lantern,

'Since Faisca can't come, I'm taking Pedro with me to São Luis.'

# CHAPTER IX

Antonia spent the night lying motionless in the hammock in case the creaking strings should disturb Severino in the room next door and let him know of her distress. At times her eyelids would close, heavy with sleep. Then she would start up again, broad awake, and shift and turn, restless with anxiety and grief, and pray.

'If only Faisca was going along! I wouldn't have to worry so. But he can't, poor man. Severino'll have to work the boat alone. How can he do it? What if the pain comes back? I don't believe he'll be able to do it. When the pain comes, he goes as white as a ghost, he can't breathe! Next time he'll probably faint, and then what'll become of him, all alone in the middle of the sea! Oh, dear God, who's going to steer the boat for him and manage the sails? Who's to know what course to set for São Luis, or coming home? Oh, dear Lord, holy saints in Heaven, I can't bear to think of it. Blessed Virgin, look down on me, give me your help, deliver me from this trouble, for the love of Christ, by His Holy Wounds!'

Outside the wind has changed and is singing a song of bad weather. Antonia's fear seems to grow, she lies huddled beneath a choking weight of terror, twisting the end of the sheet between her fingers while her prayers turn to a mutter of anguish. Next door Severino coughs, and clears his throat raspingly.

'It's madness! But once he's made his mind up, there's nothing anyone can do about it. If he said he's going, go he will. He'll go, and take his grandson as well. Even if I were to kneel down at his feet and beg him to leave Pedro with me, I wouldn't do it. He's a hard obstinate man, and never goes back on his word. It'd take a miracle to make him see reason! Please, Lord! Sweet Saint Lucy, for Jesus' sake! Oh save me, save us all!'

Since Mercedes' death Antonia had slept in the room next to the main bedroom and the child slept there with her. At first he lay in his mother's old cradle; then she hung a hammock for him near the window that overlooked the yard. At night she would get up to see whether the bedclothes were still in place; the winter nights were chilly. Drawing up the covers around the boy she would plait the fringes of the hammock over him, so that he lay in a cocoon of warmth. Then she would make sure that the window was properly shut, and go on tiptoe to Severino's door, open it soundlessly, and look at him lying quietly asleep in his hammock. All was well; she would murmur a prayer of thanks and go back to sleep.

Toward morning she would hear Pedro get up, and after peeping at him from beneath lowered lids, close her eyes again and listen for the tinny rattle and splash of her old chamber

51

pot as he made water. Lying there, her cheek in her hand, she would say to herself with pride: 'He's a man already! And yet it seems like yesterday that he was born!'

He hadn't been an easy child to rear, in spite of the goat's milk she gave him, milking the beast herself, every morning. She watched him grow strong and rosy, turn into a plump child taking his first unsteady steps; she watched him play and run, go on errands for her, start for school, always biddable, gentle as a girl. Whenever he was late coming home Antonia waited for him at the sitting-room window and only settled to sleep when he was safely in his hammock. She would sit in her room, swaying lazily in her own hammock, smoking her pipe. When he came in at last, she would rise, kiss him on the forehead, draw the hammock fringes about him, turn down the flame of the small oil lamp, and then go to her own rest after saying the Lord's Prayer and a Hail Mary.

And now all this was over. She would be left alone in the emptiness of the silent house. How could she live without Pedro to care for?

She pressed her fingers to her eyes. 'He's never been away from me in his life!'

Yes, she had always known how to keep him by her, she had been good at finding first one reason and then another, putting off the day when he would have to go on his first voyage, afraid that the treacherous sea would take him as it had taken his father. After all, why did Pedro have to be a boatman? There were so many other things he could do, things that ordinary people did. He could work at the chemist's, get a job with the city council, keep a shop on Market Square. Perhaps old Balbino the notary would take him as a clerk.

'He writes a beautiful hand, why it's almost like print, it's so clear! And he'd be a quick learner,' she murmured, as though talking to Balbino already.

What she had always feared had happened at last. She would never be able to stop Severino from taking Pedro. What could she do, whom could she get to speak to Severino, make him give up the idea of sailing to São Luis? Antonia thought of

Father Dourado, and then remembered how old he was, almost senile; he would hardly have the strength to cope with Severino. What about the Mayor? She didn't even know him by sight. And did the Mayor have any special powers that could force that iron-willed, wrong-headed old man to listen to him?

No, there was no help anywhere; she must put her trust in God.

Next morning, as she watched the boy wash his face, grief and fear rose chokingly in her throat; just a few more days and he might be lost to her forever. She fought to keep back her tears.

'Your grandfather wants you to sail with him to São Luis,' she said huskily.

Pedro looked at her in surprise.

'Did he tell you that ? When are we going?'

The boy's face shone with pleasure. Minutes passed before she could trust herself to speak.

'Next Tuesday.'

'Good for Grandad!' Pedro said gaily.

Alone in the kitchen, waiting for the water to boil, her tears fell silently. Pedro was a child, he saw only the novelty, the adventure, he could never understand what it really meant. Back in the dining room she poured him his cup of coffee, trying to keep her hands from shaking. A little later, when Severino passed her his cup she summoned up the strength to handle coffee-pot and milk jug and wait on him with the same self-effacing care that she had always shown, even during the days when Celita sat across from him at the table.

Breakfast over, Pedro went whistling down the yard, a bird-cage dangling from his hand. Antonia began to clear the table, praying for courage to speak to Severino.

'What about the doctor, Severino? Hadn't you better go to see him before you leave?'

Severino wiped his mouth on the back of his hand and cleared his throat. Frowning, he looked up at her.

'I've been to the doctor.'

'What did he say?'

'He said I'm done for. Ready for the grave. If he had his way I'd stay at home and lie in my hammock until I'm laid in my coffin. The fool! The stupid fool. Lie in my hammock, give me this, give me that, shut the window, bring my broth, like a woman who's had a baby!'

He got to his feet, scowling, and hit the table with his fist.

'I'm going to show that conceited simpleton that he knows nothing, nothing at all. I'll never make it, is that it? I'm going to die between here and São Luis! Die Indeed! I'm going and I'm coming back, sailing my boat myself, just as I did when I was young.'

Antonia stood motionless and numb. Suddenly she felt incredibly old and defeated, as if she might collapse at any moment. Oh, God in Heaven, what now? She leaned heavily on the edge of the table and watched Severino walk to the end of the dining room and back.

'Didn't he give you any medicine?' she asked weakly.

'After all the nonsense he talked, do you think I'm going to pay any attention to him? The man's an idiot!' Severino's voice was harsh with anger.

'I threw his rotten prescription in the gutter where it belongs! And I should have told him what I thought of him! But never mind, I'll do it yet. He'll be hearing from me.'

Antonia let him rage; all she could think of was that nightmare trip to São Luis, Severino, lying mortally ill and helpless in his boat. Terror gave her strength to rebel; she said:

'You're still taking the boy? Even after what the doctor said?'

'I've told you, woman, I'm going, and I'll be back. That's exactly why I'm taking Pedro. If I weren't *sure* I'd be all right, I'd leave him behind. Or have you got the same maggot in your head as that damned doctor? You believe I'm going to drop dead, do you? Well, you're wrong.'

The veins stood out on the old man's thin neck, his face was twisted with fury; he stood in front of her, his raised hands clenched. The lines at the corners of his mouth seemed deeper than ever in his tanned face, and the white stubble hiding the obstinate chin made him look much older. His eyes had a fevered brightness.

Antonia turned pale and drew back; what if he were to die now, before her eyes, felled by the heart attack brought on by some thoughtless word of hers? She clasped her trembling hands.

'Severino, for God's sake, don't get so worked up! Forget what I said!'

He put his hand to his heart, panting for breath.

'I'm going,' he muttered between clenched teeth, 'Going and coming back.'

'Yes, yes!' She hurried to get him a glass of water.

Severino turned away, still scowling, and walked down the slope to the beach. Antonia, leaning on the back of a chair for support, watched him anxiously until she saw him reach the end of the pier. Then, dragging her feet in their old slippers, she shuffled toward the rocking chair and sat down, her hands in her lap, ice-cold.

It was a fine sunny morning, the sky was cloudless and serene; the hanging ferns swayed gently in the breeze. She had hung the pots herself, from hooks in the verandah roof, above the cage where Pedro's *corrupião** fluttered and sang. But she could only sit, trembling with exhaustion, oblivious to the beauty around her. She felt worn out. It occurred to her that possibly Severino might outlive her. The thought added to her torment. She was seventy, she had lived long enough, she longed to close her eyes and be at rest; nonetheless, during these last few years, she had prayed daily to be spared long enough to see Pedro started in some respectable (and safe) profession, where he could make his way. It would have made up for her long hard life of uncomplaining suffering, those wearing years of silent bitterness. But that hope was over. The old man had taken Pedro from her, perhaps to be lost at sea, forever.

'Oh, my God! Saint Lucy, pray for me!'

Looking toward the beach she could see, beyond the green fans of the coconut palms, the 'Fair Weather' at the end of the pier, and the sparkling crests of the waves; in the distance two sails stood out clear against the horizon. But a different

* Corrupiao: Songbird native to Brazil.

picture came in flashes before her eyes, a picture of the 'Fair Weather' drifting helplessly with no one at the helm, alone in the endless wastes of water. The waves reared up, higher than the mainmast; Severino lay unconscious on the steersman's bench. The 'Fair Weather' would soon vanish, sucked down by the insatiable ocean. Was there no help anywhere? Drops of sweat rolled down her forehead, she put her hands to her eyes to blot out the sight and set her teeth to stop the tembling of her chin. And then a fiercer anguish clutched as she thought, what if it happens at night, impenetrable darkness all around; inside the silent cabin only the glimmer of the swaying storm lanterns.

'Oh, no, dear God. No!'

Sobs shook her thin body bent forward in despair. If there had been any one else to see to the house and the meals she would have stayed there all day, weeping the slow painful tears of old age. But there were things to be done. Dragging herself to her feet, she looked away from the sea and toward the street. Where could Pedro be? She had seen him go down the yard carrying a birdcage. Why didn't he come now, since, in a few days, he was going away for always? Obsessed by the thought that she was about to lose him, helpless before the threat of death, she wanted him there, beside her, for every moment that was left to them. Antonia looked out of the living room window, went into the street; Pedro was nowhere in sight. She went drearily back to the kitchen, dragging her shapeless old slippers, sat down on a stool in front of the stove, and began to fan the embers. She felt defeated, shattered, sick of life. She thought of her own death, and found a seed of consolation in the thought. Once Pedro was gone, she would die. Old, weary, with nothing to live for, why go on suffering?

'I'd rather die. May God in His mercy please take me from this world.'

And before the day was over, weeping without sound, she packed Pedro's clothes in his suitcase. From time to time, crushed by the knowledge that, for her, all hope of happiness was over, she would stop and hide her face in her hands, stifling her sobs.

# CHAPTER X

Severino's eyes were on the glowing end of his cigarette, of which the morning breeze scattered the ash; the hand that held it lay quietly on his knee.

'Yes, I got here earlier today; that's because I came straight from home, didn't stop to see the boat. And would you believe it, the Cemetery gates were still locked. I waited a bit outside — I did think of climbing over the wall, but then I thought, 'Better not', and walked about the street awhile, smoking a cigarette, for company, you see, while I waited. People tell me I've got to stop smoking. Foolishness; no man dies before his time. Then, when I'd finished my cigarette, I though I'd ask the Keeper to let me have the key of the gate. He lives right beside the Cemetery, in that little house with two windows, next to the entrance. Oh, he was very polite, 'Not at all,' he said, 'I'll go and open it for you.' And he came along with me, begging my pardon and all. He wanted to know when I was going to São Luis. 'On Tuesday,' I told him. 'Well, Skipper,' he said, 'I'm going to ask you to do something for me. My daughter's going to São Luis to have her baby, and I want you to take her in your boat. We've already written to the Maternity Hospital and they're expecting her. She could have flown over in the Cessna, but she doesn't like flying, and, besides, it's so expensive! And the plane only goes over once a fortnight.' Poor girl, she tripped, you might say; it was a shotgun wedding, she was four months gone and beginning to show already. For all the good it's done her, poor child! The husband took off after the ceremony and nobody's set eyes on him since. Some people say he had a wife already. She cries all day long, her father said. And pretty, too. She doesn't deserve such bad luck. I said to her father, 'All right, I'll drop her off at Coronation Quay.' 'That's fine,' he said, 'She knows her way

57

about the town.' But this is just gossip. Let everyone mind his own business and God'll look after us all. About my health, now. It's not good. I'm a bit worse than I was, last time I came here. A tired feeling, and that pain, as if everything was tearing loose inside my chest, and I can't breathe. Nobody knows what it feels like. Antonia's on the watch night and day, she worries, and worries, and nags me to go to the doctor. 'All right,' I said, 'If it gives you any pleasure.' A fat man, wearing spectacles. Doctor Estefanio; you never met him. When he first came, you should have heard what people said, he could heal this, he could cure that, and books he had, and magazines, a real Doctor Know-it-all. Well, my dear, just as big a fool as the others. I'm sorry I ever went there. If regret could kill I'd be tucked away in the ground, like you. He took his time, poking and prodding, and there I stood, stripped from the waist up, with a black girl wearing a white cap staring at me. I even had to undo my trousers, I still don't know what for! I did all he told me to do, like a child. 'Show me your tongue!' he said. So I showed it to him. He asked me I don't know how many questions, I answered the best I could. Then he pulled my lower lid down and shone a tiny flashlight in my eyes. After that he told me to stand up and shut my eyes. Very well; I stood up and shut my eyes. Then I opened them when he told me to. He put his ear to my chest and said, 'Take a deep breath,' I felt like saying, 'Thanks, Doctor, good day to you,' and leaving, just like that. But I held my tongue and waited; I wanted to see what it would all amount to. Well, he made me lie down again and put something round my arm, something with a kind of watch on it, and he kept on looking at the hands. Then he felt for my pulse and kept his finger there, moving his lips as if he were praying, and looking at the watch thing on my arm. Finally, he told me to sit up on the couch with my legs dangling over the side, and you know what? He got a little hammer and tapped me on the knees, first one, then the other. And there I was, as meek as can be, and you know me, pretty short on patience, my dear! And when it was all over, do you know what he said? 'No travelling!' He said. 'No more sailing! You're to stay at home and rest.'

Rest! A man like me, Celita. You'll never know how hard it was to keep from knocking him down! I didn't go there so as to be told I was going to die. We're *all* going to die some day, the doctor as well. I went there to get something for the pain and the tired feeling. And all he did was scribble on a bit of paper and tell me to take it to the chemist's, and then swallow a pill every night before going to bed. What do you think of that? I wanted something to take the pain away; without the pain I can sleep all right, don't need any pills for that. Oh, but I was angry! But I kept a straight face, and nobody noticed anything. I was halfway across Market Square, still holding that bit of paper before I realized it; then I crumpled the thing up and threw it where it belonged, with the rubbish in the gutter. Now I'm going to show that doctor that I can go all the way to São Luis and come back, alive and kicking!'

Severino threw his cigarette away and looked at the burn on his finger. He licked it with the tip of his tongue, blew on it, laid his hand back on his knee.

'I wasn't paying attention, Celita, and let my cigarette burn down. Silly of me. That's another thing the doctor told me. 'Stop smoking,' he said, as if I were a boy, and he could tell me what to do. I pretended not to hear; no point in having a fight. I've been in plenty of fights in my time, but now I want a little peace and quiet, that's all.'

He crossed his legs and lit another cigarette absently, watching the bird hopping on the stone slab that covered the grave.

'It looks like Pedro's *corrupião*,' he thought, drawing deeply on the cigarette.

'I haven't told you the most important thing yet: Pedro's sailing with me on this next trip. Faisca's ill and can't make it. That's his business; *I'm* not giving up just because I'm sick. I've said I'm going and that's that. Besides, I want to show that doctor — he surely deserves a lesson, don't you think? If I didn't have Pedro, I'd go by myself. Before I went to jail I was always a loner. I was a loner when we met, remember? Oh, yes, I'll show that doctor all right, Celita, you can rest easy. By God's mercy, I'll make it to São Luis and back.'

59

He uncrossed his legs, examined the end of his cigarette, glowing brightly in the breeze.

'Antonia made such a fuss about Pedro's going with me that I lost my temper. She said the doctor was right, can you believe it? Just to stop me from taking the boy. I saw red then, I can tell you! Then afterwards, I felt sorry for her. Poor woman, she's old, part deaf—very different from the Antonia you used to know, Celita. And Pedro—well, Pedro's the apple of her eye. She never lets him out of her sight. Of course she does it for the best, but it can't be good for the boy. No, it can't be good for him! I want my grandson to be a *man*, Celita, tough, fit to take over the 'Fair Weather' once I'm gone. And it's time he started learning; how old was I when my father took me to sea for the first time? Thirteen! Just the same age as Pedro—no, he'll be fourteen come next month, and he's taller than me. When I was his age, I could hoist a sail, lower it and stow it away. But he's clever; he'll soon learn. If it hadn't been for Antonia, he'd have been to sea with me already. But she thinks up excuses all the time, so as to keep him ashore and home, idling. He's a good boy, it's a shame that he should spend the day just fooling about, and killing birds with a sling. At least, he's given up that crazy idea of being a priest! A priest, Celita! There's something else; his teacher at school gave him a box of coloured pencils, and he went mad about drawing. I managed to get rid of the pencils, by taking out one at a time and throwing it away. Not that he didn't draw nicely. But there he was, the sea in front of his eyes and he never drew a boat, a raft, nothing! Butterflies, a doll (you remember that trouble we had about dolls when he was little? A bad business!), a house, a bird, a church door, Saint George on horseback—they were all very good; people said they were pretty good, and Antonia, of course, thought they were wonderful! Well, that worry's about over. He only draws once in a while now, with an ordinary pencil, too.'

He noticed a group of people at the entrance to the Cemetery, and throwing away his cigarette looked at them curiously.

'There's a funeral coming,' he said to the grave. 'They must

60

be strangers, I don't recognize any of the family. They're coming this way. No, they've turned off, near Colonel Juvencio's mausoleum. The coffin's all white, it must be a young girl; God rest her soul in peace. Amen. Before I forget, I told the Keeper to have Mercedes' headstone whitewashed; yours is fine, dear, I always see to it that it's kept clean and tidy. And I asked him to take special care of this tree, I don't want you to have to lie in the sun. I told him, 'Seu* Neco Torres, I planted that tree myself.' And he said I wasn't to worry. After all, it's no trouble for him, and I'm taking his daughter to São Luis, aren't I? One good turn deserves another.'

He looked round at the group that followed behind the white coffin. They were slowly moving up an incline some distance away. He folded his hands on his knee.

'I didn't see Father Dourado at the funeral. They must be Protestants. Or else he wasn't able to come; poor old man, he's getting very low. After all, he's over eighty, eighty-two or three, if I'm not mistaken. I knew him when he first came here, still a young man, and he's always been my friend. We had that quarrel about Pedro, when he wanted to make a priest of the boy; we weren't speaking to each other after that, for quite a while. Then he came to see me, and we made it up. He's a good old man, a saintly old man. I always remember the day he married us—do you know how long ago that was, Celita? Thirty-nine years! Like yesterday, it seems; I can still see you going to church wearing your red straw hat. How time flies! Nearly forty years! But when I was in jail, time went so slowly; as for that Public Prosecutor, well, as far as he was concerned, I was a marked man. He did his best to make my life hell, even after he got to be Judge. His family hate me to this day. That swine, he never gave me any time off, like the others had; I was only allowed to come here once a month, to put flowers on your grave, and with a guard standing beside me. Twenty-two years shut up in a cell with a water jug, a tin trunk, a couple of old books. Faisca had a dozen deaths to account for; I had only one. But Faisca was allowed all sorts of

* Seu: Abbreviation for 'Senhor', a respectful form of address.

61

privileges that I never had. Well, it's over and done with, and here I am, my own man again. If it weren't for having to bring up Pedro and teach him how to sail the boat, I shouldn't worry about being ill. Except I wouldn't want to linger; I'd want to get it over with, and go where you are, through the mercy of God and Our Lady's intercession. Sometimes I wonder whether you'll know me again, Celita? Old as I am, and full of wrinkles? Why, I might be your grandfather, my dear! An old wreck, that's what I am. Time's been hard on me, girl, and I've never looked in a mirror since — I have myself shaved at the barber's and try not to look. Old age makes a mess of a man, believe me. Once Pedro's fit to take over the boat, I hope I'll die. Why should I live on and on, get to be like Father Dourado? That's no life for me. Sick, weak, my wits gone. God forbid it should happen to me. I'll go and see the Father before sailing; I do it once in a while and tell him my sins, although they're nothing to make a fuss about, Celita. I tell you everything I tell him.'

His bony chest lifted in a sigh.

'What I'm going to tell you now is a simple truth, my dear. You know me — I'm not a man to tell a lie. I want you to know that when I'm here, by your grave, sitting on the roots of the tree I planted with my own hands, I'm happy, I'm at peace, such a peace, Celita! I haven't found it anywhere else. And I believe that's what death is: peace. No wearing oneself out with longing, no struggling and hurrying. Life tires one out, you know, dear. And I'm getting very tired indeed. It looks like rain, I think — it *is* raining. I'd better be going. I'll come again when I'm back from São Luis. Sorry about the flowers; they're the only ones I could find, and I had to give some to Mercedes. I'll bring you more next time, prettier than these.'

As he left the Cemetery Severino met the Keeper, who was sweeping the pavement in front of the gates with a broom made of dry twigs.

'So you're leaving on Tuesday for sure, Skipper?'

'Yes, late in the afternoon. There'll be a moon that night, to see by.'

# CHAPTER XI

Father Dourado pressed the toe of his shoe against the concrete floor and pushed slightly to start the hammock swaying. His head rested quietly against a little pillow without the covering of a pillow-slip. He sat in the hammock, hands folded together, thumbs twiddling, and lifting his head, peered at Severino who had drawn his wicker armchair back, out of reach of the rocking hammock.

'Thank you, no, I don't want anything from São Luis at present. But if you should see our Archbishop, tell him that I'm getting ready to travel soon, very soon.'

Severino was startled.

'You're going on a trip, Father?'

'Yes. Yes indeed. But not by boat, Skipper. If I were going by sea I'd go with you, naturally. No, I'm just going—like this—' and his hand pointed up to the ceiling. Severino was still perplexed.

'You're taking the plane, Father?'

'Me? I'm not the kind of priest who flies about in airplanes, my son. God keep me from any such madness. No, the wings that are coming to fetch me are quite otherwise, Severino. Can't you guess? Take a good look at me. They're angel's wings, Skipper. I'm going to close my eyes down here and open them up there, before the face of God. Do you understand now? I'm on my last legs; at any moment—phtt—and nobody can say it isn't time. I've done what I had to do. Now I can rest. So tell the Archbishop to start looking for the man who'll take my place. But don't let him send one of these frivolous, vain young fellows. I want a priest, a real priest, a priest like me, Severino!'

Father Dourado raised a finger, measured off the tip.

'You've never heard that much gossip about me, have you?

I've never pissed outside my own pot, the Lord be praised! I can go any time, with a peaceful conscience. Yes, I can appear before God's divine mercy without a blush. Not that I haven't had opportunities to follow the path that leads to perdition. Oh, there've been plenty of those. But let me tell you, whenever the Devil tried a bout with this old man who's talking to you, he lost, hands down! He had the worst of it everytime, Severino! Yes indeed. I bested him every time, and gave him a good kick in the tail as well.' His dry chuckle was followed by a fit of coughing. When he had cleared his throat and gotten back his breath, the old priest sighed deeply, crossed his hands on his shrunken belly.

'Ah, my old friend, I need to get away, leave this planet behind me. There're things going on which I don't understand, and they upset me. Such shamelessness everywhere! There's never been a time like this. Sodom and Gomorrah were nothing, nothing! Look ahead, aside, behind, what do you see? Whoredom, whoredom! I've had enough, Severino!'

He put his hand to his head. 'Up to here, Skipper! In the old days, girls didn't as much as show their feet. Nowadays, it's foot, leg, thigh, everything, every bit of them's on show. Every bit, Severino! Even in church, in the presence of Our Lord Jesus Christ Himself. When I have to preach, God only knows how I manage to make sense. They can't even sit down with decency; the old women, who ought to know better, are just as bad. I don't know whether you're aware of it, but nobody comes to confession any more. I'm only needed to give them Extreme Unction — yes, they don't want to go without the Last Sacraments. But that's all they want of me, my friend. And I'm sickened by the evil gossip people bring me, whispering in my ear. Enough! I can't bear any more of it! There's only one thing I'd like to do: sit in the confessional with a good, strong whip and give them their penance myself, *crack*, right on those old women's backsides! Oh, it's enough, it's too much. They're worse than savages, they don't know the meaning of shame! Sin, nothing but sin everywhere, the sin of the flesh. *Retro me, Satanas!* The Devil is loose in the world, Severino, take my word for it. And have you seen the Rio magazines? Well, don't look at them. Naked women, nothing but naked women, showing their breasts. Yes, Severino! Making a show of their breasts, their navels, everything they've got! And who's behind it all? Who should it be? Old Sir Satan himself, no less. The sly old scoundrel, after sowing his seeds of perdition in the big cities, here he comes to destroy what he can.

'When he found that his temptations were wasted on me, and that he was face to face with a real priest, one who could take him by the horns and wrestle him down, he took his revenge by spreading his filthy plagues through my flock. Yes, my friend. Yes indeed. Out, foul fiend! Out! *Vade retrum!*'

In his growing excitement, Father Dourado had risen to his feet and pushed his spectacles askew. Now he sat down again in the hammock; the wizened face, red with rage, softened as the flush faded; he began to smile, showing two yellow teeth that overhung his lower lip. He felt in the folds of his cassock for his battered old silver cigarette case and matches, and Severino, for a minute, saw him as he used to look years ago, in the little adobe house behind the Cathedral, close-shaven, spruce in a a clean cassock, the silver shimmer of the case in his hand as he said,

'A cigarette, Skipper?'

Severino had walked into the room twisting his hat nervously in his hands; his shirt clung to his back wet with sweat. He had been there a couple of days earlier to let the priest know that he had been married in São Luis — a civil marriage only — and that he wanted to be married in church as well, as soon as possible. Father Dourado had agreed and everything had been arranged; the marriage would take place next Sunday, just after Mass. Why had the priest suddenly sent for him? Had he changed his mind about marrying them? Perhaps he had listened to lying gossip, some piece of ill-natured scandal such as rumour often started in small towns like this one. Still, the wedding couldn't be put off; what about the desserts glowing richly in the glass dishes, the turkey already seasoned, the sucking pig dressed for the oven?

Severino crushed his hat in his hands, straightened the soft

65

crown and crumpled it up again. He thought angrily,

'He'd better not tell me it's off. What kind of scamp does he think I am? I gave my word I'd marry her, and so I shall. You said you'd do it, Father, and you can't go back on it now.'

The priest got up from the hammock without saying a word, pulling at his lower lip with thumb and forefinger. He looked disturbed and somehow uncomfortable. He walked up to Severino, fiddling with his cigarette case, the silver gleaming brightly in his nervous fingers.

'You sent for me, Father.'

'Well, Skipper; it's this way: when we set a date for your marriage to the young woman you brought back from São Luis, I believed that you had put away the woman you had been living with up to now. Last night I was told that she is still with you. In fact both women are living under the same roof with you. Is that true, Severino? Are the two of them living with you?'

Severino met his eyes challengingly.

'Yes, it's true. They're both with me.'

'But, Severino! To keep your wife and your mistress in the same house, in everybody's sight! And you want me to receive you in church, for the solemn Sacrament of Marriage, knowing all about it? We aren't blasphemers, Severino!'

Severino stood amazed, his arms hanging limply at his sides, his mouth half-open; slowly his tanned face turned pale. Then his eyes flashed, and his words came pouring out, in a mixture of shock and indignation.

'Father Dourado! Don't you know me by now? Do you really think I'm such a scoundrel as all that? If I was really living with both women I wouldn't have come here and asked you to marry me to one of them. No, Father. I've got only one wife, and that's Celita, to whom I was married by the Judge in São Luis, last week. The other one, Antonia, she's what you might call one of the family now. She has her own room. If she thought she could live in the same house as the other one, what was I to do? She's got no home, nowhere to go, how could I turn her out into the street, a woman who's always been good to me, a faithful honest creature? As long as I live she can share my roof and my food, Father! And if, after what I've told you, you still won't marry Celita and me, very well; I'll take the girl and we'll get married somewhere else, by some priest who's not so ready to think the worst of me. I'll leave this place, Father, I'll sell the house, the pier, turn my back on you, and everybody else, and put my wife and Antonia aboard the 'Fair Weather' and just go and not come back, ever.'

Father Dourado's frown relaxed and the beginning of a smile played round his mouth. Severino was almost at the door when the priest spoke.

'Wait, Severino, we haven't finished our talk yet. And unless we talk things over, how can we agree? You're not going anywhere, my friend. You're not selling your house or anything of the kind. No indeed! Certainly not.'

He opened his cigarette case.

'A cigarette, Skipper?'

'No, thank you.'

The priest's cigarette hung loosely from his fingers, unlighted. 'You tell me Antonia accepts the . . . situation?'

'Yes, sir.'

'And so does the other young woman?'

'Yes, sir.'

'Each of them knows her place, and is content to stay in it?'

'Just so, Father.'

'In that case,' the priest said amiably, as he blew out the match and threw it away. 'Since both young women are in agreement, and no offence against public decency is being committed, I'm prepared to trust you, Severino, and perform the marriage. Bring the girl to Mass on Sunday. But no veil, no wreath, remember; a plain dress, my friend, the plainer the better. Right?'

'Right it is, Father.'

'Very well. Then you can go now, and God be with you.'

So many years had passed and now Father Dourado was a worn-out old man in a rusty cassock, with scanty wisps of white hair framing his wrinkled face. The cigarette case in his hand was the same, although the silver had dulled and turned almost black with age and use. His withered hand still held it

67

firmly, however, and snapped it shut with the same decisive click. The room, too, was the same; the glass-fronted bookcase, crammed with books, the old chest of drawers whose top was cluttered with medicine bottles, magazines and newspapers; along one wall was a little cane settee; there was a chair for visitors to sit in, and a ragged piece of carpet on the floor beneath the hammock. An English china spittoon stood by the wall.

The old priest raised his head to look at Severino, peering through the lens of his spectacles; smoke drifted up from the cigarette between his fingers as he gestured. With the tip of his shoe he pushed the hammock to and fro.

'Severino, you spend your days at sea, sailing between here and São Luis; you haven't a notion of what the world has come to. A horror, my friend. A horror! There's no room in it for me any more; I've got to leave this planet for good, since I can't understand it any more. No indeed. Not a thing. Why, even the priests are losing their heads, Skipper. Don't you believe what I'm saying? Well you ought to. Things are worse, much worse than you can imagine, Severino. Have you ever seen a priest wearing shirt and trousers instead of a cassock? Well, that's what they're doing now. And nuns don't wear habits either, Severino. Yes indeed. How can you expect me to understand such follies? Tell our Archbishop that I'm ready to go. Any time now, Skipper. You know — phtt — like that!'

His indignation gave way to a tremulous gaiety; he gave a little laugh, full of unexpected mischief. He put both feet down on the frayed carpet and the hammock ceased to sway.

'My friend, you know Dona Zita, the wife of Jeremias Pinto who's got that shop on Market Square. Always looking for trouble, remember? Well, I had to chase her out of here last night, and give her a piece of my mind as well.'

Severino wrinkled his forehead in thought. Three or four years ago, as he was sitting by Celita's grave, he had watched a funeral pass by, followed by a crowd of mourners. Surely it was Dona Zita who was being buried that day.

'Are you sure it was her, Father Dourado?'

'Perfectly sure, Skipper.'

'But Dona Zita's dead, Father.'

The old man stood up.

'How can she be dead if she was here last night? Yes indeed! She came in through that door while I was reading, she said, 'Please may I come in?' And there she was. When I saw her, I lost my temper, Severino, and let her know what I thought of her! Her dress, in front, was open all the way down to her belly. Every time she moved, you could see her bare breasts, served up in the shop window, you might say. 'Go and put on something decent, you old cow!' I shouted, 'How dare you come here like this? Get out!' And she went out without a word, her tail between her legs! Serve her right!'

He began to laugh, showing his two big yellow teeth, his hands on either side of his shrivelled little belly. As Severino got up to go, the priest squeezed his hand with all his remaining strength, and said gravely.

'Listen, Skipper; if you find a good strong whip, of the kind I asked you for, in São Luis, buy it for me. I'll keep it by me underneath the hammock, just in case. And I'll take it with me to the confessional, handy for touching up the backsides of those shameless old gossips!'

# CHAPTER XII

It is still night, deep and dark, but soon there will be a streak of brightness on the wall, thrown there by daylight shining through the crack of the window overlooking the yard; through the room's flickering shadows he will be able to see the outlines of the big wardrobe, Aunt Tonia's hammock, the chest of drawers on which the nightlight stands with its sinking, fluttering flame; then the wooden stool and tin chamberpot will become visible, and the dark shape looming on the wall turn into clothes, his and Aunt Tonia's, hanging from the rack by the door.

Before this happens, however, Pedro will lie quietly listening to the shrill singing of the *saracuras*\* and the lively crowing of the cocks. He is fully awake now, a night's sleep behind him. Usually, he falls asleep as soon as his head touches the pillow; sometime during the night he will stumble toward the chamberpot, still in a drowse, and back in his hammock, sink deep into sleep once more. When he opens his eyes again, he can hear the *saracuras*\* crying in the distance, where the woods are. He concentrates on listening, wondering how many have been caught in the snares he set for them yesterday evening. Or are they flying low over the still waters of the lagoon?

Through half-closed lids, Pedro watches the light grow stronger, while the shadows fade and disappear. The morning breeze ruffles the branches outside and blows between the tiles of the roof and beneath the door, heavy with mixed scents of wet earth and blossoming jasmine. An ox-cart moves slowly down the road beyond the yard, its wooden wheels groaning, as it does every morning at that hour.

When he was small, and afraid of the dark, Pedro would wet the hammock rather than get up to use the chamberpot. Full of terror, he fancied that if he opened his eyes he would see the white shapes, trailing transparent robes and dragging their tenuous chains, of the ghosts of the dead. And he would press his cold little hands to his eyes and hide his head beneath the covers so as to shut out the sight. Sometimes he could not sleep, and had to lie, rigid with fear, listening to the night noises he had learned to expect and dread: the hoot of an owl coming from the eaves of the roof, the whisper of the wind in the bamboo thicket, the sudden slam of a door, steps going slowly down the passage. He would call Aunt Tonia's name, softly at first, and then louder and louder until she came to him, in a bustle of alarm. He would ask for a drink of water but the old woman would guess his fear.

---

\* Saracura: A water fowl belonging to the Aramides mangle (Spix) species.

70

'You're not thirsty at all,' she would scold, straightening the covers, 'You're afraid. Whoever heard of a man being afraid? Nonsense!'

One night, Severino, in the room next door, lost patience.

'The boy's old enough to get up and go get his drink of water in the dining room.'

But on the following night, Aunt Tonia found a better way; she would leave the clay jug and beaker on the marble-topped chest of drawers, beside the little oil lamp. Before she went to rest, she sat down in Pedro's hammock and talked to him, stroking his hair.

'My son, it's silly to be afraid of the dark. Look here, through my hand at the nightlight.' And she hollowed her hand so that he could look through the curved fingers. 'See? Now if I close my fingers, there's only a little space left, here on top, where you can look, but the light's gone, isn't it? Are you afraid of looking? No, of course you aren't, it's only my hand, isn't it? Well, that's what God does to the world; he sends us night to make the dark for us to rest, just in the same way that I close my fingers and shut out the lamplight. If you're not afraid of things in the daylight, why should you fear them at night? They're the same things, Pedro; it's the same world.'

She looked straight at him, and her tired voice sounded stronger.

'I'm only a woman, an old woman, whose strength's nearly gone, but I'm not afraid. You're almost a man, Pedro, young and strong; no more foolishness, my son. If a weak old woman isn't frightened of the dark, well, neither are you. A man has to *be* a man, Pedro.'

And in fact, after that, his night fears began to seem comical, even though, when he woke just before daybreak, he continued to lie waiting anxiously for the first streak of brightness on the bedroom wall. Each day that dawned, even the misty, chilly mornings, held a special enchantment; he would listen to the twitter and chirp of the birds while he thrust his feet into his leather sandals and washed·his face, swallow his breakfast hastily, clean the *corrupião's* cage and give it fresh water and birdseed; then he would run down the

71

slope and out of the yard, and not come home till lunch time.

Seeing him at the dining room door Antonia would say:

'I wish I knew what you've been up to all morning.' Pedro would smile and shrug his shoulders.

'I've been here and there, Aunt Tonia.'

Once, when the Bishop was on a pastoral visitation to the little town and had ridden into the crowded Market Square, mounted on a splendid white horse, while church bells pealed a welcome, Pedro's half-forgotten dream of becoming a priest came alive again. Lost in the crowd, he saw the Bishop alight from his horse at the foot of the Cathedral steps, and minutes later found himself standing by the sacristy door, without knowing in the least how he had reached it, enthralled by the pomp and colour of the episcopal vestments, glittering in the lights of the High Altar. On the week following Pedro was back in the sacristy, asking for Father Dourado. The priest came and listened to him in silence. Then he said firmly:

'The last time I spoke to your grandfather about this, he turned me out of the house. No, my son, I'll never mention it to him again. Wait until you're grown up; you can come to me, then, and if you have a real vocation, well, so much the worse for your grandfather. I'll put the cassock on you with my own hands! Yes indeed! Myself I'll do it, and no one else.'

However, before a month had passed, the fabulous American Circus came to town and paraded through the streets, complete with brass band and tame elephant. And Pedro had to admit to himself that it would be even more exciting to be like the tall blonde broad-shouldered man in breeches and boots who flourished his whip in the middle of the ring, and made the seal balance a large ball on its nose! As for the acrobat in his spangled tights, swinging through the air to the rub-a-dub-dub of portentous drums! The boy watched breathless with parted lip and wide eyes — what a glorious life, wandering from town to town surrounded by music, brightness and applause! It was just as well that a few days later, as he leapt from branch to branch of the jackfruit tree he missed, fell, and nearly broke his arm; but in spite of the bruises, he still dreamt of owning a trained seal, some day.

They sat together in the dining room one evening, Pedro and Aunt Tonia. She was hemming a dress by the light of the storm-lantern hanging on the verandah; he was sitting at the table, leafing through an old magazine.

'Aunt Tonia.'

She stopped sewing, looked up at the boy with her dark soft eyes.

'How can one get hold of a seal, Aunt Tonia?'

'A seal?' she said in astonishment. 'You mean that big fat fish with whiskers?'

'That's the one,' he agreed.

"You want a seal? To keep here at home?'

'Yes, I do.'

The old woman returned to her stitching. 'Now, Pedro, please! The bird's quite enough, it gives me plenty of trouble as it is.'

During his four years in school, Pedro learnt easily, so much so that, during his last year, if it had not been for the extra drawing lessons his teacher gave him, pleased to find a pupil of more than average gifts, he would have cut a lot of his classes so as to be able to climb to the top of one of the crags along the beach and sit there dreaming and watching the colours of the afternoon slowly change to the broken purple lights of evening. When he was given a box of crayons as a prize for school work, he tried to put down on paper the subtle shades of all the beauty garnered during those long afternoons of patient watching, while the taste for solitude took root within him.

And then he lost his cherished pencils one by one; how it came about he could not think. All he knew was that he was left eventually with an empty box he could not bring himself to throw away, and an aching memory of the quiet hours spent at the dining room table, intent on line and colour, while Aunt Tonia hovered over his chair, and murmured admiringly,

'Whatever'll he be up to next!'

Her footsteps fell softly on the bare wooden boards. Sometimes she would say gently,

73

'That's not what your grandfather expects of you, my son. You were born to be a boatman, like your father, and your grandfather. Your family belongs to the sea, and you mustn't forget it.'

He could hear the old woman's deep-fetched sigh break the silence of the room.

'If I had my way there'd be no more going back and forth between here and São Luis. The sea was made for fish, let them have it then. The land and the man; they were meant for each other.'

Pedro's hand stopped, left the drawing unfinished. He looked up at Antonia.

'Auntie, what was my father like?'

'Well, now, you've got me muddled. If I knew how to draw the way you do, I'd draw his picture, and you'd like the look of him, of that I'm sure. He was a big man, like Nagib who owns the haberdasher's shop on Market Square, but without the moustache and the belly. And much younger, of course. Oh, a fine young man, as handsome as could be . Once your mother had set eyes on him, during the procession in honour of Our Lady, Help of Sailors, she never looked at another man. It had to be him, or no one. And the Lord knows, there were plenty after her. The street outside was never quiet, young men coming and going and making eyes at her; and she would get annoyed and shut the window in their faces. But they always came back, wouldn't give up until she got married. And then, when your father was lost at sea, they came back again.'

A silence fell; Pedro rested his hands on the drawing that lay on the table-top.

'Aunt Tonia,' and he raised his eyes to her face, 'did nobody ever hear of him again?'

'Never again. We were having a spell of bad weather, it rained and rained, the waves reached higher than this house, the wind never stopped blowing. There were boatmen in plenty who stayed ashore, waiting for better weather. But not your father; he'd made his mind up, and put out to sea, storm and all. Your mother, poor girl, kept a candle burning before Our Lady, Help of Sailors, until the hour of your birth, always

74

hoping that he'd come back; there were nights when she'd get up out of her hammock, crazy with joy, crying, 'Vicente's back!' But the house would be dark, no sound anywhere, the door shut; it had been only a dream. Back she would go to her hammock without a word. I'd feel so sorry for her, I'd lie awake and cry and cry, trying not to make a sound so that she wouldn't know.'

Pedro sat without moving, his eyes on Antonia; another silence fell.

'A boatman's life isn't easy; he's always in danger.' She said finally, looking out towards the sea.

The salt breeze blew softly, playing with the graceful fronds of the hanging ferns.

'Were you never afraid that Grandad wouldn't come back?' He asked, getting up from the table.

'I got accustomed to his coming back.'

Antonia held back the sigh that lifted her breast.

'He always came back; he might be a day or two late, sometimes a week, but in the end, he always came, and I stopped being afraid.'

Pedro walked round the table and picked up a magazine that lay on a wooden rack. He sat down in the rocking chair and began to turn the pages. Antonia rested her hands on the sill, her back to the window and the sea beyond it.

'Your grandmother Celita used to spend hours in that chair, reading magazines, just like you.'

'Why did Grandad kill her?' The boy asked abruptly. Antonia straightened up and put her hands to her face.

'What was that you said?' She quavered, trying to gain time.

'Why did Grandad kill her?' He repeated stubbornly, raising his head so as to watch her face.

'Who told you that?'

'I've known it a long time. At first I thought it was a lie, and I hit the boy who said it to me at school. Then—then there were other people—the only thing I don't know is why he did it.'

Antonia felt her hands grow cold and her thoughts whirl in confusion. Mercedes, as a little girl had asked her the same

75

question. She tried to remember what she had told the boy's mother. Twisting her fingers together, she answered slowly.

'Nobody really knows why, and I never tried to find out, myself. The truth is, your Grandad loved her very much. And she was beautiful; really beautiful. She looked just like one of the girls you see on the magazine covers. Anything she wanted your grandfather gave her, he did whatever she asked him. And then, one day, he lost his head and killed her. But that's an old story; let it rest. It's over and done with. I can tell you one thing, though, there's not a man fit to be mentioned in the same breath as your grandfather. He's one in a thousand. What happened to him might happen to anybody; there's no going against fate.'

The sunlight fell upon the birdcage and the *corrupião* began to sing. The old woman turned in the direction of the verandah.

'You're giving him too much birdseed, Pedro, this is the first time I've heard him sing all day. Aunt Noca says that a bird that's fed too much won't sing.'

# CHAPTER XIII

Loose sand creaked and spilled beneath Severino's feet; his tall thin shadow kept pace with him, step for step, as he walked toward the house. His long legs seemed to move of their own volition, their owner's thoughts far away. Unconscious of the quiet street down which he walks, oblivious to the illness that is a torment to his tough old body, unaware of the present, he is back in the small whitewashed police station, sitting hunched in a chair, his bowed face resting on his hands. Father Dourado arrives as though driven by a whirlwind, his spectacles pushed back on his forehead, the ankle-strings of his drawers hanging down over his shoes.

'Godofredo', he says imperiously to the Police Commissioner, 'you must leave me alone with the Skipper for a few minutes. And don't let anyone in. Not anyone!'

The Commissioner moves away heavily, his loosened tie hanging from his open collar, making for the room next door, and beckoning to the clerk and the two policemen to follow him. The priest closes the door and turns the key in the lock; then he turns to Severino, who, motionless on his chair, has been watching him all the time.

'But, my dear friend! What is this? What happened? Antonia came to me in tears, and I ran here as fast as I could, but I can't—I don't *want* to believe what she told me! Say something, anything, tell me what happened!'

Severino glanced at the window, his eyes blank with grief. On the pavement outside, beneath the blinding sunlight, he saw a crowd of inquisitive faces peering into the room. When, almost at a run, he had reached the police station to give himself up the Commissioner, who sat listening to him open mouthed, letting his cigarette go out, the street had been empty. Then he had seen Nagib arrive, the fat owner of the haberdashery shop, in his shirtsleeves, his braces hanging down over his trousers, his eyes alight with curiosity. Then the newspaper seller, Anastacio, his shabby cap pulled down to his grey eyebrows. Suddenly the freckled face of Dona Cleonice, the school teacher, appeared between the two men, her prominent bloodshot eyes, like a gamecock's, fixed on the windows. Severino turned his head away so as not to see who else might come. But when the Commisioner called in the clerk to take his statement, he glanced dazedly at the window again and saw that a crowd had gathered already buzzing with gossip, their eager eyes glued to the window.

Severino rose from his chair and faced the priest.

'It's true, Father Dourado. What Antonia told you is true, to my grief. My Celita is no longer of this world, Father. She's with God, and it was I who killed her.'

A sigh gathers hugely in his chest, his face is haggard. The

77

priest closes the window, shutting out the prying eyes. He cups his chin in his hand; his eyes are bright with a mixture of indignation and pity.

'But the Lord had said 'Thou shalt not kill,' Severino! And you know that we must *all* obey God's commandments!'

Severino sits down again, his body stooped, his head in his hands, blinking his eyelids.

The closed window has darkened the room but there is still light enough for the priest to see his way as he walks to and fro between the clerk's table and the Commissioner's, and the two chairs with their cane seats. Severino shrinks back into his corner, his elbows on the arms of his chair, his face hidden in his hands, rocked by a storm of sobs.

Outside, cartwheels bump over the gaps in the stone-paved road; the carter cracks his whip and curses his donkey.

Severino said strongly, above the noise,

'I've wrecked my own happiness, Father, I know that, but there wasn't another way out of it. If I hadn't killed Celita now, she'd have gone back to being — what she was before. I had to chop it down to the root — the evil. There was no other way.'

The priest turned sharply round and faced Severino in silence, looking at him with eyes gone suddenly hard.

'What do you mean?' he shouted suddenly. 'No other way! Of course there was! Why didn't you come to me first? Was it too much trouble to walk over to my house? Haven't I always shown you the right way, the Lord's way? In God's name, Severino, answer me!'

Severino held his aching forehead in his hands. His voice shook as he answered.

'You would have told me to wait, to be patient, that I was making too much of it. And I'd have given in; I'd have agreed with you. And Celita would have become a whore again, gone with one man today, with another tomorrow, and my name, that I gave her, mocked, dishonoured. No, Father, it was too much. And I loved her. As I never loved another woman. Oh, I thought it all over, before making up my mind. When I saw that there was still time for me to take *that* way — I took it, father. I accepted the ruin of my life, the sorrow — and now, here I am.'

The priest pushed his spectacles down on his nose and clapped his hands to his head.

'But why, Severino? Why didn't you speak to me? I'd have opened your eyes for you, shown you what to do!'

Severino shook his head slowly.

'There was no other way, Father.'

Suddenly Celita was there before his eyes, her long hair dripping, her pale lids half-closed, stretched on the big double bed with, on either side, a candle burning, that Antonia had lighted. His bowed body shook; tears ran through the fingers hiding his face. Beneath the knitted brows the priest's eyes were wet also, as he walked slowly toward the window and back again.

'Father, it hurts . . . it hurts so,' said Severino, lifting his ravaged face.

'It was I who told Antonia to ask you to come here. Don't be too hard on me.'

He felt the priest's hand on his shoulder and his voice saying gently:

'Forgive me, Severino. It was a shock to me, you see. But it's over. Trust me, my friend.'

He drew up one of the chairs and sat down facing Severino.

'Tell me everything. Show me your poor sinner's soul all bare, Severino. Confession brings God's comfort with it.'

Severino passed his handkerchief slowly over his face. He began to speak hesitantly, twisting the handkerchief in his hard hands. Then the words came in a rush.

'Father, when we married, we took an oath; if she was unfaithful to me, ever, I would kill her. I swore I'd never look at another woman; she gave me her word she'd never look at another man. If she ever caught me with another, she'd have the right to kill me, too.'

'You had no right to take such an oath,' the priest said softly.

'But we did, Father. Taking God to witness.' There was a silence. Father Dourado leaned back in his chair; there was a jingle of spurs in the room next door.

Severino went on,

'I gave her everything a man can give his wife. Love, money, food, a home, new dresses, magazines, high-heeled shoes, a hat, I took her out to enjoy herself, for a year and a half, she had everything, Father. I just didn't take her to São Luis with me on any trip I made because we had agreed it would be better not to. You know very well what she had been in São Luis, a common whore. I couldn't have borne to walk down the street with Celita holding my arm and meet the eyes of the men who had slept with her. So I told her once and for all, and she agreed. 'We'll get married,' I said, 'but you'll never set foot here again.' I wanted to keep her away from temptation, Father, and that's the truth. What the eyes don't see the heart doesn't long for, they say. At first, it all seemed strange to her, living in such a small place, after São Luis. That was only natural; life was slower, she wasn't accustomed to it. And I always brought her back a present from São Luis; a dress, a bag, a pair of shoes, and plenty of magazines for her to amuse herself with while I was away. And every time I came home, it was like a celebration; Celita would be waiting for me at the pier, in her best dress, her earrings, her pretties, everything.'

Once more Severino wiped his face with his handkerchief; he took a deep breath and faced the priest again; Father Dourado put a hand on his knee encouragingly.

'Go on.'

'If you'll excuse me for mentioning it, Father, she'd no reason to complain of me—as a man, I mean. Whenever she wanted to, no matter how often, I was ready for her. And she liked it, Father. Forgive me; these are things I shouldn't be telling you, things a man ought to talk about only with his wife. But I've got to tell you everything, every single thing, so that you can put yourself in my place.'

The priest settled his glasses so that the lens fitted centrally over his eyes.

'Quite right,' he said gravely.

'As for cooking and housework, Antonia did everything; quiet, kind, helpful, you know what she's like. Celita had nothing to worry about, she lived like a queen, waited on hand and foot, with me always trying to guess what she wanted, so that I could get it for her. And then, when she was expecting the baby, there was nothing I wouldn't do. Mangoes, you know, Father, December's the time for mangoes. Well, it was August and she wanted to eat mangoes. I found mangoes for her, in August. I don't have to tell you more. I wanted a boy, to take the boat over from me, when the time came. The child was born, a girl, I was so disappointed I could have cried, seeing that God's will was so different from my own. But I hoped for another child, and God would surely send me a son, next time. Celita said 'No!' She couldn't face giving birth again. I felt something thick in my throat, the blood buzzed in my ears, but I remembered her screams when the child was born, and I said to myself, Wait.'

Severino paused for breath, his damp hands lying on his knees.

'After our daughter was born, Celita never waited for me at the pier again. I thought, 'She's not well yet, besides, she's got eyes and ears only for the baby now, her husband's been forgotten for a while, never mind.' It hurts, but I got over it. And when I saw the baby lying in her cradle, that round pink little face, and waving her fists about, I felt — well, if I felt that way, and I was the father, what didn't her mother feel?'

The priest nodded, and moved in his chair, crossing his legs.

'That's where I was wrong, Father. Celita hardly ever looked at the child. It was Antonia who cared for her, night ånd day. When the child cried in the middle of the night, it wasn't her mother who got up, in the cold dark, to see to her, it was Antonia. Celita went right on sleeping. I began to ask myself: if she doesn't come to wait for me any more when I come back from a trip, who does she dress up for? It took me a couple of days or so to come up with the reason. Before Celita was well enough to get up, she made up her face and did her hair as if she were getting ready to sit by the window looking into the street and showing herself off. Well, I told myself that she liked to look pretty, that was the way she was. For a little while I felt better, and tried to forget that I was jealous, that I

81

was sore with jealousy, Father. But I was wrong once more. As wrong as could be. You'll see.'

He passed his hand over his face from forehead to chin, breathed deeply through his open mouth, as if he were choking.

'It was a little while before the baby was due, that *Dr*\* Genesio, married, father of two children, was sent here to be Public Prosecutor. I brought him over, with his family, from São Luis. On the way over I felt uneasy, noticing what a careful dresser he was; his trousers without a wrinkle, a fresh pair each day, his shoes shined, his curly hair full of brilliantine, initials on his shirt, a big gold watch, a fine ring on his finger. You know why I was uneasy, Father? I had a feeling Celita would take a liking to him. I never said a word about it to anyone, a man doesn't talk about such things, and I'm not given to talking anyway. Now, listen. When the boat came up to the pier, Celita was there waiting for me, big belly and all. Dr Genesio got out, then his wife and children, then the other passengers, while I was stowing the sails away. When I came ashore, what did I see? There was the son of a bitch talking to Celita — I didn't even have to introduce them, they were joking and laughing together like old friends! I kept my temper, not wanting to give people anything to gossip about. And anyway, she was pregnant, so I had to be patient with her. All right, so I was. Anyhow, there's no harm in talking and laughing. I made as if I saw nothing, said not a word, and we went home, she and I, arm in arm, as if nothing had happened.'

Severino stopped, drew a long breath.

'Am I tiring you, Father?'

'No, my son. Continue.'

'A few days later, just before dawn, the baby was born. Before she was really fit to get up, Celita was on her feet, painted, scented, wearing her earrings and tortoiseshell comb, one of her Sunday dresses, and buckled shoes. And with a new trick of standing by the window and looking out into the

\* *DOCTOR*: In the interior of Brazil, any man who has taken a degree whether it be medicine, law or engineering, is known as 'Doctor'.

street. That's when I grew really jealous, a married woman, young and pretty, at her window all day that's a bad business, Father. The first time I caught her at it, I told her what I thought of it. She cried, she screamed, she sobbed that she was dying, and ended up by fainting. So I gave in.

'What harm was there if she looked out of the window awhile? It's such a quiet street, just someone passing by now and then. So there she was, always at the window, like a picture in its frame. She wasn't interested in anything else. First thing in the morning there was Celita at the window. She took to putting a chair next to it, so she could sit down when she got tired of standing. And there she stayed until the afternoon sun shone full on that side of the house. She'd go away then, but come back as soon as the sun had moved on. And always dressed and perfumed, painted and jewelled—she might have been going to a party.'

Someone outside the door tried the handle; the Commissioner's voice asked,

'Will you be much longer, Father?'

'Wait a little, please. I haven't finished yet,' the priest said irritably. He gestured Severino to go on.

'Now, Father, can you imagine what I felt when I heard that Dr Genesio had rented a house near mine, and that the window of his living room—a room full of books, with a hammock hanging in the middle of it—its window faced the window of my living room, the window where Celita spent all her time. I tell you, Father, my blood turned to ice. I felt as if I'd been knifed in the back. I thought, I'll get the rifle and shoot him now—that son of a bitch, that devil. It's what he deserved. I went out into the yard and walked along the wall, keeping my head low, so as not to be seen, hoping he'd come out and then I'd let him have the bullet that'd send him off to settle his accounts with God. You'd have thought he'd been warned; he never showed up at his window at all. It was better that way. He'd have been a dead man otherwise, and me in jail and Celita free to run wild all over again. I let the days go by, I went to São Luis and came back, once, twice, three times, and I suffered, Father. I suffered, as

I've never suffered before. I couldn't get my food down, and as for sleep — I went about, my head in a whirl, without a word to say. And Celita at the window. After the baby was born she was even lovelier, her eyes bigger and the lids full and smooth, her bosom rounder. As for waiting for me at the pier — never again! And it hurt, it felt like a raw wound inside my chest! One afternoon, as I was coming into the house through the back door, I heard a horse galloping down the street. I looked out through the dining room window: it was that scoundrel, on a fine sleek horse with a chestnut mane, his feet in silver stirrups, curse him, riding by my front door, while Celita was at the window. I ran to my room to get the rifle-and then thought better of it. I called Antonia aside and asked what she knew of it. But Antonia hadn't spoken a word since my wedding day; she would never so much as open her lips except to eat. I begged her, I threatened her, not a word would she say. Mumble in her throat and shrug her shoulders, that's as far as she'd go, in spite of all I could do. That was another sleepless night, things going round and round in my head. The worst of it was, Father, I wanted Celita, I wanted her worse than ever. It must have been just before dawn, I couldn't bear it any longer, I got out of my hammock and felt my way over to hers, I said her name and asked her to come to bed with me. And she refused me. Father Dourado, Father Dourado, that was the first time in my life it had happened to me! I can still hear her voice, soft and sleepy, saying, 'No, Severino, not now, get back to your hammock!' And so I did. But not to sleep. I sat and watched the darkness fade and the morning grow bright. And I knew the truth at last: Celita didn't love me any longer. She shouldn't have done that to me! It wasn't right, was it? All day long I thought, My God, what'll I do now? Until I was sure that unless I put a stop to it then and there, I'd end up with horns sprouting from my head, like poor Norato; you know him, Father, he can't show his face anywhere without people jeering, making jokes — My God! And so today, not an hour ago, I killed Celita, my poor Celita. Better to see her dead, as I saw her, than to know that Dr Genesio had lain with her. That can't ever happen now. And now here I am, the unhappiest man on earth, as you can see, Father. I thought of sailing off in my boat, the world's wide, after all; but then there's the baby, and poor Antonia, who shouldn't suffer, she's not to blame for my misfortune. At first I thought I'd get rid of the scoundrel as well, but he's got a wife and children, why should they pay for his sins. Celita's dead, and I'm finished. And I came to give myself up, before they went after me to catch me, as if I were a runaway Negro. I killed and I must pay for it. I didn't kill in hot blood, a moment's madness, I thought it over carefully before deciding; I admit it, and I'm not going to try and find excuses. I'm not sorry for what I did; Celita died before she could go back to being a lost woman, a lost soul, Father; that's all.'

Father Dourado said:

'Did you know that she went to church today and made her confession?'

'Yes, Father, I know. She died with her soul as clean as a new-born child's. This very minute, by God's mercy, my Celita is in Heaven, while I'm still here on this earth carrying such a load of sorrow, it's as if all the grief of a lifetime were weighing me down.'

Severino was staring fixedly at nothing, as though his body were quiet as stone. Then he bent forward convulsively, his face buried in his hands, his shoulders heaving. The priest pushed his chair back and once more began to pace backwards and forwards, striking his open palm with his clenched fist.

'What an awful thing, dear God! Dear Lord, what an awful thing!'

He stopped in his walk, pushed his spectacles up on his forehead and laid a compassionate hand on Severino's shoulder.

'Courage,' he said, 'you still have much to bear; yours will be a long expiation, my son. But ask God to forgive you the crime you've committed, and trust me to help you carry your cross.' He paused, his hand still on Severino's shoulder, and added, 'I'll arrange for the burial.'

Severino's eyes were like dark bruises, as he drew the back of his hand against the swollen lids.

'I've already done it, Father. Before coming here, I went to the undertaker's and then to the Cemetery. And I've ordered flowers — a lot of flowers.'

Father Dourado turns the key in the lock, twists the metal doorknob and opens the door; the clerk, the Commissioner, and the two policemen file back into the room. The Commissioner walks over to the window and throws it wide, and Severino, raising his eyes for a moment, sees the crowd outside the window, every face in it turned to his.

As he walks down the long street the sand continues to creak and spill beneath his feet. When he turns aside, further ahead, his shadow keeps up with him, a slender, transparent, tireless companion, slipping along the bamboo thickets on his right.

## CHAPTER XIV

He had nearly reached the house when he felt that the pain was about to squeeze his heart once more. He could have hurried on and called to Antonia for help, but he preferred to lean on the fence and wait for the spasm to pass. He stayed there a long time; he might have just been watching the light sparkling on the water.

'When I'm at sea there won't be anybody to help — I'll have to look out for myself,' he muttered, and then held his breath as the claw of pain struck deeper.

Luckily, it was soon over, and he could feel the air come slowly back into his lungs while he went on leaning against the fence waiting for his pulse to steady.

There was the 'Fair Weather' at the end of the pier, its sails clewed up, ready to put out to sea and head for São Luis. Away, where the bay opened out into the ocean, two dark sails stood out against the skyline; it was too far to make out the smaller jib sails. Gulls swooped between sea and sky, linking the green of one to the blue of the other in delicate arcs of flight. And the sunlight broke into spangles on the crests of the waves.

Severino stood and looked at the blue and green stretching to infinity before his half-closed eyes. He might have feared it; he felt instead the quiet confidence that always came to him when the wind filled his sails and he made for the open seas, his hand on the helm of his boat. He had been doing it for more than fifty years; he had been in danger, often, fought his way safely out of many storms, without ever the thought of dying at sea entering his mind.

Back at the house, the *corrupião* was singing in the corner of the verandah, and Antonia came into the sunny dining room to greet him, drying her hands on the hem of her skirt, her eyes bright with a joy she tried to hide.

'It looks as if you won't be able to sail after all, Skipper,' she said.

'Why not?' he asked in annoyance.

Antonia's smile disappeared, but she could not hide the relief in her voice.

'As soon as you left, Souza's daughter came to say she's changed her mind about going to São Luis. Then Rufino, the ironmonger, he's not going either. The Tax Collector's daughter came by to say the same thing. Ruth, Dona Paula and Seu Artur's stepdaughter, Norma, and Aristides, who was so crazy to go last week, they've all left you the same message. And even Dona Eufrasina left just now, saying to tell you she was sorry but she can't go over this month after all.'

Standing at the door into the passage, about to take off his hat, Severino understood in a flash what had happened. Dr Estefanio had talked; he had spread the news that he, Severino, wasn't fit to sail; he might die before the journey was over.

Antonia let go the hem of her skirt and straightened up. Joy

87

had gone and fear took its place.

'Don't go, Severino', she begged.

He took a step forward and hung up his hat on the peg. Looking at her over his shoulder, he asked,

'Have you got Pedro's bag ready?'

'Yes.'

There was an interval of silence. Finally she said,

'Are you going just the same?'

'I'm going.'

'With only four passengers?'

'There's the cargo to deliver as well.'

Antonia sat by the window sewing; there was still light enough to see by, and she concentrated on her stitching, trying to forget her wretchedness. But sewing did not help; her fingers trembled and her stitches were in the wrong places. At times she tried to straighten her drooping shoulders, and steady her quivering lips. Finally she sat idle, her needlework forgotten, in a kind of dull despair, while the light dimmed and shadows gathered about her.

'Oh, God! What will become of me, left all alone!'

Growing older, she had put on flesh. Not much, but enough to add a fullness beneath her chin above the long neck ringed by two deep grooves.

Sunk in the armchair, dressed in a loose white bodice edged by a lace frill and full gathered skirt that reached to her ankles, her small figure seemed stouter. Between the wrinkled eyelids, her eyes looked out, dark and without lustre.

The night wind filled the room with the heady scent of jasmine, hanging in clusters on the wall. Presently the sound of the waves breaking on the beach would grow stronger, as fireflies drifted through the dark and the first stars began to shine beyond the growing moon. It was time to light the lamps. But Antonia sat on; she was weary of work in vain, of hope cheated, of life itself. As the last light faded from the sky the *corrupião* began to sing. Tears stung behind her lids, she took up her needlework and dropped it again. Her lips moved and a faint murmur disturbed the silence.

'I was so relieved! I thought that God Himself had sent

them, all those people who came to say they wouldn't be travelling after all! Now there's no help for it. Nothing'll make him change his mind, not even if there's only Pedro left to go with him. And I can only sit here, doing nothing to stop him! Dear God, what's going to happen? Oh, please, show me a way to stop him. Have mercy on an old woman! What have I done to deserve this, Lord!'

The slow tears came heavily from beneath her lids, and she wiped them away one by one. Then she gripped the arms of her chair abruptly and sat up, staring into the dusk with eyes gone suddenly dry. What if Severino were to die before putting out to sea? Pedro would be safe then — but she shook her head, fighting temptation. How could she have wanted to buy the boy's life with his grandfather's death? She crossed herself. 'God forgive me for such a thought!'

But in spite of herself the thought returned, insidious, insistent. She strained her ears listening for the stir of Severino's hammock in the bedroom next door, but the rustle of the guava tree's leaves shut out all other sounds. What if he lay dead there already? A shudder of guilt shook her; she wished for nobody's death, least of all Severino's. She got painfully to her feet, her heart thudding, and felt along the walls in the dark toward the bedroom. A red streak of light shone through the partly open door, and she looked in, seeing first the little oil lamp burning on the chest of drawers, and then Severino himself, lying with his head resting against the head of the hammock and his feet on the straw matting that covered the floor. She ran into the room in panic, calling out his name, and praying incoherently to Saint Lucy.

'It's my fault, oh, it's my fault if he's dead!'

But the hammock swayed and Severino turned his head toward her. She smiled in relief.

'How do you feel?' she asked, still tremulous with fright.

'Much better. I had a nap and it's rested me.'

She stood beside the hammock looking down at him with an anxious tenderness she did her best to conceal.

'Would you like me to make you some herb tea?'

'Yes, I'd like that.'

89

Slowly she went to the kitchen, feeling the weight of weariness returning to her body. But first she lit the storm lantern, peered into the yard and then down the passage. Where had Pedro gone? He had eaten his supper in a hurry and left; probably he was up in Market Square, hanging round the door of Neco's bar, watching the men play billiards.

'He'll be back late, I'd better leave the door on the latch so that his grandfather won't hear him come in,' she said to herself, fanning the embers of the stove.

The lump of charcoal grew red, little flames sprang out from the short lengths of wood. For the hundredth time she wished he was beside her, safe in the circle of her arms, as in the old days when he would cling to her in fear while she pretended to scold the ghosts away, saying in an angry voice 'Go away from here! Leave my boy alone!' And traced the sign of the cross over herself and the child.

The child was now a man, taller than his grandfather, and no longer feared the shadows that danced on the wall, beyond the lamp's weak glow. He had grown up all of a sudden. From one day to the next his trousers shrank above his ankles, his voice broke and a fine down grew at the centres of his mouth and on his chin.

'Nobody would think he's only thirteen,' she thought, fanning briskly. 'And he still hasn't stopped growing. Why, he'll be having to stoop to get through the door!'

Her hand fell quiet. How could Pedro go on growing when in the next few days he might be drowned at sea? She made an effort to shake off her obsession.

'God is great, God is good. The boy'll come back to me.'

But what if he didn't? Once again she closed her eyes and saw Severino lying unconscious, the 'Fair Weather' reeling before the wind. Our Lady, Help of Sailors, hear me! Blessed Jesus, have mercy! Nothing but sky and water, and a boat with a dead man aboard, and Pedro.

Antonia waited for the water to boil and went on with her prayers. Without them she felt lost in a gloom as deep as night itself. It was so dark that she could no longer see the trees in the yard outside. The long sigh of the waves along the empty beach reached her through the blackness. Her lips moving without sound, she dropped a pinch of herbs into the pot and waited for the water to simmer. Her bones ached, she was too tired to stand. She sat down on a stool in front of the stove, her eyes on the brewing tea, murmuring the Lord's Prayer under her breath, intent on supplication; bubbles winked in the water, a small cloud of steam began to rise, the pot boiled over, hissing. She started up, seized it by the handle, and reached for the strainer. 'There won't be anyone to do this for him,' she thought wearily, 'when he's away from home and the pain gets hold of him — what then?'

Slowly she shut and barred the window, rinsed the pot and put it away, and let the fire die out. She picked up the mug of tea by its handle and went through the dining room into the passage; her steps quickened; as she stood by the hammock, holding out the mug to Severino, the expression on her small wrinkled face was almost cheerful.

'Drink it while it's hot,' she told him, and smiled in happiness as he took the mug and sipped the fragrant tea. 'I want to ask you to do something for me,' Antonia said, as he handed back the empty mug. 'No, it isn't about staying home,' she added hastily, meeting his eyes.

'Well,' he said at length, 'what is it?'

Antonia lowered her eyes and held the mug tight in both hands, as though wondering what to do with it. Then she lifted her head and looked straight at the old man.

'Take me with you.' She said imploringly. 'Don't leave me here all by myself. I want to be near you if the pain comes back. Who'll make your tea for you, if I'm not there? Let me come too!'

Severino stretched out his bare feet, feeling for his slippers. His forehead creased in a frown as he looked up at Antonia.

'I know what you're after. It's Pedro that's on your mind, he's never let go of your skirts before, has he? You'd never let him, if you had your way. Well, this time he's going with me: two men together, you hear? You've managed to put it off long enough — much too long! I said he's going, and so he is; with me, away from your coddling. He belongs in the boat; you belong here, in the house. That's the way things are, and don't you try to change them.'

# CHAPTER XV

When Antonia saw Doctor Estefanio beckoning to her from the door, a shiver ran up her spine and her feet turned cold. A fat man in a white overall, his eyes small and bright behind his spectacles, was nothing to fear but she felt her stomach contract, and the thoughts she had so carefully built up into words broke up and scattered, leaving blankness behind them.

'Come in,' he said as she stood motionless in the corridor. 'It's your turn now.'

The neatness of the white room and its unfamiliar objects made her feel worse. This was a place where sick people came hoping to be cured. There was nothing wrong with her, thank God; so how could she answer him when the doctor asked her what her illness was? Her legs grew weak, and as she sank into the armchair placed in front of the doctor's desk, beads of sweat sprang out on her forehead; her hands rested limply in her lap. She watched the doctor sit down at the desk opposite her, and look back at her, smiling.

'I know what you've come to ask me for, Dona Antonia,' he said, chuckling. 'You want me to give you something that'll make you young again, isn't that so?' His plump cheeks creased with laughter.

His manner made Antonia feel better. She put her hand before her mouth to hide her answering smile.

'If only that were all, Doctor!' She replied easily. 'But I haven't come here to ask you to prescribe medicine for me.

No; it's something quite different.'

Doctor Estefanio sat back in his chair and picked up a pencil. Tap-tap, tap-tap, went the pencil on the table-top. Drops of sweat rolled slowly down Antonia's face, and she fidgeted, smoothing her skirt above her knees.

'It's this way,' she said, her restless hands moving aimlessly in her lap as she looked up at him, and then looked away again. 'I'm Antonia—Skipper Severino's Antonia,' and her eyes slid away once more, 'and I know he's been to see you a couple of days ago. He told me so himself. I'd asked him to come, you see. Obstinate—well, that's hardly strong enough, Doctor, you know him! He's always been like that. Once he makes up his mind, nothing's going to change it, not even if Our Lord Himself were to come back to this world and speak to him in person. May God punish me if I'm lying! But I'm telling the truth: that's the way he'll be until he dies. You saw him, you looked him over and gave him a prescription, didn't you? Well, he threw it away, and as for resting—he'd rather die than take a day off. And the worst of it is that tomorrow afternoon, at sunset, he's sailing for São Luis—alone—as ready to face the sea on his own as if he were still a boy in his twenties! So you see how it is, Doctor; perhaps you can tell me what to do about it?'

'Dona Antonia, I must tell you the truth. Severino isn't fit to sail. I told him so. But he didn't believe me. And yet, he's in a bad way; his illness is very serious, very serious indeed. I must be frank: if he tries to go to São Luis, it isn't just madness—it's suicide. I listened to his heartbeat through the stethoscope; shocking, Dona Antonia! Shocking! His heart beats once, hesitates, stops, and begins again; then the same cycle starts once more. One of these days it'll stop for good; what if he's at sea when that happens?'

Antonia gathered her failing strength and looked at him intently.

'What do you think I ought to do, Doctor? Please, please, think of something! I've begged him not to go, but it's no use, he won't listen to me. And now he wants to take the boy along, his grandson, who's only a child! I've asked the blessed Saints to help, over and over again, and now I've come for your advice!'

Doctor Estefanio took off his glasses slowly and laid them down on the desk.

'It's a delicate matter, Dona Antonia. Professionally, I've done all that I can. The trouble is, people know all about Severino's temper, and they're afraid of provoking him. One can't very well use force to stop him from sailing; it would have to be his own decision. Why don't you speak to Father Dourado? Coming from a priest, his advice would have special weight — maybe Severino will listen to him; he certainly won't listen to me.

Market Square lay white and dusty in the sunlight; it occurred to Antonia that before going to Father Dourado's, she might look in at Faisca's house. Perhaps he had shaken off the fever. If so, she need worry no longer, Severino would have an experienced companion, who could take over should the old man be suddenly stricken.

There was no answer to her call, so she pushed open the door and entered the house. Lucas Faisca's voice sounded feebly from the bedroom.

'Excuse me for not getting up, Dona Antonia,' he said tremulously as she came into the room, 'I'm in a bad way; sometimes I think that I'll never get up again. The fever's got hold of me all right, this time; it goes off sometimes, for an hour or so, but then I'm so weak my legs won't hold me up. Poor Chica, she gets no rest at all. She's out now, looking for some herb or other she thinks'll be good for me. She's wasting her time, Dona Antonia! Short of a miracle, nothing's going to do me any good!'

His face had fallen in and the skin had a greenish tinge. His eyes looked back at her dully from their sunken pits.

'Saints in Heaven! He's nothing but skin and bone.' thought Antonia, horrified. She tried to think of something encouraging to say and could find nothing.

'The Skipper's not well either, Faisca. I'm so worried.'

Sunk deep in the hammock Faisca struggled to draw himself higher and shivering pulled the fringes of the hammock over

94

his wasted body. The afternoon light fell on the waxy pallor of his face, the thin sharp nose and sparse pointed beard.

'At least he can still swallow his food,' he said breathlessly, peering at Antonia from between shrivelled lids. 'I can't get anything down at all. Chica tries her best, but the food just sticks in my throat.'

Antonia drew her shawl closer about her shoulders. Shaken by disappointment and exhaustion, she yet would not give way to the weakness that made her hands tremble and her legs unsteady. There was still Father Dourado; she would go to him now. Quickly she took her leave.

'I only came by to see how you were getting on, Seu Lucas. Please tell Chica that if she needs any help, she's only to ask me; that's what friends are for! I've got Severino to look after, but I can always come over if you need me; just let me know.'

In the doorway, she stopped for a moment and turned toward the sick mam.

'You know that he's sailing for São Luis tomorrow, without anyone to help him. His mind's made up, and that's that. I don't know what to do, Seu Lucas! Dr Estefanio told me it was madness, plain madness, for Severino even to think of it. He might die on the way! So I'm trying to find someone who can help me in this trouble, talk to him, make him understand. I'd hoped you could have done something about it, he thinks a lot of you, you know.'

'Me?' He moaned feebly. 'I'm helping myself, Dona Antonia!'

'You could at least give me some advice,' Antonia persisted, paying no attention to the sick man's groans.

'If he's set on going, let him go. In this life it's each man for himself and God above us all, Dona Antonia. I'd go with him if I could; we can only die once, what does it matter where it happens?'

'But he's taking Pedro along.' She had said it at last.

'So much the better, it's time the boy learnt his trade. Leave it all in God's hands, Dona Antonia; no man dies before he's called.'

Back in the street she looked about her, trying to find a short cut to the priest's house that would save her going all the way uphill to Market Square. But the steepest way was also the quickest, and the old woman eventually reached the top out of breath and hardly able to stand. Slowly she made her way along the side of the Square until she reached the little house tucked in beside the Cathedral where Father Dourado lived. She clapped her hands loudly outside the door as a signal to whoever might be within.

'Who's there?' came the priest's cracked voice.

'It's me, Father. Antonia.'

'If you want to go to Confession, wait inside the Church. If you just want to speak to me, come in!' he called back.

Father Dourado lay in his hammock, cassock pulled up above his knees, plaited leather sandals dangling from his feet which hung over the edge of the hammock. He was holding a newspaper close to his eyes; other papers, neatly folded, lay in a heap on his lap and were stacked beneath the hammock. He looked up at his visitor over the top of his spectacles and waited for Antonia to come nearer.

'Things are a bit untidy, Dona Antonia, but please take no notice. Old people's houses always smell of mice, haven't you noticed? How are you getting on? And the girls? Tell your son-in-law that I haven't been to see you all because I'm getting too old for going out!'

Antonia stood beside him wondering how to put him right.

'Father Dourado, I'm—you're mistaken, Father, this is Antonia. Skipper Severino's Antonia.'

'Severino?' The old man repeated doubtfully, 'Are you sure? Well, sit down at the table, but be careful, one of the legs is loose. Antonia! Yes indeed! I can see you properly now. How you've aged! More than I, even; time hasn't been kind to you, child. Or is it Severino that's too hard on you? One or the other, isn't it? But you look a wreck, my daughter, and that's the truth. What a difference, my friend, from the young Antonia!'

He beckoned her nearer. 'Come closer, I can't see your face, your back's to the light. There, that's better. All right, now you can talk. But don't tell me your sins, please! I'm sick and tired of listening to people's sins.'

Antonia sat uneasily on the edge of her chair, plaiting the ends of her shawl between her fingers. The priest's voice, suddenly loud and harsh, frightened her.

'Come on, speak up! We're both too old and ugly to sit staring at each other without a word! What have you come here for? I hope you're not going to ask me for money. Money! No indeed. Nor for an introduction to the Mayor, who's a nasty little man, I want as little to do with him as possible. Speak up, here I am — don't keep me waiting; I want to finish reading my newspaper.'

Antonia blinked, forced a smile, and began to speak.

'I need your help badly, Father. Severino wants to — it's madness what he wants to do! I've come to ask you to stop him!'

'Madness? Severino? He's lost his mind again, has he? Isn't that what you said?'

He turned sideways in the hammock and half the pile of newspapers on his lap slid rustling to the floor. His mouth had fallen open, showing the two yellow teeth that stood forlornly in his lower jaw.

'Madness, you said?' Antonia nodded, her wrinkled cheeks quivering, her eyes full of tears.

'Yes, Father! It's sheer madness, that's what everybody says! He's sick, very sick, and yet he wants to go to São Luis, all by himself, without anyone to help. And he means to take his grandson along. Pedro, Father Dourado! For the love of Christ and Our Lady, help me to stop him! He's going to die at sea, and Pedro'll be drowned, Father!' The tears brimmed over and rolled down her cheeks; she paid no attention but continued to look at the priest, her face distorted by grief; Father Dourado, calmer now, and more collected, looked steadily back at her.

'Is that what you mean by madness, Dona Antonia?'

'Yes, Father.'

'I thought you meant something worse, much worse. Dry your eyes, daughter, it upsets me when people cry.'

But the tears continued to trickle, shining in the creases of the haggard old face. The priest said firmly:

'Come, Dona Antonia; let's consider it carefully. In the first place, who said that Severino was so ill?'

'The Doctor said so.'

'Doctor Estefanio?'

'Yes, Father.'

The old priest smiled crookedly, and held back a chuckle.

'Well, well; the Doctor knows as much about medicine as I do about astronomy! It's due to him and his knowledge that I've given Extreme Unction to a lot of people who've since risen from their deathbeds and are going about their business every day. If he's told you that the Skipper's at death's door, lift up your hands to Heaven in thankfullness, Dona Antonia! All it means is that Severino's going to be with us quite a while longer! I'll be leaving this world before him, daughter, and so will you. He'll be one of the mourners at our funerals, you may be sure!

'There's only One who knows when death'll come for us, Dona Antonia, and it isn't the doctor, with the bits he's learnt in books, here and there, it's Him, with His arms spread out wide on the Cross there'—he pointed to the Crucifix on the wall—'Looking down at us all. Until He calls you home, stop worrying and tell Doctor Estefanio to—well, pay no attention to him. Yes indeed. Just tell him so.'

A smile began to show through the old woman's tears, she no longer sat slumped in her chair. The priest got to his feet, letting the papers fall carelessly on the floor. He sat down again in the hammock, still facing Antonia.

'Severino came to see me, yesterday or the day before.' he said, 'He looked fine to me; as hearty as I've ever seen him. Strong, colour in his cheeks, the picture of health. Let him go; I'll be responsible for his safe return. Let him take his grandson, too. And peace be with you, daughter; Our Lord Jesus Christ, who can hear me as I speak, will be with them.'

Antonia patted her eyes dry, smiling, her eyebrows raised in surprise and hope.

'Oh, Father! Are you quite, quite sure?'

'Absolutely sure. As certain as you and I are talking here together. Severino'll see his hundredth birthday, Dona

Antonia, and very likely go beyond it. I'm telling you the truth as an angel might speak it. Now wipe your eyes, you look even uglier when you cry!' He rocked in his hammock and laughed, the cracked old voice full of mischief.

'Tell Severino that he'll find the whip I ordered at Santos' shop, on Long Beach. I want a good strong one, the best there is. There'll be a discount if he tells Santos it's for me.'

Antonia, her hands busy with her shawl, forgot her worries and grew curious. 'Father, may I ask you why you want a whip?'

'Didn't Severino tell you? I want that whip beside me in the Confessional; instead of giving them so many Hail Marys to recite, or telling them to say the Lord's Prayer, when they start talking to me about their mean little sins—unchaste thoughts, evil thinking, evil speaking—out I'll come, whip in hand, and lay it on their backsides as hard as can be, the miserable sinners!

'One, two, three! One, two, three! And there's an end to sinning, Dona Antonia! We'll end up a model parish, you'll see!'

As he said goodbye, he exclaimed, looking at her from beneath bent brows,

'Tell me something, daughter. Has Severino ever married you? I want the truth, now. Remember, you're speaking to a priest.'

'No, Father. He never did.'

'So, after all these years, you're still living together in sin? After you brought up his daughter and his grandson;'

'Yes, Father.'

'There you are,' shouted the old man in his harsh voice, 'living in a state of sin all these years! Can that be right? Of course not! No indeed! Well, daughter, what with my good whip ready to my hand, let's see if he doesn't marry you. Oh yes, he will! I'll whip him into marriage, never fear!'

# CHAPTER XVI

One small window overlooked the prison courtyard, but through the other a glimpse of sea showed between the bars; Severino, his world reduced to the four walls of his cell, would stare at the strip of blue and then close his eyes and make believe that he was back in his boat, alone on the ocean's broad breast, surrounded by sky and water beneath the 'Fair Weather''s wide sails, spreading in the wind that blew fair for São Luis. But his lowered eyelids would grow heavy and he would drift into a doze, only to wake suddenly from an interval of short and troubled sleep. It was with a shock of surprise that he would become aware once more of his surroundings; the hammock slung in the angle of two walls, the old trunk, full of his clothes that Antonia had brought him, standing below one window; underneath the other, a table of cheap wood, with his oil lamp and pitcher, some old magazines, two books that had lost their covers, and the tide time-table from his boat which he had asked for at the beginning of his imprisonment. From a nail on the wall hung a calendar, its gaudy picture the only note of colour in the cell; half the pages had been torn off already.

At first he used to tear off a leaf, each morning, and put it away in the table drawer. That way he could count the days he had already spent in the cell, he counted them over and over again, but soon wearied of it, and threw them all away, crumpled into paper pellets, through the bars of the window. Twenty years. Was he to count every day, for twenty years?

'I killed. Now I've got to serve my sentence, that's all', he would think, trying to force himself to accept the monotony, the loneliness, the loss.

His body needed exercise, so he would walk the length of his cell, up and down, until he tired, or else did a few exercises,

100

push-ups, knee-bends, before the cold bath, taken in company with the other prisoners, in the bathroom at the end of the courtyard. Back in his cell, overcome by the old longing for the sea, he would stand at the window peering through the bars at the bright streak of blue until his eyes ached, watching the *igarités* put out to sea. At sunset he would be there again, watching their return, one by one.

When Severino's prison life began Antonia came to see him nearly every morning; she brought him food, told him about his daughter, gave him news of his old trade. Remembering how far it was from his house to the jail, he felt the effort would be too much for her. One visit a week would be enough; however, she always found a reason for coming unexpectedly, to ask his advice or tell him of some new happening, sometimes with a flower in her hair, or wearing a new dress, her best shoes, her gold bracelet and chain.

Severino kept his usual morose silence, and never seemed to notice the flower, the dress, the bracelet. Little by little she went back to wearing her faded old dresses, her hair drawn back plainly, caught at the nape by a cheap tortoiseshell clasp. As for the gold chain and the bracelet, she put them away in her trunk for Mercedes to wear some day.

She came one afternoon, obviously with something important on her mind, and called out to Severino through the window opening on the courtyard.

'I couldn't wait for my usual day, Skipper; I've got good news for you! The black marble slab for Celita's grave has arrived, that you sent to São Luis for, and I've had the epitaph carved on it; Father Dourado wrote it himself. It's been put on her grave already, and it looks fine, Severino! Just what you would want!'

He wanted to thank her for her care, her zeal, her strangely innocent thoughtfulness, but the words would not come. He felt for a cigarette, struck a match, and squinted at her silently through the smoke.

The truth was that, in spite of his misery, Severino had to admit that he had nothing to complain about. Outside, Antonia looked after his affairs, showing such tact and attention, that he could hardly believe it. Nevertheless, the first week of his imprisonment had been appalling. Away from his home and his boat, shut into the tiny room in the cellar of the police station, his unhappiness had been such that he had thought of killing himself, knowing he could not bear much longer the dark solitude between the damp oozing walls, stifling in the stench of rotting excrement and sour urine that came from the privy next door, a single privy for all the prisoners, of which the overloaded plumbing had ceased to work.

He was taken down to it, that first night, by a policeman who never said a word and silently locked the door once he was safe inside. He had accepted it as a deserved punishment, sitting elbows on knees, and head buried in his hands, on a hard wooden bench; against the background of darkness he could see, over and over again, Celita's look of terror as she died between his powerful hands. Once dead, peace had returned to the delicate features; memory worked both ways and could also summon back the serenity of the girl lying as if asleep on the big bed, wearing the pink dress she would be buried in. He blew out the lamp so as to weep more freely; the darkness seemed to ease his tears. Bent double in the blackness of the stinking cell, he wept as never before for his loss, untouched by regret. He had planned her death deliberately, with cold foresight, seduced her by trickery into death, out of a love which he had never felt nor ever could feel for any other woman.

Father Dourado came to him again before the week was out. After one gulp of fetid air, he rose up, calling for the guard.

'Go up and tell the Commissioner to come to me *here*. Right now. At once. No excuses!'

'My friend', he said to the Commissioner as the man arrived out of breath, 'How can you lock up a human being in this unspeakable place? I haven't been here more than a few minutes, but I'm already half suffocated. Can you bear this stench? No! No indeed! Of course you can't; nobody could. Severino can't possibly stay here, it's out of the question!'

'I'm only carrying out orders, Father.'

Father Dourado lost his temper.

'Orders? Whose orders? Who told you to leave Severino to

breathe this poisonous stink? Whose orders, my dear sir? Who was the monster who was cruel enough to give you such an order?'

The Commissioner hesitated, looked about him for inspiration, and finding none, said reluctantly,

'It was Dr Genesio, Father.'

'The Public Prosecutor?'

'Yes, Father. He came here and gave special orders that Severino should be put in this cell. I told him that the privy was blocked up; none of the prisoners would put up with it. He shouted 'A convict does what he's told. Put the man there. I'm the only one who gives orders around here.' So what could I do? He's got the authority, we just do what he tells us.'

Father Dourado clenched his fists, trying to contain his rage. Finally he said through clenched teeth.

'Kindly tell Dr Genesio that unless Severino is removed from this hell-hole to the big jail, this very day, and given a cell in which he can survive, I shall preach a sermon tomorrow — Sunday — which will teach him a thing or two.'

Severino was taken to the jail two days later; he stood at the window of his new cell, watching the *igarités* make for home in the fading light of sunset, and tears of thankfulness dimmed his sight.

Little by little he lost all notion of time, and became accustomed to his walled-in existence. The sea was infinite and that was where his real life took place, between sky and water. But would he be strong enough to endure the endless empty hours that stretched ahead, ten years, twenty years, perhaps thirty years? Or would he give way to the temptation of the noose hanging from the hammock hook and end it all at once? There were days when the thoughts of escape became torture, as he watched the sails leaving the quay. Head bowed, he would tell himself softly again:

'I killed. Now I must pay for it.'

The nights passed, either in timeless stretches of dreary insomnia, eyes open and staring at the dark, or curiously brief and restful; there were nights when once he had settled himself in his hammock, lying sheltered beneath the plaited fringes, the lamp extinguished, he would open his eyes to the light of another morning, splashes of sun on the walls of his cell. But the days were bad; his existence in that tiny space, useless and unproductive, was agony to him. He had hung his old pocket watch by its cheap metal chain from the hammock hook. He would take it down, wind it, put it to his ear, listen to the tick-tack, tick-tack, and yet he could have sworn it had stopped. Even the second hand circled with infinite slowness. Worst of all, he did not know when his trial would take place. Who would undertake his defence? Nobody had told him anything. He lived out his days and nights, ignorant, idle, good for nothing.

Often a sickening feeling of loss came over him, the memory of Celita, gone for ever. He would shrink into a corner of his cell, his head in his hands, fighting to keep back his tears. In his unspeakable desolation, he would try to re-create the very texture of her body, the look in her eyes, the mouth so eager for his own, the long loose hair, the subtle intonation of her voice. She seemed to flow from his memory's open wound, taking shape with merciless clarity, so that he would squeeze his eyes shut so as not to see her, his thoughts in confusion; the only thing that seemed clearer and grew stronger with every day that passed was the bitterness that seized him at the thought that he had been compelled by fate itself to kill her.

A few days after Mercedes' first birthday Father Dourado got permission for Severino to be given two hours' leave of absence from the jail, so as to visit his daughter. Instead of going home Severino chose to spend the afternoon by Celita's grave around which the roses had begun to bloom behind the marble coping. He had spent more than he could really afford on the elaborate tomb under which she lay, in the shade of the casuarina tree, surrounded by flowers. It was not only a monument to death but a memorial of love; the thought was a comfort to him and his guilt seemed somehow lessened. Even when he was back in his cell the feeling persisted; all hope of happiness was over, but his misery seemed less crushing.

It was that same night, quite late, when all was silence, that he began to sense that Celita was there with him in his cell. The lamp's small flame flickered suddenly; he looked about him in surprise. The air was still, with no breath of wind. And yet suddenly his nostrils were full of the scent of her body. He breathed in deeply, and looked about him once more. It was stronger than ever, the penetrating odour, as of flowers after rain, that used to cling to her after her bath. Had there been a sudden gust of wind, heavy with the scent of rain-washed gardens? Any why had he never noticed it before? Beneath the lamp's glass shade the flame wavered again, responding to some unknown breath. A shudder ran coldly up his spine. His heart beat crazily, his eyes widened and shone suddenly with a strange light, half fear, half joy. He sank down into the hammock, shut his eyes and began to speak.

'I know it's you, Celita', he said softly, with absolute conviction. 'I can't see you but I can feel you near me. Oh, I would have known you, no matter how far you were. I remember. I *know*. It was your breath that made the lamp flicker. I pray for you night and day, asking God to give you peace and wisdom. Above all, wisdom, my dear. Where you are now, they've no use for scatterbrains. Watch your step; take Our Lady for your model, stay as near Her as you can. Stick to the really good souls, Celita, forget the others. And don't hold it against me, my darling. You'll see I was right to do what I did; you'll see it more clearly every day. If I hadn't put a stop to your love affair — it *was* a love affair, Celita, I saw it with my own eyes — what would have happened in the end? All right, let's say that that swine of a Prosecutor (if I were to tell you how badly he's treated me, you wouldn't believe it), let's say that he really was in love with you, which I don't believe. He'd have left his wife and children and gone off with you. Did you stop to think what it would mean? All the trouble, all the scandal, it would have caused? Would it have been right? No; never! You'd have ruined two lives, mine and his wife's, not to mention the children — what about them, Celita, and all the suffering they'd done nothing to deserve? I'd be willing to bet you never even gave it a thought. And Mercedes, Celita? Did you think I'd let you take her away — my own daughter? How could you ever think it! Never, hear me now: never. If you'd gone to the end of the world to hide, you and that man, I'd have followed, I'd have found you out, I'd have killed you first, and then him, and brought my daughter home. Yes, Celita! I take my oath before God that's what I would have done.'

He peered through half-closed lids at the lamp; its bud of light shone steadily. His head sank back against the hammock and for a while there was silence. The odour of flowers, freshened by rain, grew stronger, and he shut his eyes and went on, his low voice heavy with sorrow.

'Celita, that son of a bitch meant to make a fool of you, that's all. He was from São Luis, he knew you'd come from a brothel there. All he wanted was to make a whore of you again. Was that right? No, never! Did you think that once I'd given you my name, you could go back to your old trade? Well, if you ever thought so, you didn't know anything about your husband, my dear. And you were the mother of my child. Was I going to let Mercedes' mother become a tart? Sit down with my arms folded and wait for my horns to sprout? Ah, Celita, how wrong you were! But I warned you, didn't I, before we were married. I told you what sort of a man I was, I never tried to make out that I was an easy, good natured fellow. I told you, in plain words, that if you ever betrayed me, I'd kill you. And I gave you the right to do the same to me. Didn't I? And didn't you cling to me, crying and swearing by God and Our Lady that you'd always be faithful? How could you, how *could* you, after being married to me by the Judge and in Church, after having borne me a daughter, and never anything to worry about, with Antonia to look after everything, how *could* you look at that man twice? I killed you, Celita, and I'll say it again: I have no regrets. There was no other way. I had to do it before it was too late. Oh, I thought it over a lot before making up my mind. Many a night I lay awake, with you sleeping quietly beside me. ·I would look at you, rosy in the lamplight; so lovely, Celita! Oh God, I'd say to myself, how can I ever do it. But it had to be done; it had to be done. God Himself could see that I *had* to do it. I prayed, I begged the Saints to make you wise in time. But no;

106

day after day there you were at the window, all dressed up and full of smiles. And what was I? A tame cuckold. I, Severino, a boatman, like my father and grandfather before me! It was more than I could bear. Only death could put an end to the evil: so I killed. And now, here I am, I don't know for how many years. Did I deserve this? No; I didn't. But I broke the law and must take the consequences.'

Slowly he raised his head and looked around him. Each thing was in its accustomed place, enfolded by silence. The breeze touched him lightly, he saw the flame of the lamp quiver and sink. Beyond the open window, the courtyard was a rectangle of shadow pressing against the iron bars. Faint with distance he could hear the notes of a guitar? fainter still, the far-off barking of two dogs. And always the sound of the sea, rising and falling incessantly, with now and then a muffled crash as a wave reached up and broke against the rocks that raised their spires above the beach.

Severino leaned back against the head of the hammock, looking absently at the calendar on the wall. Still that tantalizing scent of rain-wet flowers; he breathed it in as deeply as he could.

'It's the same every night,' he went on in his monotonous undertone. 'Just the same, Celita, except when there's a storm. I try to pretend that I'm in my boat, at sea, alone; it helps me to bear the life I have to live here in jail. But there're times — well, I don't know how I can stand it. I try to keep busy during the day; you'll never guess what I'm doing now. Building ships in bottles! That's the truth, Celita! I used to do it as a boy and now I've gone back to it. Time goes so slowly, each hour's as long as a week of days. I pray to God they don't send me to jail in São Luis? I'd rather die. Here, at least, I'm near your grave, I can see Antonia and the child, and when I look out of the window, I can see a bit of sea. In São Luis I'd have nothing, and there isn't a soul there who cares about me. Not one. Here I've got Father Dourado, who helps me in every way he can. The man's a saint, believe me. A *good* man — there're no bounds to his goodness. It was he who told me that I'm to be tried next week, please God. Get this

107

waiting over with. Do you know what Dr Genesio is up to? He's going to try and get me the maximum penalty: thirty years in jail. Thirty years!'

He put a foot to the floor, gave the hammock a shove to set it swaying, and lit a cigarette.

'Well, those two houses I bought, when I was making enough to save, they're both let and the rent'll keep me going. It isn't much, but it'll do. I've had offers for the 'Fair Weather', but I'm not selling. Not my boat. If I get a short sentence, she can wait for me at the end of the pier. If not, let the sea rot her, and take her. I'll buy another boat once I'm free. And Mercedes has grown into a beautiful child, Celita! She was a year old last week.. Looks just like you. Plump, rosy, and Antonia says she's no trouble at all, almost never cries. I hope she'll have plenty of sense; that's the only thing I ask of God for her, to make her grow up a good, sensible girl. They gave me leave to go and see her today, but I went to the Cemetery instead, to see your grave. It's just the way I want it. And I'm going there every time they let me out. Like that, you'll know that no other man could ever love you as I do. It'll be that way as long as I live. I'll love you until the day of my death.'

He gave the hammock another shove, threw away his cigarette, and lay back. His eyelids felt heavy. The rocking motion lulled him, and gradually sleep overcame him, a sleep that blotted out his thoughts and extinguished the perfume of petals opening after rain. He never saw the lamp's tiny flame tremble and go out, blown into darkness by the cold night wind.

# CHAPTER XVII

Antonia has been deaf in one ear since last Christmas, when she caught a chill going home after Midnight Mass. She has taken to lying on that side when she goes to bed, keeping the good ear free to listen to the night noises of the sleeping house. But it happens sometimes that, in her weariness, the window slams or the wind punishes the trees in the yard, without her waking. When the morning comes, and she sees the traces left by the storm, she says to herself in excuse, 'I must have gone to sleep on my good side last night.'

But this time she wakes up with a start, a little after midnight; someone had given the hammock a shake, she was sure of it. She lifted her head, turned her good ear to the room, looked about her. Silence. The sough of the wind blended with the murmur of waves along the sand, and she could hear the ticking of the clock in the dining room. The light from the lamp's opalescent blue shade threw a ring of brightness on the chest of drawers' marble top and struck gleams from the tin plate beneath the water-jug. On the shadowed wall the picture of Saint Lucy looked down on the candle blessed by Father Dourado, which burned steadily, stuck in a saucer in a little pool of melted wax. In the angle of the room beyond the chest of drawers Pedro lay beneath the fringes of his hammock, sunk in sleep; on the floor beside him, discreetly covered by a sheet of paper, stood the chamber pot should he need it during the night.

Antonia continued to sit up uneasily, glancing around her with a frown.

'I know I felt the hammock shake. Maybe I dreamt it; but then I almost never dream. And if I had, I'd remember it.'

She shrugged her shoulders; her tired old body longed to settle back into the hammock, relaxed and cozy, but she stayed as she was, listening intently with her good ear and stretching out her bare feet, felt along the cold floor for her slippers. Sighing, she rose heavily, and took a cautious step forward, holding on to the head of the hammock. After another step, she let go of the support and moved slowly towards Severino's room.

She had gone to bed late that night, long after Pedro and Severino had gone to rest. When she finally left the kitchen, the provisions for the next day's voyage were almost ready; the big pot of rice cooked with dried meat\*, known as 'maria-isabel', the dough made from manioc flour used for making the beijus† to be eaten at breakfast, the fresh cheese and cluster of oranges, as well as the pitcher of herb tea were all there, waiting for Severino to ship them aboard the 'Fair Weather' next morning.

After her talk with Father Dourado her anxiety had ceased to torment her. She felt at peace; she could let Pedro go now, confident that all would be well. There were moments when the old fear returned with its insidious chill, her face would grow tense and her mouth droop. But they were moments only, and, reacting, she would pray the fear away.

'God is good,' she would say to herself, filled with faith.

Alone in the kitchen, cutting up the dried meat before putting it into the pot, she began to laugh aloud, remembering the priest's words and his determination to get her married, by force if need be.

'He even said that he'd give Severino a taste of the whip! Now *that* I'd have to see to believe! And why should we marry, after all these years! A pretty bride I'd make, to be sure!'

Someone clapped hands loudly in the corridor. She shaded her eyes with her hand and peered into the dark passage. A woman stood there, all in black, a scarf over her hair, holding a long-handled sunshade. Antonia went to meet her and as she drew nearer recognized her; it was the wife of the shoemaker, Noraldino.

\* *Dried meat*: ('carne de sol', literally 'sun's meat')—meat which has been dried in the sun and lightly salted.

† *Beijus:* A favourite Northern delicacy, made from manioc flour or tapioca, either in the shape of thin wafers or small buns.

'Come in, Dona Hortensia,' she called, showing her into the dining room, 'You're welcome.'

Dona Hortensia entered the room and sat down in the rocking chair, stiffly erect, hands folded over the handle of the sunshade. She spoke out without wasting time on ceremony.

'Is the 'Fair Weather' sailing tomorrow, Dona Antonia?'

'Yes, it is.'

'I heard tell that the Skipper wasn't well, there's something wrong with his heart. Is he sailing just the same?'

'Yes, he's sailing,' Antonia confirmed.

There was fear in her eyes as she looked at the other woman's long-jawed face. She felt her heart beat faster and her hands turn cold. Dona Hortensia continued to sit, immobile and severe, her head held high, the corners of her mouth pulled down, wrinkling her long pointed nose. She stared back at Antonia, her hard features implacable.

'Forgive me for saying so, Dona Antonia, but the Skipper must have lost his wits. He's not a young man any more; at his age, one can't be too careful. From here to São Luis, even with a following wind, and if there're no setbacks, it's at least a day and a half. I heard that Lucas Faisca's too ill to go along—Chica told us so herself. Well, who's going in his place?'

The angular face with its prominent cheekbones had gone tensely aggressive; the eyes developed a squint, while the nasal voice became shriller, more imperious.

'You heard me, Dona Antonia? Who?'

'Pedro,' Antonia said softly, letting her arms hang limply. limply.

Dona Hortensia tilted her head further back, raised her eyebrows with incredulous disapproval.

'The boy?'

'That's right.'

'What are you saying, Dona Antonia? That boy, that child, making the journey with Severino! Why didn't you forbid it? Good Heavens, Dona Antonia! I know Pedro, he and my son shared the same desk at school! His thoughts are always off somewhere else, he doesn't even recognize people he's known

111

all his life when he passes them in the street! And he's going to help Severino? If anyone but you had told me, I wouldn't have believed it! Pedro! Oh no!'

Antonia's face had turned to a livid colour. She tried to speak, contracting the flabby muscles beneath her chin. Confused and terrified, she tried to think of any answer that would silence her inquisitor. Suddenly Father Dourado's words came back to her, rising triumphantly from some unknown depth within her.

'Everything'll be all right, Dona Hortensia,' she said, after a moment's anguished silence. 'God is good.'

'May He hear you, Dona Antonia! But whether He does or no, I've come to tell you that my sister-in-law, who was leaving tomorrow for São Luis on the 'Fair Weather', has changed her mind, she isn't going after all, and neither would I, in her place.'

After her visitor had left Antonia took her place in the rocking chair, her hands lying laxly in her lap, her shoulders bowed, gazing towards the door as if the tall gaunt black-gowned figure were still in sight, going down the passage toward the front door, the thick knuckles clenched on the sunshade's handle. It took some time for her to rouse herself enough to walk with dragging steps back to the kitchen and listlessly complete her work of provisioning the 'Fair Weather' for the next day's trip.

Back in front of the stove where the pot bubbled and steamed, her hands busy with the meatchopper, she began to talk to herself, repeating her arguments until they brought a measure of tranquillity. Father Dourado, when he spoke, did it in God's Name; nothing could have made him conceal his real thoughts behind a veil of untruth, no matter how much she needed comforting.

Whose word counted the most, Dona Hortensia's, or the priest's?

'How silly can an old woman be? The priest's, of course!'

But now, as she felt her way towards Severino's door, Antonia's fear returned, weighing her down oppressively, constricting her heart. What if Dona Hortensia was right after

112

all? Father Dourado was old, wandering in his wits—there were times when his words were nonsense, neither more nor less.

'Oh, dear God,' she whispered, as her legs began to shake beneath the weight of her body.

Severino's hammock was empty, the flame of the lamp nearly out; she could distinguish a tumbled book and a couple of magazines thrown down on the floor beside the hammock, and a saucer on a wooden stool was full of cigarette butts. She stood there for a minute, her lips apart. Before calling Severino's name, however, she glanced down the passage and saw the yellow light which came from the dining room and lost itself in the shadows of the corridor. She walked toward the light, still shaky, but with quickening steps.

'Dear Saints in Heaven, I hope there's nothing wrong!'

Moonlight streamed into the room from the verandah and the yard beyond. Severino, his face ghastly in the colourless silver light, sat in the rocking chair, his hands clenched on the armrests, his shirt torn away from his bare breast that rose and fell in the struggle for breath.

'Why didn't you call me,' Antonia cried, racked with pity, as she ran toward him. Should she stay there fanning the air back into his tortured lungs, or ought she to seek out a neighbour for help? Inspiration came of a sudden and she turned toward the door.

'I'll send Pedro for the doctor!'

Severino summoned up strength to shake his head, and gesture weakly: No. No doctor.

'It was a bad one,' he managed to say eventually between gasps, as he pressed his open palm to his chest. 'I feel as if everything here inside was getting too tight, and then it hurts as if it was breaking to bits!'

Antonia asked him whether he'd drunk his herb tea.

'Yes, I did, but it wasn't any good. I came out here to see if I could breathe any better. But I can't, not yet, anyhow.'

'You'll soon feel fine', she said with conviction, 'God is good. I'll make you some more tea. Hot, strong, and fresh, it'll make you feel much better.'

113

But at the kitchen door she paused, looked back at him and begged again:

'Let me call the doctor, Skipper.'

Severino was obdurate. 'No!' He gasped. 'I'm bad enough as it is.'

The wind, heavy with moisture off the sea, rocked the ferns hanging in the verandah. Far off, the yellow lantern of the 'Fair Weather' shone into the blank spaces of night and was reflected from the smooth tops of the waves, shimmering like the slide of water over rock.

'All right, all right,' Antonia said feverishly, 'I'll manage by myself. For God's sake, Skipper, don't worry!'

She struck a match, there was a crackle, and a small red flame shot up from the dry straw, edged the dark lumps of charcoal with a coronet of fire that grew ruddy with the sap oozing from the lengths of wood piled between the bricks of the oven. Above the flame water began to bead and bubble in a little saucepan. The same reddish glow shone upon Antonia's features as she bent above the fire, feeding it with twigs and blowing it up with rhythmic breaths. Straightening, she picked up the fan of plaited straw* and stood before the stove, alternately fanning the flame and looking anxiously toward the dining room.

Meanwhile Severino continued to fight for breath, his mouth open, his hands beating the air. At times, he would lie back exhausted only to lean forward again, stretching out his neck and gasping. His bare feet scuffled on the floorboards as he clutched at the arms of the chair, his eyes wide and staring. Like a drowning man who sinks and rises and sinks again, he would subside into immobility for a few minutes until his limbs resumed the grim battle for air. The pyjama jacket lay open on the breast covered with grey hairs just visible in the moon's pale light, as the meagre chest rose and fell, rose and fell, in its terrible effort.

Outside, the wind began to turn; it blew in damp gusts, heavy with brine, and the moonlight grew and dwindled in

---

* Bellows are almost unknown in the North of Brazil, a small plaited straw fan is used instead.

114

uncertain intervals of light and dark. A gale sprang up suddenly, the *corrupião's* cage danced wildly back and forth beneath the wind-lashed green streamers of the hanging ferns.

Antonia came back into the dining room carrying the steaming cup in both hands which she was doing her best to keep steady. She stood in front of the sick man waiting until he should be able to drink; her lined old face was tense with pity and pain; it seemed as if she longed to reach out, draw the agony from his body and take it into herself instead.

'If only I could suffer in your place', she said brokenly.

Somehow she kept back her tears, put the cup down on the little table by the chair, and praying under her breath with shaking lips, went to fetch matches to light the lamp. The wind blowing into the room extinguished the tiny flame as she tried to light it; finally she bent over the lamp, sheltering the wick with her body.

'The wind's so cold, it's bound to be bad for you', she said as the flame sprang up and grew steady. Antonia went back to stand beside Severino, who was quieter now, his head resting against the cane back of the chair. She held out the cup to him, and watched him drink it in cautious sips.

'Don't be angry with me now, but listen to what I'm saying, Skipper! What's happened may well be God's warning to you not to sail tomorrow. Don't go; leave it till next month. You know how strong the August tides are, especially when the moon's at its full. Who will there be to help you if you have another attack like this, Severino, out in the open sea? Pedro's big, but he's only a boy, he's got no experience; wait until Faisca's better so that he can go along with you. Why shouldn't you listen to me just for once? Is it such a sacrifice, Severino? I shan't have an easy moment until you're back; I'll just be sitting here, my head full of nonsense, fearing the worst! Oh, please, do have some pity on me! Don't leave me here to watch the sea, like Mercedes! She was young, strong, she could bear it, without losing hope; I can't. I'm only an old woman with one foot in the grave already. If I don't see your boat come back, I'll lose my wits, Severino! Don't go! For God's sake, my dear! What'll I do, who'll look after me, if I were to lose you and Pedro?'

115

Severino finished drinking his tea, put the cup back on the table, still in silence. Little by little his breathing steadied, but his profile, where the lamplight fell on it, seemed older, the wrinkles deeper, as though the old man were still locked in an interior struggle, while he listened to the whistle of the wind, growing higher and keener and the patter of raindrops turned to a downpour.

Later, as Antonia helped him to draw the hammock fringes over his weary old body, she said once again, humbly, hoping against hope:

'You never answered me. Please, please, think about what I said, and don't tell me you're going no matter what. I'll beg you on my knees not to do it.'

'That's enough,' the old man replied surlily. He put his cigarette down on the cracked saucer. 'If God didn't want me to go, He'd have taken me now; wouldn't He? Well, I'm still alive, woman! Now go to sleep!'

# CHAPTER XVIII

As darkness gave way to light and the first gleams of dawn began to show between the tiles of the roof, Severino sank at last into sleep, sleep so heavy it was almost a stupor. Antonia could hear the noise of his breathing; twice she crept into the bedroom: when she first got up and then much later, tiptoeing up to the hammock, unsure of what she ought to do. Should she wake him? No, let him have his sleep out. The day was cloudy, drops of water fell from the branches still laden with last night's rain, the room swam in dimness, it was a good time for sleeping. Softly she backed into the passage and closed the door, taking care to keep the rusty hinges from creaking.

Perhaps when he woke up, after such a long sleep, Severino would agree to put off his journey. Once in the kitchen, however, she went on with her work of preparing provisions for the 'Fair Weather', mixing the chopped-up dried meat with the rice.

"Let be — things'll happen as God wills,' she muttered to herself again and again as she struggled with the long wooden spoon, stirring the mixture in the big cooking-pot.

In spite of the mist which hung over the houses like a thin veil spangled with persistent raindrops, Pedro had gone out immediately after breakfast. Full of love and care, she had thought to keep him by her, those last few hours before he was due to sail. But then she changed her mind; let him do whatever he felt like. From the sitting room window she saw him go up the street, skirt the bamboo thicket and disappear round the bend, tall and thin, an old waterproof hanging on his skinny frame, cap tilted over his eyes. Would she ever see him walk away again, intent on his boy's business, safe, and hers?

'God will be merciful — He'll surely have mercy on an old woman.'

She turned away from the window, and went down the passage that led to the dining room. Severino was standing at the head of the table, drinking the last of his coffee.

'Sit down, Skipper! Why should you stand up to eat your breakfast?'

She noticed the untidiness of the table which had been so neat a little while ago; there were stains of coffee freshly spilled all round the cup and saucer; the cheese had been taken from its plate and put back carelessly on top of the table-cloth, and the *beijus* lay limply at the bottom of a deep dish. Mechanically she began to put things straight, without taking her eyes from the old man who was still eating hurriedly, the flour of the newly-cooked *beijus* powdering his unshaven chin.

'Are you quite all right now, Severino? No more pain, no more breathlessness?'

Her eyes lingered on his face, seeing the dark circles round his eyes and the swollen purple flesh beneath them, the deep-

117

bitten lines. Pasty beneath the half-grown beard, drawn with fatigue, his face looked older than she had ever seen it. Should she ask him once more to give up the thought of travelling? Her lips opened impulsively and then the moment passed; his dark eyes looked back at her grimly and she was afraid.

'You're really leaving today, then?'

'Why shouldn't I?'

Antonia watched him open the gate of the yard and go, almost at a run, down the slope toward the pier, wiping his mouth on the back of his hand. She began to clear the table, her eyes heavy with unshed tears.

'I've begged him again and again, I just can't do it any more', she murmured despairingly to herself.

The mist, thickening, hid the horizon but here and there sunlight broke through, showing blue patches of sky; while Severino went on down the slope, the rifts widened and light poured through, so that he was able to see the last *igarités* sailing out of the bay.

On board the 'Fair Weather' he went over the canvas of the mainsail, inch by inch; all it needed was a patch or two strengthened, after which he hauled it up the mast, still furled. Then he examined the stays and the jib sheet, looked to the stepping of the mast, and carefully checked the boom, and the rest of the gear. Going forward, Severino inspected the helm and tiller, and sitting down on the steersman's bench, looked the boat over again with his keen seaman's eyes, missing nothing: fore and aft, all was in order; he felt his strength return and with it, his old confidence. The violent onslaught of his illness, in those dark hours before dawn, had left him exhausted and almost hopeless; he had nearly given up his resolve to sail at any cost. Then sleep had come, deeper and longer, except for once or twice, than he had ever known in his long life of hard toil. On waking he had felt slow and heavy in mind and body, but by degrees his vitality increased; and now he felt sure that he would be able to journey to São Luis and back to his home.

Resting his wet hand on the tiller he thought things over quietly.

'It's an ill wind that blows no good. If Faisca had been well enough to come along, people would have said he'd been in command of my boat; he'd get all the credit for sailing it. It's better this way; I'll do it myself, by God's help, alone.'

On the day before he had already dealt with the cargo; part of it stowed away in the hold and part on deck beneath the tarpaulin shelter. He hadn't asked for aid to do it, either. Neco Viola had offered to give him a hand, but he had said no. Perhaps the day's hard work had brought on last night's spasm.

'Well, it's over, and here I am again.'

He turned his dark face seaward, where the broad waters of the bay glittered in the sunlight that had dispelled the morning mist. He breathed deeply, filling his lungs with the salt air. Pain flashed briefly in his chest, just a twinge, nothing to worry about; he could breathe. Everything would be all right.

As he sat by the helm gazing out to sea, an old memory stirred within him and he saw himself descending the wooden steps of the court house, between two policemen, on the day of his trial. It was already twilight, and he was forced to lower his head so as to look where he stepped. In the street he raised it again defiantly, unafraid of the crowd that had gathered to see him pass. He walked on steadily, somber and calm, mutely challenging the world and time itself to do its worst. Twenty-two years. Twenty-two years shut up in a cell, like a caged beast.

Down the dark little streets he went between the two policemen. 'I'll serve my time and go back to my boat', he said to himself silently, again and again, with fierce conviction. On the other side of the town the jail stood waiting.

And so it had been. Here he was, master of his own boat, with enough strength to make his accustomed voyage to São Luis, and then home once more, God be praised.

At noon he walked back up the pier, preparing himself to hear that yet more passengers had cancelled their journey. How many were left of the ones who had taken passage? Three? Four? He had lost count. All right; he would sail without passengers, taking only his cargo of cotton, rice, manioc flour and dried shrimps.

Halfway up the slope he was forced to stop, his heart hurried and tripped in his breast, and little hammers beat an irritating rhythm on his temples. He put a hand to his chest, drew a long cautious breath—no trouble there. Standing motionless, he looked up and down the beach, empty beneath the burning midday sun, and waited for the flurry in his breast to pass. After a while, he continued his slow climb, bathed in the full heat of the sun which had chased away the last wisps of mist.

As he neared the house, his step slowed, grew deliberate and firm. 'Be damned to the passengers! I sail this evening and I'll be back!'

The house had been tidied, the table was laid for the midday meal; Antonia sat in the rocking chair, her chin resting on her hand, looking straight before her with dark grieving eyes. Her drooping shoulders and the fatigue of her drawn and wrinkled face added years to her age.

Severino paused at the dining room door and looked about him. 'Where's Pedro?' He asked.

'He's eaten and gone out again', Antonia replied listlessly.

Severino approached the table, a heavy frown drawing his eyebrows together. She quickly thrust her feet into her slippers and got up from the chair.

'He asked me whether he could eat earlier, and I said yes', she said mildly; and going to the kitchen she added, glancing over her shoulder: 'It's his last day. Why shouldn't I do what he asked me?'

Sitting at the table, Severino turned his plate right side up* and picked up his knife and fork, letting his hands rest on the edge of the table. While he waited for the food he talked to himself under his breath, his thick eyebrows knitted above his nose.

'It's all her fault; she's ruining the boy. It's always the same thing! If I've told her once I've told her a hundred times; but

* In the North and the interior of Brazil, plates and cups are placed face down on the table until they are needed, to keep them free of dust and flies.

120

what good does it do? There, now I'll lose my temper and be ill again! Pedro should have been on board with me, that's where he belongs. On the boat, instead of creeping about the woods trapping birds! When I was his age, I was in charge of stowing the cargo, and I did a good job of it, too. I've always done a good job of any work I had to do. So will the boy, God willing. It's an ill wind, as I said before, if Faisca wasn't ill I wouldn't have had the chance of getting Pedro away from the old woman's apron-strings. In January, I tried, didn't I? I got him away, got him aboard for a few days, and then what? Mumps! He comes down with mumps, for God's sake! His neck swollen up to twice its size, so sick he nearly died! So what does Antonia do? 'Oh no, the boy's still delicate, you've got to be careful, leave him with me.' Weak, I was! I gave in, but I shouldn't have. Well, that was the last time it'll happen. I'll not weaken again. He's going to sea with me; he's got to go — why shouldn't he? If he won't come willingly, he'll come *any* way, that's all. He's got to come.'

In his mind's eye he saw Pedro aboard the 'Fair Weather', wrapped in silence, the adolescent face blankly, looking away into a distance Severino's eyes could not reach. Slow, awkward, he hardly seemed to know where he was. Severino tried to teach him everything at once, how to handle the sails, how to work the helm, make the most of the wind and the way the sea was running. And Pedro stood in silence, his eyes far away.

'Are you listening?'

'Yes, sir.'

Two weeks; during those two weeks he had tried to pass on to the boy all his dearly-earned knowledge. However, Pedro needed practice; what good was knowledge without experience? But there had been the mumps, and a month spent lying feverish in his hammock, and Antonia saying the boy had fallen ill because of a chill caught at sea!

'Stop your nonsense,' Severino would growl, while Aunt Noca sprinkled the room and hammock with drops from a twig of rue* steeped in water, the best remedy against the evil eye.

* *Rue*: 'Arruda' (Ruta Graveolems), used for medicinal purposes in various ways, and considered an infallible defence against ill-wishing.

The aroma of the stew Antonia placed before him brought Severino back to the present. He helped himself slowly, in sour silence. Only when he had finished did he ask her, 'Why aren't you eating?'

'I'm not hungry', she said, and then added hastily, 'I had a bite to eat with Pedro.'

Severino, without answering, relapsed into his habitual withdrawn silence. Leisurely he drank his coffee, put the cup back in its saucer and lit a cigarette, then crossed the room to the rocking chair, and closing his eyes against the glaring light, drifted into his noonday doze, a chewed match hanging at an angle from the corner of his lips.

Some time later he woke with a start, afraid of having overslept. But it was still early afternoon; the *corrupião's* cage was bathed in sunlight, and the bird's song trilled loud and sweet from the verandah. As he went down the passage which led to the front entrance he saw a man at the open door, one foot still on the pavement outside. A stout high-coloured person with bristling eyebrows, a blue beret clinging to the side of his round flat-topped head, who hailed him effusively, his fat cheeks wreathed in smiles.

'Have I the pleasure of addressing Skipper Severino?'

'I am he', the old man said gravely.

The fat man was already halfway down the passage, holding out his small plump hand with a beam.

'Clementino Pinto, my dear sir, at your service always!'

An irresistible self-content shone in his eyes, surrounded by folds of fat, and ripened his voice.

'Your boat's leaving this evening for São Luis? Might there be room for your humble servant? Excellent! I shall have the honour as well as the pleasure of being conveyed by my worthy friend to our fair capital! We leave at five o'clock, do we not? That is the information I was given at my boarding-house. At five o'clock. Punctually. They assured me that the Skipper is famed for his punctuality. If I may say so, so am I. Time is sacred, do you not agree? In fact, I always arrive a little beforehand. Nobody need wait for *me*! I was able to see your boat from the top of the street there. Beautiful boat, beautiful!

122

My congratulations! The kind of boat that gives passengers that feeling of safety; and what's more, with a master like yourself, my dear sir! Very well, then. Punctually at five. I shall arrive a little earlier. We shall meet again then. Thank you! Many thanks! Your servant, sir!'

Seizing Severino's bony fingers in both his plump hands, he shook them cordially, turned briskly around and went out into the street, almost skipping down the shady side of the pavement, happily bouncing, fat and content.

Severino lingered for a moment in the street in front of his door, his hand still mechanically extended, not knowing what to think of the stout figure stepping lightly down the strip of shade. A travelling salesman? A Government inspector of something or other? He shrugged, smiled, and watched the man disappear behind a cluster of banana trees.

He admitted to himself that he felt grateful to the fat man; when so many others, who were personal friends, had lost their faith in him and cancelled their passage, this man had especially sought him out, determined to sail on the 'Fair Weather' . . .

'And at this time tomorrow, God willing, he'll be in São Luis', he promised himself, throwing his cigarette stub out into the middle of the street.

He looked up again at the brilliant blue sky, clear except for a few feathery clouds drifting in the east, and imagined what it would look like that night, stretching wide, clear and serene, bathed in the light of the full moon. To his right, the land mass would show up as a dark line in the lucid silver night. He had only to look up at the Southern Cross or the Three Marys* glowing dimly above his head, to find his course and follow it, as sailors have done since the beginning, manoeuvring in obedience to the wind, holding the tiller steady while the 'Fair Weather's' prow slipped between the glassy hills and valleys of the ocean.

'Everything'll be all right, the same as always,' he told

---

* Three Marys – 'Tres Marias': the three stars in the Constellation of Orion, which make up the pattern of the Archer's cross-belt.

Before going on board he had to stop at Carvalho's the ship chandler, two blocks beyond the Cathedral, to pick up the bill of lading. He took his hat from its peg in the corridor, crossed over into the shade and walked rapidly away. The certainty that he would make a safe crossing shone in his narrowed eyes and lent springiness to his step, as the sand creaked beneath his sandals and the high note of the cicadas sounded from among the bamboos.

As he neared Carvalho's he slowed down unconsciously. The windows of the court house were open; someone's trial was about to take place. Severino stopped opposite the door and raising his eyes recognized the entrance to the room where his own trial had been held; then he heard feet coming down the steps, strong and steady, the buzz of the crowd in the street, the policemen's shrill whistles, and realized it was himself that he saw coming out of the court house and down into the street.

# CHAPTER XIX

Father Dourado strode up and down in indignation.

'Yes, my friend! That man has become my enemy exclusively on your account! When I try to hold you up on one side, he comes along and tries to drag you down on the other, without giving me time to breathe in between! Never have I seen a Public Prosecutor behave like this — stubborn as a mule, to say the least. Mind you, I'm stubborn too, and it's just as well: if I hadn't dug my toes in, you'd already have been judged and sentenced to thirty years! Yes : thirty years! He's doing his best to get you the maximum the law allows. Thirty years!'

Severino stood with his back to the window watching the priest as he came and went in the cell, his face red with anger, the bare boards creaking beneath his elastic-sided boots. He emphasized his words by pounding his open palm with his fist.

Abruptly he stopped and faced Severino, eyebrows raised, thumbs stuck in the armholes of his cassock.

'And the worst of it is, *you* gave him the weapons to use against you, Severino! You, my friend! Yes indeed! I read the statement you made to the police — dreadful! If hanging was still lawful in Brazil, as it was during the Empire, you'd end up on the gallows, and I assure you, the Prosecutor would be there to set you swinging himself!'

Severino could not understand what the priest meant.

'All I did was answer their questions, Father', he said, straightening his shoulders. 'I told no lie. I swear to you that I never lied to them. You've known me all these years — I'm no liar, Father, you're sure of that. I only answered what they asked me, and I told the truth!'

Father Dourado uncrossed his hands and pointed an accusing forefinger at Severino.

'That's just it. That's where you made a fool of yourself! You told the whole truth to the Commissioner while the clerk wrote it down word for word. It was to me you ought to have told it, under the seal of confession, Severino. To me, not him! You put the noose round your neck with your own hands, and you can be sure they'll draw it as tight as they can!'

Severino, still at sea, put a hand on either knee and bent forward. He tried once more to explain.

'The Commissioner asked me if I had killed Celita, and I said yes. How can I deny it? And I wouldn't have, even if I could. All I do, I do in the open, and I'm ready to answer for it. That's the way I've always lived, and I'm not going to change. Afterward, he asked me if I had planned the crime before Celita and I left the house. 'Yes', I said again, and told him that for two whole months I'd had this thought of death in my head, the right time, the loneliest place, and the quickest and surest way to do it. I told him everything. What I do, I do, and I'm not hiding anything, thank God. He listened to me, his eyes as big as saucers, he didn't know what to think! He scratched his head, he stopped me, he asked me to repeat the whole thing again. So I did it. After listening to me the whole afternoon, he asked me whether I was sorry for what I'd done. I told him the truth — 'No', I said, 'I'm not sorry, not one bit, if Celita were to come back to life I'd do it all over again.'

The priest leaned his chin in his right hand, resting his elbow in this hollowed left palm.

'All that should have been said to me,' he exclaimed, 'to me, not to him! And what now, Skipper? You may well ask! Thirty years; thirty years between these four walls. And thank the Lord if they don't send you to jail in São Luis, where you'll have to go out with other prisoners and weed the streets, with people pointing at you and whispering!'

At that Severino's control gave way.

'For God's sake, Father, don't let them do that to me!' It's the only thing I ask, I'll bear anything, anything but that. All right, let them give me thirty years; I killed, I've got to pay for it. But go away from here — No! I've got to stay here — this is where Celita comes to me.'

Father Dourado, who had resumed his striding back and forth, turned round of a sudden.

'What did you say, Severino?'

'Celita comes to me here', he repeated obstinately, setting his back to the window. 'It's the truth. She's been here with me more than once.'

The priest approached him, eyes round in his flushed face, divided between incredulity and belief. He sat down in the hammock and folded his arms, bending his head sidewise the better to hear.

'Tell me about it properly, Severino. Take your time; I must know all. How does Celita come to you here? Do you really see her with your own living eyes? In here?'

'No, it's not like that — I don't see her the way I see you now, Father, before me. But I can *feel* her near me.'

'Do you hear her voice?'

'No.'

'Well then; if you neither see her nor hear her, how can you know she's been here?' A crooked smile pulled at the corner of the priest's mouth.

Severino answered him with deadly earnestness.

'By her smell. The way she smelt, coming out of her bath. The smell of flowers in the rain.'

The priest threw his head back in irrepressible laughter. Slapping his thighs, he exclaimed, still laughing.

'Don't talk such nonsense, Severino! The dead are at peace; they don't return to this troubled world.'

'Christ Our Lord came back, Father.'

This shocked Father Dourado.

'You can't compare Celita to our Our Lord, Severino. Easy does it, man. Use your wits.'

There was a moment of strained silence. Then the floor creaked beneath the priest's boots as he stood up, while Severino, fingers shaking, felt for his cigarettes.

'You must pray for her, my friend, that's what you must do', Father Dourado said, slowing in his walk. 'Ask God's peace and mercy for her, as I have done. This very morning, at Mass, I said a prayer for her. And for you too, Severino; I prayed for you both with all my heart.'

Severino sat listening, with his head down, looking at his feet. He felt the priest draw near and lay a hand on his shoulder.

'I can promise you that you shan't go to São Luis. Even if I have to see the Archbishop and the Governor of our State in person. Put your mind at rest. Dr Genesio's stubborn, but so am I! And what's more, God's on my side!'

After the priest had gone Severino stayed where he was, on the hard wooden bench below the window, for a long time, still holding the cigarette he forgot to smoke. The little room seemed emptier than ever; and its solitude weighed him down and bowed his shoulders. It was only when the last light of evening faded that he moved away from the bench to light his lamp.

And yet late that same night, when quiet lay over all, he felt Celita's presence again; she was there with him, in spite of all the priest could say. From his hammock, even with his head turned away, he could tell that she was by the window which let in a glimpse of the sea, looking at him with her long dark eyes. Without turning round, he felt for his cigarettes and matches which lay on the floor beside him.

'Yes', he said slowly, 'it's a good thing that you came tonight, Celita! When Father Dourado came to see me today, he managed to convince me that you'd never been here; that I'd imagined it all. The dead want peace, he said, I felt crushed, Celita! I could only sit like a fool, staring at nothing. Oh, what a relief it is, how happy it makes me that you're back! My trial's set for tomorrow; the Father tried to have it put off, but he didn't succeed. It's better this way, I'll get it over with sooner. I hear they're going to give me thirty years. The longest sentence that the law allows, thirty years, my dear! Just think of it, thirty years in this room, away from the sea except for the bit I can see from the window. If you didn't come to me from time to time, how could I bear it?'

He lit his cigarette and watched the smoke drift away.

Aniceto's going to defend me; he's no genius, but he knows his job. A light-skinned mulatto, who got himself a pair of spectacles and a lawyer's licence in São Luis, years ago. A bit too pleased with himself, but a good fellow, all the same. He did his best to convince me that I'd killed you in a fit of rage, blinded by passion, some nonsense of the sort. Of course I didn't agree. But he kept on insisting, until I had to shout at him to make myself clear. I'd already told the Commissioner how it happened; was I going to go back on what I'd said? No; I killed, committed a crime, and I'll answer for it, by God! Aniceto didn't know what to do; when he got to the door, he turned round and said to me, 'Skipper, you'll ruin everything! Admit you weren't in your right mind, or else they'll have no mercy on you.' Father Dourado thinks the same. They'll let me have the lot: thirty years. Well, what can I do about it? Be patient, that's all. A prisoner can't dodge his sentence, and I'm in jail already. I took your life and now I've got to pay the price; if I had my way, I wouldn't even bother with a lawyer to defend me. Defend me—from what? That's what I asked Aniceto.'

The night breeze, cold, salty, moist with the breath of the sea, sighed through the barred window, and made the flame tremble within its glass .

'One thing I'm sure of. Some day, I'll get back to my boat. Serve my sentence, and go back. Don't think that I'll try to escape, Celita. Oh no, my dear! Ten, twenty, thirty years, whatever it is, this is where I'll stay until my time is done.'

His eyelids drooped, he stretched an arm out of the hammock and let the cigarette drop to the floor. When he awoke day was breaking and he could see the brightening sky, streaked with red, through the window. The flame of the lamp had shrunk, become a tiny seed of light. He blew it out and went over to the window, filling his lungs with the dawn wind, trying to visualize the *igarités* slipping out to sea, still in darkness, guided by the lighthouse's beams.

He remembered that he was going to be tried a few hours later, and felt a shiver crawl up his spine, cold as a snake, and his hands grew clammy; however, he fought the feeling instantly, clenching his fists and knitting his brows. Would it last all afternoon? Stretch on endlessly after nightfall? And would he have to watch Dr Genesio all the time? Nobody had told him at what time they were coming for him. He thought of shaving but changed his mind; he would go as he was. And instead of wearing the suit and tie Antonia had brought, he would wear his working clothes; no boots, either, his everyday sandals.

It must have been about ten o'clock that he went up the steps to the court house, an armed policeman on either side, his ears burning underneath the brim of his old felt hat. He had come all the long way from the jail to Holy Cross Street holding his head high and looking straight ahead, so as not to see the people who gathered at the windows, leaning out to stare at him; some of them came out of their houses and stood in little groups on the pavement. Now and then he would hear a whisper: 'He murdered his wife!'

He went up the steps between two rows of staring faces; people had been there since early that morning, waiting greedily for the sight of the murderer — a man who had seemed so respectable, an honest, passionate, obdurate man, who had taken a beautiful whore from a 'brothel, married her, and killed her to keep her from falling back into sin. Setting his feet down firmly on each step, ignoring the support of the stone balustrade, he reached the entrance to the court room and only then took off his hat, his head as high as ever.

Sitting on the bench where they had placed him, still between the two policemen, he began unconsciously to swing his legs and twist his hat in his hands; his eyes kept wandering, not knowing where to look. Fixed to the ceiling above his head, an electric fan turned lazily round and round. All about him there was a murmur of voices that reminded him of a wake, and through it, the clack-clack of the generator. From time to time he risked a glance at one face or another, but looked away at once, overborne by the hostility of the crowd. A savage impatience took hold of him. Why didn't they begin? He wanted to leave the place and get back to jail; didn't he know already that they would condemn him to thirty years of imprisonment? Twice he took his watch from his pocket; he had been there for more than half an hour, it was almost noon. Oh yes, they would be at it all the dreary afternoon and half the night. Then he saw the Judge enter, followed by the Public Prosecutor and Clerk of the Court. His guards gestured for him to rise. He rose; what for? As he sat down again he heard the mutter of voices rise excitedly and then subside once more. Aniceto came in at the other door, professionally severe in his high starched collar and spectacles, an old leather briefcase under his arm. He greeted the Judge and Dr Genesio unhurriedly and took his place beneath the Judge's bench, putting his briefcase on the table in front of him, and waited for the trial to begin, his eyes expressionless, his lower lip thrust out; the room was hot, beads of moisture gathered on his bald forehead. Severino glanced at him, then looked again at his watch. There was nothing else to wait for: would they never begin? He heard his name called and stood up; the Judge's small hairy hand motioned for him to sit, while he spoke the opening words of the trial. Silence fell, broken only by the sharp click of the blades of the electric fan and the noise of people settling into their chairs. Severino, his hard hands kneading his old felt hat, tried to ignore what was happening to him, blot out the sounds, wipe out the sight; but the more he tried, the more acute his perceptions became. The rustle of papers, the scratch of the Judge's pen as he signed the documents brought to him by the Clerk of the Court sounded loudly in his ears. Physically, he felt half-suffocated by the pressure of the people in the room; he raised his head defiantly, filled his lungs with stale air, while his unconscious hands continued to punish his hat. The strong light hurt his eyes, and he shifted continually on his chair; it was all he could do to go on sitting there, alone and exposed. The Prosecutor stood up, looming in his black gown, one hand on the papers lying before him, while the other held a crumpled handkerchief. Severino froze; his hands lay rigidly on his thighs, his eyes were fixed on the tall black figure who had begun to address the jury in full rich tones, choosing his words deliberately, trying to give drama to a performance that succeeded in being pompous.

'The crime which has today come up for judgment', he began, 'is without doubt the most revolting that has ever occurred in this jurisdiction. I have made an especial study of crimes committed since the days when our country was still a Portuguese Colony, and can assure you, gentlemen, that no other violation of the law ever took place in similar circumstances of cold premeditation, deliberate choice and extreme cruelty.'

Severino's face began to flame, his mouth dried up and his heart thundered in his chest. Each accusing word was like a whiplash across his face laying open the burning flesh. How much longer must he endure it? He had to fight down the crazy impulse to leap from his chair and strike down the man who stood there, his features congested, the veins bulging on his neck, his voice raised to a shout.

'Beast!' He muttered, biting down on the word in a spasm of frustrated hatred and disgust.

His hat fell from his hands, he stooped forward to retrieve it, and as he stooped, tensed, his feet seeking equilibrium for the leap that would let him clear the barrier between them and take the man by the throat. The impulse ebbed and he leaned against the back of the chair, feeling his lips cracked dry as if under torture. From beneath his brows he shot a look at Aniceto who was listening impassively to the mixture of personal insults and exaggerated accusations, one hand curved round his ear, the other busily making notes. The jury, on their raised bench, listened in silence, while the Judge, his double chin resting on his starched collar, kept his patient eyes solemnly turned on Dr Genesio's gesticulations, as though the latter's arguments reached him through the bright lens of his spectacles rather than through his bodily ears.

As the trial progressed, Severino's hat lay forgotten beside him. Anger and contempt had reached their peak of concentration and shone piercing in his narrowed eyes; his jaw clenched and unclenched, his hands, writhing in emptiness, battled to master his rage as if it were something material and endowed with a life of its own; his Adam's apple moved convulsively in his throat. At times he moistened his chapped lips with his tongue, without moving a muscle of his face, expressionless except for waves of red that came and went on the high cheekbones.

It was mid-afternoon; Dr Genesio had reached the high point of his oratory and was describing the crime with a flow of pathetic detail. Severino leaped to his feet, shaking off the policemen trying to restrain him, and shouted with all the strength of his lungs, eyes on the Prosecutor, while the Judge rang his bell in vain.

'Yes, I killed her, you swine, and I'd do it again, as you know very well, you scoundrel! And whose is the loss? Mine, you hear—mine! It's my wife that's lost to me, I'm the one who's being judged, not you, who's the only one to blame for it all! You're a rascal, a son of a bitch, who can stand there insulting me because you're stronger than I am, although the strength's not your own! Man to man, you'd never have had the guts to say half of what you've said here!'

Late that night Severino heard the Judge sentence him to twenty-two years of imprisonment without blinking or bowing his head. Afterward he marched out of the court house, a policeman on either side and four others behind him, his head high, his eyes fierce, treading unafraid the narrow wooden steps which led to the crowded street.

# CHAPTER XX

The first passenger to turn up at the pier was Clementino Pinto, his beret clinging to the side of his head, a silk scarf round his neck, full of bounce and as garrulous as ever. A fat black briefcase was tucked under one arm and in his other hand he carried a neatly-rolled umbrella; he was followed by a boy who balanced on his head a large wooden chest* with highly polished metal clasps.

* These wooden chests known as 'baús' are used in the place of leather trunks, in the North and interior of Brazil, good quality leather goods being an expensive commodity.

Before boarding the 'Fair Weather' he turned to Severino with an elaborate bow, puffing out his fat cheeks and smiling.

'Four o'clock and thirty-six minutes, by my watch,' he cried triumphantly. 'I'm right on time, am I not? May I come aboard?'

He went down into the hold, stowed his chest where it would be out of range of chance drifts of spray, and going back on deck produced from his briefcase a book whose covers were protected by cellophane. Before taking his seat he walked up and down examining the boat, testing the condition of the rigging and cables, measuring with his keen eyes the height of the mainmast, inquiring whether the sails were new, had a look at the flying jib, in fact, went over the boat's gear piece by piece and finally installed himself on the bench next to the tiller, leaning his elbow on the taffrail with a happy and self-satisfied expression.

'A fine boat, Skipper. Why, it looks like new, straight from the shipyard. I had already heard how demanding you are, and I see that I was not deceived. My congratulations. It's a pleasure to sail on a boat as well kept as this one. A bench for passengers aft as well, I see. And clean—why it positively sparkles, sir!'

A tall thin boy with fiery hair jumped down from the pier into the boat, a canvas holdall in his hand.

'Your son, Skipper?' Clementino's benevolent smile grew wider. 'Ah, your grandson! I'd have guessed it at once, the resemblance is unmistakable. And a boatman too? Well done, sir! Yes, he really does look like you, Skipper, especially the colour of the hair.'

Severino was busy tightening a stay; he answered the man's volubility in monosyllables and with occasional nods, without turning his head, a cigarette dangling extinguished from the corner of his mouth, his deft hands busy among the ropes.

'You should send him to join the Merchant Navy,' Clementino went on, leaning back against the taffrail. 'Plenty of opportunity for advancement there. Many of my friends have done very well in it; some study, a lot of travelling and seeing the world; promotion follows as a matter of course. In

134

your place, I shouldn't waste any time. Why don't you make up your mind to it? Young men, these days, want a more spacious life; when all's said and done, they're right, aren't they? A civilized atmosphere, comfort and interest. Why look at your town, Skipper: you people are just beginning to change over from oil lamps to electricity! Your boat ought to have an engine; you could get to São Luis in less than six hours instead of taking a whole night and half the next day.'

Severino, with a dour look, cut short the man's remarks.

'Keep your advice to yourself. I've lived longer than you and I've got my own ideas. If you'd rather sail in a boat with an engine, you're free to get up and leave. I can get along without you.'

'Now, Skipper. I meant no harm! I'll take it all back if you wish; certainly I had no intention of criticising you', Clementino said hastily, as he wriggled his bulk, flushed with embarrassment. 'Quite the contrary! It's due to your reputation as a seaman and master that I've taken passage on your boat; there's no one in Maranhão who can stand up to you, Skipper. And mind you, I'm not one to praise indiscriminately. Oh no; I always think twice before I speak; everybody knows that.'

Severino had finished with the stay. He made his way along the deck toward the prow of the boat, filling his lungs with deep slow breaths. Halfway along he stopped: Neco Torres' daughter was coming down the pier, followed by her father. Her skirt hung unevenly, pulled up in front by her swollen belly.

'Here she is, Skipper', Neco Torres called out, and Severino went aft to the poop, holding out his arms and waiting until the wave that rocked the 'Fair Weather' had sunk away. The pale girl, pressing a handkerchief to her lips, settled herself in the hammock slung in the cabin; she wore stockings and shoes; a patent leather handbag lay in her lap, Neco Torres gratefully took Severino's calloused hands in his own.

'I can't wait for you to sail, Skipper; I've got two funerals this afternoon. I'll leave her to you, as if she were your own; look after her, friend. I'll see you when you get back.

The morning had been cloudy and dull, by contrast the evening sky shone wide and bright above the *igarités* slipping homeward into the bay. The tide was rising; it would soon be at its full.

Clementino Pinto waited until the girl's father was out of hearing, and then beckoned to Severino, speaking in a whisper that emphasized his anxiety.

'My dear friend, what if she gives birth here on board? That baby's due in a few hours! Do you know anything about delivering a child? Personally, I'm completely ignorant! The only birth I ever saw was a cow calving. But it's different with people, surely! Have you thought about it, Skipper?'

Severino heard his name being called. He turned toward the pier and saw fat Abdalla, the two upper buttons of his trousers undone, forced apart by the prominent belly, the leather belt buckled at its extremity, his shirt sleeves rolled up, sweaty, unshaven, looking as if he were about to weep.

'Remember the last time we met, before the Cathedral,' the Turco* said, between gulps for air, as Severino joined him on the pier. 'I said I wanted to ask you to do me a favour, something terribly important, Severino, it's life or death to me!'

Abdalla gripped Severino's arm and told his story, hoarse with emotion.

'Only you can help me, Skipper! I'm in such trouble I don't know what to do, which way to turn, I'll go mad if I don't find a way out! Believe me, my friend, I'm paying for all my sins at once! You remember my youngest son, Jacob? The one who enlisted and then was kicked out of the Army? Well, he's turned up again! From one minute to the other, without a word of warning, he's been home for two weeks, and the things he's done —! You won't believe me, Skipper, but it's all true: he's used my name to borrow money, he's given half-a-dozen people worthless cheques, taken money from the till in my shop, stolen my wife's jewelry — God knows where it's got to — he stole a lorry-driver's wallet as well. A criminal,

* 'Turco': term applied to natives of Syria and Lebanon, of which there are many in the various states of Brazil.

136

Severino; my son has become a thief and a swindler! Just put yourself in my place! My wife, poor soul, begged him with tears to go away before the police caught up with him, and he agreed to go provided I let him have money, Skipper, I had to run here and there, borrowing from friends as to make up the amount; I still don't know how I managed to do it! But I've got it, and then I remembered you'd be leaving today. I ask you on bended knees, Skipper, to take him with you. Just take him over to São Luis and leave him there. It would be an act of charity, of compassion for me in my trouble, Severino! But I can only pay you when you get back; He's taken every penny I had!'

Severino looked at him in silence, underlip thrust out. Abdalla believed he was strong enough to make the journey and come back safe. He put a hand on the fat man's shoulder.

'Make your mind easy, Abdalla, I'll take him over free. You've already spent enough on him.'

Abdalla's huge bulk trembled with feeling, he mopped his swollen eyes with his fat fingers. Dona Corina Soares was coming down the pier; she wore a bright blue dress and had tied a flowered scarf over her grey hair; in either hand she carried a canvas holdall crammed to bursting. Severino went aft to help her down on to the deck.

'I almost didn't come, Skipper! Duda, my youngest daughter dreamt last night that the house had caught fire; so she took it into her head it was a warning that something bad would happen to me. She wouldn't hear of my travelling today, I had to dig my toes in, I can tell you! What nonsense! One dies when God wills, not a minute before!'

Severino had gone up on to the pier. As he turned back to the boat, carrying the old lady's holdalls, he felt a stab of pain in his chest that stopped him in his tracks. Afraid of fainting then and there, he made himself jump down to the deck, staggered, and pulling himself together with an effort, handed Dona Corina's bags to Pedro. His heart still gripped by that claw of pain, he sat down on the passenger's bench, furtively put his hand to his breast beneath his shirt, and turned his haggard face away toward the sea.

137

Clementino Pinto stood leaning against a bale of cotton, his watch in his hand.

'It's five o'clock, Skipper. Aren't we leaving?'

It was high tide and a light breeze ruffled the waves. The fishing *igarités* were on their way home; a few were already just off the beach.

Severino sketched an answer with his left hand. 'We're waiting for one more passenger,' he managed to say.

'The last one aboard is usually the bad apple in the barrel', Clementino said sententiously, putting away his watch. He began once again to pace back and forth along the deck, looking about him knowingly.

Pedro turned his eyes away from the fading sunset and looked at his grandfather. The drawn features told him what was happening. He hurried over.

'Would you like me to get you your tea?' He asked anxiously.

'No, no, I'll be all right.'

Daylight was nearly extinguished and the sun hung just above the horizon, with streaks of red, bright as blood, staining the west. A thin boy with a head of dark curls, shining with hair-oil, reached the pier. His eyebrows seemed permanently arched in mockery, he wore shoes with gleaming silver buckles, skin-tight trousers, a jacket slit behind; there was a gold chain bracelet on his wrist and a printed silk scarf tucked into his open shirt-collar. He came down the pier without haste. His eyes, deep black and slanting, were shadowed by long glistening lashes. Their blackness and brightness seemed heightened by make-up. The aquiline nose, with wide fluttering nostrils, curved toward a pointed chin, and his black hair reached down onto his forehead in a deep widow's peak; there was something artificial about his looks; give him cloven hooves and a tail and he would have looked like an imp out of a nineteenth-century operetta.

'May I come aboard, Skipper?' he exclaimed, laughing. 'Now don't tell me that I've kept everybody waiting!'

He looked at Pedro who was staring at him in amazement.

'Now, sweetie, help your chum down', he said, and tossed him his suitcase. 'Oh, well caught!' Pedro, without moving from his place, had reached up and taken hold of the case as it flew through the air.

He skipped down onto the deck and went up to Severino with a smile.

'I'm Jacob, Skipper, Jacob, whom people speak so ill of—unjustly! Abdalla's son, Jacob! I bet you've already heard awful things about me!'

His shrill voice became shriller as he whirled round on his heel, arching his waist and throwing his hips forward.

'I know people say horrors, simply *horrors*, about me! Horrors.' He repeated, smiling and pronouncing the two syllables with mocking emphasis. 'But there! They'll have to eat their words again, that's all! Because *nothing* that people say about me is true. Not a thing, I promise you! I'm telling you all this as we're shipmates on this trip and I don't want any one here to think badly of me, especially you, Skipper—God forbid! I'm only a poor sinner, like everyone else.'

He looked about him, wheeling slowly round.

'Where shall I put my case? And my trunk? Where is my trunk? Oh God, where's my trunk? I can't bear to lose it! My most *precious* belongings—it's a big yellow leather trunk with a metal lock—that one! Oh! What a relief! Just to think that I might lose it—I could faint! I wouldn't have let you set sail without it, Skipper—not even if I had to squeal like a stuck pig. Oh, what a blessing! Thank goodness I've found it!'

Severino, wrinkling his brows, tried to draw the air into his lungs, slowly, beneath Pedro's worried look,. Little by little the claw in his chest relaxed its grip. The attack was over. He got to his feet, began to hoist the mainsail.

Jacob spoke to him without turning his head, his bright black eyes on Pedro.

'Is this good-looking boy your grandson, Skipper? I'd already heard of him. How handsome he is! What's your name? Pedro? That's my godfather's name, too; Pedro, yes, that's a real fisherman's name, and the name of the Keeper of Heaven's keys as well, eh? There's Dona Corina simply *glaring* at me! You needn't kill me, Dona Corina! I'm just a boy, I'm beginning life, this is springtime for me! And

139

you, Skipper, don't frown at me so! I'm a good boy, I really am, I hate to make trouble, I'm only too ready to help. Well, my friends, I can see I'm talking too much; if you don't want to listen to me, it's all right, I won't mind. You shan't have another word from me.' His fingers drew a rapid Sign of the Cross over his lips.

As he walked by Pedro, he glanced at him from beneath his dark eyelashes, sighed long and deep. 'Oh, what gorgeous eyes! Don't look at me that way, sweetie, you *tempt* me so!'

Pedro watched his grandfather hoist the mainsheet; the wind filled it with a rush and the boat's prow lifted, timbers creaking, as the 'Fair Weather' rose on the crest of a wave and slid down into the trough, while Severino, agile as a boy, manoeuvred to get the wind on his port bow. Again the boat rose and sank, the mast swayed and leaned to starboard, the wind sang in the taut stays and wave after wave broke in foam against her sides.

'Splendid!' exclaimed Clementino, as Severino sank down on the steersman's bench: 'Perfectly handled, Skipper! Congratulations!'

Jacob stood in the entrance to the cabin clinging with both hands to the beam above his head.

'Mercy, Skipper! Please don't do that again or I'll be sick — I feel queer already!' Severino shot him a look of loathing as he tightened the stays.

'You're lucky', he thought, drawing his eyebrows together in a scowl, 'I promised your father I'd take you to São Luis for nothing, otherwise I'd put you ashore right now. All the money in the world wouldn't buy you a passage in my boat. If I were your father I'd have made an end of you already — filth that you are! Well, I'm not your father, so let's get on with it.'

140

# CHAPTER XXI

Poor Antonia, leaning against the verandah's arched porch, eyes wet and shoulders drooping, tremulous, helpless, defeated, fearful of the gathering night: the boy is far away somewhere on the sea that heaves and darkens out there. You didn't go with him to the pier to bid him goodbye, afraid that your own pain might cause him suffering. And on the way back your trembling legs might have weakened; how would you have climbed the slope with no one to lean on? You were right to stay at home; that's where Pedro took his leave of you, and you gave him the pennies you had saved, dropping them into the painted clay pig. You can still feel the pressure of his arms. And you said goodbye without crying.

He spoke, and suddenly it was a man's voice.

'That's right, Aunt Tonia, if you stand here you can see us put to sea.'

You tried to walk toward the passage but your old slippers (it's time you had new slippers, Antonia) seemed glued to the tiled floor. You looked through the door and saw Pedro striding down the long corridor, tall and straight-backed, carrying his suitcase in his right hand. Quietly he went out of the door and into the street, without looking ; then he was gone, and you had done nothing to stop him, although the old agony surged through you again: he won't come back, he won't ever come back.

Poor Antonia; you still found strength to say, 'Lord, be merciful!'

The tears came then, and you went to the end of the verandah, waiting to see him pass along the curving street to the spot where the planks of the pier came up onto the sand. He turned round, saw you half-hidden by the trailing green fronds and waved his free hand gaily, bathed in sunlight. You were able to say it: 'Go with God.'

Severino's rocking chair was waiting, dark with age and shiny with use; the same chair in which you had lulled the baby Mercedes to sleep, and later, Mercedes' son, half-asleep yourself, the baby warmth against your breast, its weight sweet in your arms. Now you sit motionless, your hands in your empty lap. It can bring you no comfort today. The *corrupião* began to sing and you began to weep again. What difference did it make that you were not quite alone in the still house? The loneliness within you overflowed, you became at once the source and centre of its pain.

Around you, the daily voices of your little world: the squeak of a passing ox-cart's wooden wheels, evening cockcrow in the distance, the rustle of palms and cooing of doves: a whisper of fallen leaves ruffled by the breeze, the ticking of the clock keeping time to the waves breaking on the sand. They told you, those voices, that, whatever happens, life goes on. But you, sitting forlorn in your corner, did not know how to go on.

If you looked, wet-eyed, at the sea, it was brief consolation: the 'Fair Weather' still lay at anchor off the end of the pier. Time was passing, passing, the tide nearing its full, daylight would soon begin to fade. Night would come too quickly, its darkness broken only by the blades of light sweeping over the sea from the lighthouse. Your eyes would never again see him, your tall boy with the fiery hair.

The boat's mainsail filled with the wind: Antonia could make out Severino's thin figure standing by the mast. She left the chair and ran to the verandah, leaning against the arched entrance. The 'Fair Weather's' prow rose to the swell of the waves as she headed for the open sea. Antonia's heart contracted, she steadied herself with a hand against the wall. Her quivering lips held back a cry: there were only gulls to answer, swooping between sea and sky.

'What'll become of me? What shall I do?'

The boat grew small with distance, a soft haze, not quite twilight, settled on the waters. Now that it was done and the parting over, she realized that somehow she must find a hope to cling to, no matter how frail, no matter how small. Or else she could not live. Father Dourado's words came back to her

142

and she clung to them doggedly, trying to root herself in the priest's strong faith. He spoke in God's Name, he *could not* lie; but he was old, his wits astray—more than once he hobbled away from the altar, his Mass half-said, and sometimes wandered in his speech, said nonsensical things. She fought her doubt and fear as if they had been live things, crushing her physically now that age, loneliness and grief had robbed her of strength.

What if she did die? She had lived enough, surely, and could close her eyes, knowing she was no longer needed. Ah, if only our Lord in His mercy would call her to Him that very night. If she lived, how long would she have to endure? One week? A fortnight? If they weren't back after a fortnight, they never would return, that was sure. Better to die and get it over, clean and quick, than cry her eyes out, day and night until—

Far away the 'Fair Weather's' sails stood out against the bank of grey clouds low on the horizon. It was not yet quite dark but the lighthouse was already sending out its pulses of light. Dusk gathered inside the empty rooms and the damp wind from off the sea keened higher, and brought her wafts of scent from the jasmine hanging over the gate.

Night closed in and the boat was lost from sight. Antonia went back into the house, wandered here and there in the dark, not knowing what to do; she wasn't hungry; she didn't want to go to bed. Finally she felt her way to the table and put a match to the lamp; her fingers shook so, it took her a long time to get the wick alight.

The small red flame, steady within its protecting glass, lighted up the big room with its empty chairs and bare sideboard, the clock ticking on the wall, and the coloured calendar.
them all gathered around it, Severino at the head, Pedro beside him and herself just beyond; shadows dark on the wall behind. She felt her heart shrink again. Why did she think more of Pedro than of Severino? Surely that was unfair. Well, Severino's life had lasted for many years, the boy's was just beginning. Severino, like herself, could not complain if his hour had come.

'Like me; like me.' She muttered to herself.

But Pedro, in his first youth, the world opening for him like a flower —

'His beard isn't even grown!'

She shuffled toward her room, now propping herself against the wall, now leaning on a piece of furniture, drawing long breaths that she released again in sighs. Her eyes ached, and she pressed the back of her hand against them to dry the slow burning tears. It was to this her old age had come, she thought with bitterness, and through no fault of her own. Unjust! It was unjust! Had she lived all those years to end like this, with no one to clasp her dying hand about the lighted candle, symbol of living faith, and close her eyes after she was dead?

At the door of her room she struck another match and the first thing she saw was Pedro's hammock dangling empty from its supports. She clung to the door-frame, shaken by a storm of sobs, the match held high in her trembling fingers.

'It's more than I can bear!'

Back into the sitting room to look about her in a daze and then, once more in her room, lighted the lamp on top of the chest of drawers, kissed the picture of Saint Lucy and cast a look of silent anguish at the crucifix on the wall.

Then she hung up her hammock and sat down on it, still crying, but quieter now; she cut herself a piece of tobacco and began to chew, listening to the moaning of the wind and the chirp of a cricket coming from the passage.

Suddenly she began to talk to herself: the sound of her own voice made the silence of the empty house somehow more bearable. Rocking back and forth, while tears trickled down the grooves of her lined face, her dry lips moving:

'I'm too old, too tired, I wish God's mercy would take me from this world. What have I got to live for? Never have I suffered as I suffered today. Not even when I was living here in Celita's time, sitting still in my corner and waiting for death, I didn't die, I endured it all, the sorrow, the humiliation, everything, without a word. I couldn't sleep, I spent my nights begging Our Lord to take me but He never did for all the tears I cried. That afternoon, up and down the beach I went like a madwoman, up and down, longing to kill myself! And then I was afraid and came back here, back to my corner, my burrow, knowing that I had to see it out to the end. Since it was God's will, what could I do?'

The flame of the lamp dwindled; in the dimness, Antonia's huddled figure seemed part of the shadows that hung in the room. She chewed her tobacco, rocking slowly to and fro.

'The very next day, a dead woman was brought to this house; but it was Celita, not me, in Severino's arms, sometimes I still can't believe it. And yet I remember it so clearly! Poor soul! God give her peace. After all, she'd done nothing to harm me; it wasn't she who went after Severino, it was he that lost his head over her. I don't blame either of them. It must have been that somebody put the evil eye on me; there're wicked people in this world, God knows, who flourish on others' misery. I was happy, I had all I wanted in this world, and someone passed by and saw it all and envied me. That's when all my sorrows began. So many! Nobody knows how many and how deep. But now this, Pedro gone to sea, it's worse than anything else! Oh, so much worse!'

She swallowed a sob and looked toward the crucifix by the weak rays of the dying lamp.

'Sweet Jesus, have pity on this old woman! Look mercifully upon me and deliver me from my sorrow!'

Light came from the yard like milk spreading in a pool of ink; the wind seemed to bring it, and it spilled into the dining room and reached down the corridor into her room. There was silence except for the sigh of the wind, then Antonia took up her tale.

'When all's said and done, who was it that became Celita's child's real mother? Me! No one else but me! Who'd have imagined that she'd become my baby after all? And so she was, blessed be God! Oh, she was so lovely, Mercedes! No need to pretty her up with fine clothes! Full of life, full of laughter, gay as a humming-bird, here, there, everywhere in the house; and so fond of me, the darling! All these years while Severino was away in jail, she kept me company, did little things to please me, was so sweet. That's where she used to sleep, where Pedro's hammock is now; and when she woke up at night, she'd come over and cuddle close to me. I'd wake up in the morning, feeling her weight on my arm and her warmth next to me, and thank God for her. And so neat-handed, you'd never believe she was Celita's daughter. Mercedes knew everything a woman should know about housekeeping, and she could cut-out and sew, and embroider like a fairy! That tablecloth she embroidered, everyone admired it so! Who would ever have thought that she'd go like that, alive one night, dead the next morning! I've never gotten over it. And so unhappy, poor child, waiting and waiting for Vicente to come back, until the very moment of death. Oh, now I can understand what she must have suffered. Out there on the pier every morning, sitting on the bare planks and looking out to sea. If I didn't go and fetch her myself she wouldn't bother to come back to eat; but she'd come home with me, and rest a while in the rocking chair after she'd eaten; then back again to the end of the pier. What a business it was, in the evening, to get her to come home. She'd listen only to me; she called me 'Mother', as though I was her real mother. I told her time and time again, Celita was your mother, I said. But no, I was 'Mother' to her always.'

The milky light brightened in the passage. The moon rose slowly, huge and round, above the dark line of the horizon.

'Only God can know what one's life really is', Antonia murmured to herself. 'Mercedes died, but Pedro was left to me. Such an ugly little thing at birth, curled up in a ball! Then he got stronger, and you could see he took after his grandfather, with that hair. A good child, you'd have thought he was a girl, not a boy, and always beside me, following me like a chick follows the hen. I think he was even fonder of me than his mother used to be. Oh, dear Jesus, how is he now? What's happening to him?'

Instinctively her eyes sought out the dark shape of the crucifix on the wall.

'Dear Lord, look after my boy, for Our Lady's sake. Bring him back to me! Oh, then, I'll die of happiness or clap my hands and laugh like the madwoman in Market Square!'

Antonia let her weary eyelids drop slowly, comforted by a gleam of hope. Hadn't Father Dourado said that Severino would return?

'All things are possible to God.'

Sleep awhile, Antonia, taste a moment's peace and forget your pains. Close your eyes to the play of light and shadow about you, your ears to the banging shutters you forgot to latch. Through the open front door bright moonlight comes pouring in, the light of the same August moon hanging in splendour above the spread sails of the 'Fair Weather' far out on the open sea.

# CHAPTER XXII

The 'Fair Weather's' prow dipped deeply, shuddered, and then rose again, rushing up a towering slope of water as an enormous sea swelled and grew, huge and menacing, before her, taller than a church steeple, Pedro thought in panic, while he clung to a cable with both hands. The wall of water reared higher and the boy turned as white as a sheet. 'Jesus!'

This was nothing like the waves he had seen die out in scallops of foam upon the sand or break into spray at the foot of the rocks where he used to play. He felt his stomach contract and then relax into sick emptiness as the boat leapt at the huge wave and drove between two cliffs of water crowned with boiling foam that soaked the jib and spilled over onto the deck; another wave rose ahead, bigger than the first.

They had run into these heavy seas after hours of smooth sailing; now the ocean fought the wind that propelled them, and tried to shake them from its breast; but the 'Fair Weather' fought back, coasting dizzily down into the troughs and driving up the looming crests, her prow slicing through the torn spume, canvas swollen and straining, while the mast trembled and groaned.

Night was falling, and the vivid reds of sunset had turned to violet; there was still light enough to see the dark outline of land on the starboard bow, but the pier, the huddle of old houses, and the beached fishing-boats had been left behind.

Pedro had to some extent conquered his fear; but the thought of darkness falling on the broken water and blotting out the homely profile of land made him feel miserably small and alone, between the crushing immensities of night and sea. Even the wind sounded different, there was a wilder note to its keening; the breeze that sent little clouds of dust whirling up the street, and set the doors banging in the house, full of the perfume of jasmine, had turned into a thing of violence, blind and brutal, whipping up the waves, punishing the sails, and tilting the 'Fair Weather' crazily on to her side; it whistled and threatened, lamented and jeered. Later on, in the dark before dawn, would it still sound like the howl of a starving dog?

Aunt Tonia would have done her washing up by now and lighted the lamp on the dining room table; Seu Alipio's little daughters would come out presently to play in the street and sing about the Princess Dona Sancha, and her dresses of silver and gold.

'So we have a poet aboard!'

Pedro turned toward the speaker and saw Jacob smiling at him from a patch of shadow, one hand on his hip, the other stroking his pointed chin.

Severino had risen from the bench aft and gone to light the two lamps that hung at the entrance to the cabin. He would check the mainsail on his way back. The last of daylight shone on the thin face half-hidden by the brim of the old felt hat pulled down over his brows and secured below his chin by a length of string. His narrowed eyes were cool and steady; as always, a cigarette was at the corner of his lips. Sitting erect on the bench, adapting himself unconsciously to the rocking of the deck, he might have been a part of the boat; this was were he felt truly at home, and he seemed to have recovered his old vitality. There was confidence in the poise of his head and in the new brightness of his tired eyes, even the bony hands lying quiet on his lap spoke of strength renewed.

Clementino Pinto still leaned against the cotton bale, his beret pulled over his left eyebrow, a book tucked beneath his arm. Twice he tried to draw out Severino.

'How long have you been a boatman, Skipper?'

Getting no answer, he repeated his question, but this time veiling it in a spate of chatter.

'I love the sea. Nothing can keep me away from a boat, Skipper, as long as I've got the time. I dream of sailing round the world; no airplanes for me, I've flown once and that was enough—you won't catch me doing it again! After all, Our Lord chose the water to walk on, not the air to fly in! What about you, Skipper, forgive my curiosity, how long have you been at sea?'

Severino watched a wave rise up threateningly and divide as the 'Fair Weather's' prow climbed up the glassy wall and sliced through the mass of water.

'Not counting the twenty-two years I was in jail,' he said slowly, without taking his eyes from the sea, 'It's getting on for forty-two.'

Clementino dropped his book in surprise.

'What are you telling me, sir! You spent twenty-two years in jail? As a convict?'

'That's right; a convict; that's what jails are for. A jail's a place for men like you and me—what do you think? I killed my wife, I was judged and sentenced, I didn't complain or beg for mercy. A family matter, my business and no one else's. Anyway, what you want to know is how long I've been at sea. I was twelve when my father first took me aboard; he knew these seas like his own back yard, could have sailed anywhere along these coasts with his eyes shut. When I went to jail I was forty-one, and I was sixty-three when they let me out. I'm seventy-six years old now. You can do the sum yourself: forty-two years at sea, and always on the same course.'

Clementino, mouth open in awe, stood quiet. Eventually he picked up his book and tucked it back beneath his arm. He stroked his chin thoughtfully.

149

'Tell me something, Skipper. In all your forty-two years at sea did you ever see the ship they tell of —you know, Dom Sebastian's galleon?'

Severino shook his head.

'Never?'

'Never.'

'Well, I'm surprised to hear it. I grew up hearing all the tales they tell about it; how it's seen on Friday nights, just off-shore. Some people say that the King jumps his horse ashore, rides down the beach and comes back to the ship; once he's aboard, it disappears—simply vanishes! And you've never seen it? Never noticed anything queer? How strange! Very strange, I must say.'

The coastline was no longer. Stars shone in the darkness above their heads. The wind had fallen and the boat sailed on smoothly, rising and falling gently, in a rhythm as easy as breathing, her prow knifing through the dark waters. Toward the west the sky was impenetrably black but eastward a pale glimmer hovered, like a false dawn.

'Are there three sisters or only two? Ah, that's what I thought, just two girls. And you're the youngest; the eldest became a nun. You're Dora.'

Dona Corina Soares was indulging her weakness for talk, while her knitting-needles clicked steadily. She had slung her hammock with its wide flowered fringes near the entrance to the cabin, next to Neco Torres' daughter. The girl lay curled up in the depths of her hammock; she kept touching her lips with a crumpled handkerchief. The reddish glow of the lamps shone down on the old woman and threw her shadow on the wall in front; the outline of her head, with the long hair coiled at the nape of the neck, swayed with the swaying of the lamps. Before Severino had time to hoist his sail and take up his anchor, Dona Corina had already settled herself, opened her workbox and started to knit.

'I knew your mother as a girl. We used to sing in the choir together. Father Dourado was in charge of the choir; in those days he wasn't the poor worn-out old man that he's become.'

She stopped, lightly smacked her mouth with the back of her hand.

150

'God forgive me, I don't mean to speak evil of him!'

The needles clicked.

'Yes, he was a fine figure of a priest in those days! It was a pleasure to listen to him. A fine voice he had, and played the organ beautifully. He was tall, with broad shoulders, streaks of silver in his hair, shrewd eyes — a real priest — an example to us all! There was never any gossip about him. Yes, child, a good priest, they don't make them like that any more. I can say it because I'm old enough to compare what priests used to be like when I was a girl, and what they are now that I'm an old woman. Oh, the difference, child! The priests I knew in girlhood were something else — wine from a different barrel, believe me! Unless I'm mistaken, I saw you christened by Father Dourado. Yes, I remember it clearly. I can see you now lying in your mother's arms, in church. How long ago was it? Nineteen years? So you're nineteen! I can hardly believe it! How time passes, it might have been yesterday! And now you're expecting a baby of your own. Has it been an easy pregnancy? Yes, that's the way it is; if you feel sick to begin with, you go on feeling sick the whole nine months. I had eleven daughters — eleven girls, imagine! I felt sick all the time with the first four, but then I got accustomed to it, and never had any more trouble that way. Eleven girls, and their names all begin with the letter C, like me: Candida, Clotilde, Coralia, Creusa, Cremilda, Carlota, Camelia, Cantidia, Cacilda, Cornelia and Claudia — I think I stopped having children because I ran out of names beginning with C.'

She smiled widely, showing her false teeth, and threw back her head.

'I got them all married, and they're all alive and in good health, God be praised! Last year my eldest granddaughter got married; and now I'm going to São Luis for the wedding of my great-granddaughter! My dear, time flies — it really does! Your mother told me you'd be sailing today and asked me to keep an eye on you — as if she needed to ask! I said to her, 'Just leave her to me, I'll look after her.' You're having your baby at the maternity hospital, aren't you? Mine were all born at home; that's the way things were in my time. You had your baby and stayed at home, in your room, for four weeks, with

151

nothing but chicken broth to eat. What with my eleven girls, I got so tired of chicken broth — I must have gone clean through a dozen hen-coops! All the births were easy ones, thank Heaven, I never needed a doctor, first the pains, getting stronger and stronger, and then out popped the baby. Nothing to it, my dear! Except for Claudia, my youngest, who was a breech delivery. But people used to laugh, it was so easy; I had to laugh, myself! Is it a boy or a girl your're expecting? A girl's better; easier to bring up than a boy. I noticed when you lay down you're carrying the baby well out in front, that's a certain sign of a girl, you may be sure; I've never been wrong yet! You'll have a girl, I'm positive. If I'd had the dozen, I would have given the twelfth my own name, Corina, don't you think it's pretty? But you're right to go to São Luis to have your child; it's safer, there're plenty of doctors there. I've heard that they even have painless childbirth — *painless* childbirth, just think! Who would have thought it possible? Yes, the world has certainly changed!'

Dora pressed her handkerchief to her lips, trying to hold back nausea. Every time the boat slid down into the hollow dividing one wave from the next, she closed her eyes and hugged herself. Dona Corina rattled on while she lay in a daze of discomfort and fear, barely answering, her face so pale that the skin seemed transparent.

The old woman's needles never stopped, any more than her tongue; she never missed a stitch, even when the boat's prow seemed to plunge endlessly, reaching for the trough of the wave.

'This bit of sea's always rough; it's frightening if you don't know it. But I know it so well I'm not afraid any more. I used to get terribly nervous, the first few times I made the trip, but now I don't bother; Severino's up there, he'll take us across safely, I've sailed with him for years. So now I just sling my hammock and get on with my knitting.'

# CHAPTER XXIII

Antonia is awake after a spell of uneasy sleep. It is still early; there are children playing in the street outside but their shouts are nothing to her, any more than the voice of Ninita Porto who is sitting outside her door, at the foot of the steep little street, and singing, moved, she knows, by the beauty of the night and the full moon. Far off, a dog barks. Antonia cares for none of it. For her, it is still afternoon and she can see the 'Fair Weather's' sails filling with the wind, but she has no more tears left. She had wept until she felt weak and sick, dizzy with a faintness that loosened her limbs and darkened her eyes, but it had passed off.

Now her head nods again and her eyes close. A voice, calling in the distance, rouses her from her doze. She sits up straight in the hammock, supporting herself on her elbows.

'Well, my dear! If I hadn't come round to see you, your front door would have stayed open all night!'

Antonia smiles, raising her head. She is back in the reality of the present. Aunt Noca is standing before her, tall, thin, holding the worn pack of cards in her right hand.

'So it's you, Noca!'

'Who else? I had to come and see how you were getting along.'

Antonia got to her feet and leaned on the other woman's shoulder as they went down the passage into the dining room.

'What time is it?' She asked, peering at the clock on the wall.

'It's after nine.'

The moon was high over the sea; the leaves of the trees in the yard, ruffled by the breeze, showed glints of silver.

. 'I thought it was much later!' Antonia said, as she leaned against the door frame and thought of Severino.

'Blessed Virgin, don't let him have another attack! Have

153

mercy on us and keep him safe! Keep him safe and let him bring my boy back to me', she prayed wordlessly, in a sigh, 'don't let me be left all alone in the world.'

Aunt Noca spoke up:

'Now, Tonia, you can't go on like this. You've got to pull yourself together! I was coming earlier but I've been busy all day. In the morning they came to call me to old Seu Costa's, the poor man was dying, I could only try and ease his passing! This afternoon it was Belicia's youngest, Julita, who was having one of her attacks, you know how she always gets worse when the moon's full. She was so bad I thought my powers * wouldn't work. But praised be God, I was able to relieve her. Then I went home, tired out, ate my supper and nearly went straight to my hammock afterwards, only I remembered that you'd be needing me, Tonia. So I got dressed again and came over right away, I didn't even stop to do my hair. And if you've got a corner here for me to lay my head, I'll spend the night.'

Antonia's smile was full of thankfullness.

'Noca, it was God Himself who put the idea in your head! I don't know what I'd have done, alone tonight in this house. I haven't known a moment's peace since I saw them sail away. My poor head—the thoughts go round and round, and it's always the same thing; sometimes I think they'll be all right— they will, won't they?—sometimes I imagine the worst, lost, and everything goes black in front of my eyes and I'm alone, alone in this hard world! I can't even cry anymore, I've no tears ; my eyes are dry and hot and stinging. You're the only person who can help me bear it. Will they come back? Or have they gone forever?'

She moved away from the door, felt the giddiness return, and leaned against the wall for support, stood for a minute, fighting the wish to let go and sit down on the doorstep, her head in her hands.

Aunt Noca took her arm.

---

* *Powers*: What Aunt Noca really said was 'rezas', the literal meaning of which is 'prayers', but in this instance it means the mixture of prayers and spells used by white witches ('rezadeiras' or 'benzedeiras', literally—'Praying women' or 'blessing women').

154

'My dear, what will be, will be, nothing can change it. Everything's in God's hands, He alone knows what'll happen to each one of us. It doesn't do any good to wear yourself out imagining this or that. Leave it all where it belongs, in the hands of God, my friend!'

Antonia looked round the room, and the verandah, white in the moonlight. There was the table, there were the chairs and the oil-lamp. She could not remember having lighted it. There was a chair drawn back from the table, a plate forgotten on the cloth, the manioc-flour bowl beside it; that was Severino's usual place, and it seemed desolate.

'I can't help it,' she said slowly, 'everything I see makes me feel worse; if I look over there, I think of Pedro—something else reminds me of Severino. I feel like going away from the house and just walking, walking anywhere, like some poor half-witted creature. I've never felt like this before, never! Noca, I'll end up sitting on the pier all day, every day, waiting for the boat to come back, like Mercedes!'

Silence had fallen on the street outside and through it they heard the voice of the sea, as the long waves broke into ripples on the beach.

'Let's try the cards, Noca. Maybe they'll tell us what's happening out there.'

They went up to the table. Noca stood at one end, while Antonia sank into the chair beside her, silhouetted in shadow on the wall behind. Through the open verandah door patches of sea showed between the leaves of the coconut plams; the waves heaved gently beneath the moon which threw over them a pattern of bright scales. The two women, however, looked only at the circle of light the lamp shed on the table-top, inside which Aunt Noca was laying out her cards with swift movements of her long tense fingers.

Antonia's whole attention was given to the cards; she leaned forward, shoulders bowed, her face bent low above the table. The lamplight shone full on her worn features, she seemed to have aged in the last few hours, her wrinkles deeper, her forehead creased with anxiety. Aunt Noca moved the lamp back, so as to leave more room for her cards, and Antonia suddenly broke into words.

155

'What worries me isn't so much the crossing to São Luis, nor even the August moon, although it always brings gales—it's Severino's illness! If he had his health, I wouldn't mind so much. But he's a sick man, a very sick man, and that makes a difference! Sick, and having to work the boat alone, Noca! Mother of God! The last attack he had was frightful, I thought the end had come! He couldn't even bear to lie still in his hammock, he came out here for air, his mouth wide open! What if he has another attack? It doesn't bear thinking of! How will Pedro manage, all by himself? That's what makes me so anxious, and I can't get it out of my head.'

Aunt Noca's long fingers were busy with the cards, laying them down in patterns, quick and skilful as a spider weaving its web. Her thin hands shifted a card here, straightened one there; she never spoke. The silence gathered, grew longer, it seemed to weigh Antonia down. She bent forward, her head between her hands.

'Well? What's going to happen?'

'I can see Severino terribly alone—he has some great sorrow to bear. But you'll be at his side. Be patient. Trust in God, my dear!'

Oh, but her heart was heavy, heavy and bursting! She drew her chair closer to the table, her eyes wide with fear.

'See whether the boat's coming back', she begged Aunt Noca, unconsciously wringing her hands which were damp with sweat. Coldness shivered along her spine. 'That's all I want to know.'

Holding her breath, her whole being seemed to gather in her eyes, glued to the cards on the table. The wind, the sea, the cricket in the passage, the banging shutter, went unheard. The boat, Severino at the tiller, bowed with pain, his hand pressed to his chest. Obsessed, she could think of nothing else.

Outside, beneath the wide sky, the sea laps at the sand and seems to draw closer to the house. The breeze has turned chilly. The hanging ferns quiver and sway, their leaves breaking the moonlight into tiny silver spangles.

'For God's sake, Noca', Antonia cried suddenly, trying to rise on her trembling legs. 'For God's sake! Tell me what'll happen to them. I can't bear not knowing!'

Aunt Noca began to gather up the cards.

'Trust in God, dear. Remember, nothing happens unless it's His will. And put your mind at rest, they'll come back.'

# CHAPTER XXIV

Jacob yawned widely behind his covering hand; looking at the others, he announced that he was going to his hammock to sleep.

'The moonlight's beautiful, you're charming people, all of you — beginning with you, Skipper — but I'm asleep on my feet! Good night, chums! Sweet dreams!'

As he went by Pedro, who was standing next to his grandfather, Jacob paused, flicked his hips in a movement full of coquetry, and put out his hand as if to caress the boy's chin.

'This grandson of yours, Skipper, how many hearts he's going to break! God, those eyes — they turn me weak at the knees! *Don't* look at me that way, Sweetie!'

He slipped down the deck, still moving his hips seductively and went into the cabin.

The moon rode high in the cloudless sky, a polished globe of light sailing through the still and limpid night; the sea, calm at last, shone with reflected splendour. It was so bright that they could distinguish the low undulating outline of land under their lee. Seawards, the sparkling waters seemed to stretch out to infinity.

'It's a long time since I've seen moonlight to equal this.' Clementino exclaimed after a long silence, as he strolled along the deck towards Severino.

'What a picture, Skipper! An artist couldn't do better! For

157

my part, I'd like to stay awake all night filling my eyes with this glory! And to think there're people in this world who don't believe in God! Of course there's a God! Only a blind man could doubt it.'

Half-way to the steersman's bench where Severino was sitting, he turned, went round the cabin and up into the prow, gazing at the moon with enchanted eyes, and lingered there bathed in the cold silver light.

Severino turned to Pedro.

'Watch the mizzen-sheet. I've hauled the mainsail closer to the wind but left the stays as they are. With this steady breeze and such clear weather, we can keep on following the coastline. Later, when we're off the Long Beach, I'll take her further out to sea. And tomorrow, God willing, we'll be in São Luis a bit past noon.'

Pedro rested his head on the back of the bench in front of him. He felt tired and heavy-eyed. Through half-closed lids he watched the prow cutting smoothly through the swells. The even rhythm of their motion and the low sough of the breeze made him sleepier than ever; Severino's voice grew distant and then faded from his hearing.

'Let him sleep', thought the old man, seeing the boy's closed eyes and the hands lying relaxed on his thighs. 'I'll wake him later.'

'Yes', he said in slow triumph, pushing up his hatbrim, 'I'll take her over and bring her back and nothing'll happen to stop me. And when I get back, I'm going straight to the consulting-room and say:

'Didn't you tell me I wasn't fit to travel? Well here I am; I've been and I've come back, praised be God. And I'll do it again as often as need be until I can hand my boat over to my grandson.'

He smiled, deepening the creases in his lined cheeks as he thought of Dr Estefanio's face — astounded, indignant, ashamed — serve him right! He looked at the bench opposite and saw Pedro quietly asleep. A new feeling stole over him, like a spring of sweetness suddenly unsealed, as he looked at his grandson, resting in the moon's full radiance. The boy had nothing of his father in his looks—Vicente had been stocky and broad-shouldered—nor did he resemble his mother, who had inherited Celita's colouring of skin, eyes and hair. Pedro was Severino all over again, and Severino's father and grandfather; he had the same lean build and long-jawed face, the same way of keeping himself to himself, and to complete all, the same crown of fiery hair, so that the tradition would continue, the line of boatmen unbroken, generation after generation dedicated to the sea. Soon, he, the grandfather, would make place for the grandson. Death could come then, with its scythe and sable panoplies and carry him off to lay him beside Celita, where some day, if God so pleased, Antonia would join them.

They were all asleep except for Severino who kept ceaseless watch, one eye on the sails, the other on the helm. The knowledge that he was the only one awake filled him with exhilaration. He was still in command, still the only man responsible for the boat and the people aboard her. Without effort he drew into his lungs long draughts of the wind that blew steadily, filling the mainsail and the jib.

'That's why I was sick,' he thought with sudden joy, 'I missed being at sea! I'll be all right again, now.'

It seemed to him that the old days had come back, the days when he managed his boat single-handed, sailing to São Luis and home again without any man's help. Thinking of Lucas Faisca huddled shivering in his hammock, he said to himself: 'It's better this way, much better.'

If Lucas had been able to come, people would have given him all the credit. Severino was better off by himself. A gust of wind pushed the 'Fair Weather' slightly off-course, he got up and loosened the mainsail a little, just enough to right the boat, and walked back to his seat in the poop, proud of his mastery, sure of his skill. He thought of Dr Estefanio and wished the man were there to see it all with his own eyes; it would have taught him just how tough a real seaman can be.

Severino stoops over his grandson; he must move him into a more comfortable position, otherwise the boy'll have a stiff neck and cramped limbs when he wakes up. He'll settle him on one of the bales of cotton lying nearby on the poop deck. As he took hold of the boy, the 'Fair Weather''s prow dipped down, down, and then reared up again, riding the crest of the wave. Severino staggers, fights to keep his balance, holding the boy in his arms. He takes one step forward and then another, Pedro's weight is too much for him, but the old man is stubborn, and he moves on, step by step, until he can lay the boy down, his gaunt limbs trembling with exhaustion. The boat slides down and climbs up once again, throwing back clouds of spray on either side, and Severino puts a hand to his breast, where a thin blade of pain is stabbing deeper and deeper.

'It'll pass—it'll pass.' The old man whispers to himself, drawing shallow cautious breaths as he makes his way slowly to the steersman's bench and sits down, carefully, to wait for the attack to end.

The moon hangs in the sky directly over the boat, surrounded by a ring of yellow light, gliding smoothly between wisps of cloud. Its brightness spills over the deck and dims the red glow of the oil lamps hanging in the entrance to the cabin, shines in sudden flashes from the dancing waves, throws a net of silver scales over the boat's foaming wake, and draws stark black outlines against the background of the horizon.

The stabs of pain grow weaker, turn into tenuous threads of soreness whose trace he follows with probing fingers moving over his bare breast. The attack is over; he drops his arm and rests his head on the cotton bale behind him, letting the cold breeze bathe his chest and taking quick, short breaths until he feels his lungs are ready to drink the air in freely.

'Well, that's over, thank God!'

He sits there relaxed and lets a flood of memories wash over him, compounded of nostalgia and evocation, bringing the names of Celita, Mercedes, Antonia, and again Celita, walking towards him along the quay. But there is no quay here, only the sea, widening about him like an endless plain.

Severino the horseman spurs his mount along the plain, he is the master, his hands control the reins and the whip, and the horse lunges forward at the prick of the spur. The wind blows full into his weathered face; the horse is willing, and gallops on and on, no need to urge him with the bite of rowels in his flank. But Severino knows that no plain goes on forever. The wind freshens, shifts, and suddenly its steady keening turns to a crazy concert of shrieks and moans, while the sails shudder and flap in winged distress and the boat labours in the press of white-maned waves. He must be here, there, everywhere at once, handling the sails, clinging to the tiller, hauling on the cables, he must decide whether to lower his canvas and leave his spars bare or to run the risk of seeing his sails in shreds. Finally the waves sink and rifts of light begin to show through the clouds; once again the sea lies about him like a far-reaching plain of water, the sails swell gently and the boat sails steadily onwards, the prow stitching wave to wave, swift but unflurried.

If the sea were always as it is now, rippling like a canefield in the breeze and dappled with the light of moon and stars, Severino would never have known the joy of matching its strength with his own and conquering. But a day arrived when it came to touch-and-go between them. Up to then Severino had gone back and forth between São Luis and the town with the monotonous placidity of a woman embroidering, in and out, backwards and forwards, always the same pattern of green and blue, sea and flying-fish, sky and gulls, the sun rising and setting, and coming to an end at the port or the quay, the pier or the canal. At night, darkness lay over all, with the red blink of the lamps hanging by the cabin entrance. Or was it the moon, round and ruddy, laying a shimmering trail on the black waters? The Southern Cross twinkled in front of them, and further off, the Three Marys glowed palely; there was the long undulating coastline and always there was the creak and groan of sails and spars. When daybreak came, the eastern sky became aflame with colour. Six months went by, not a drop of rain, only a few light wisps of cloud in the sky. Then, one evening a gale sprang up and smoky clouds massed on the horizon; Severino, the down new on his lip, felt his blood tingle and his nerves thrill. His father could not leave the tiller, it was the boy who, soaked with rain and flying spray, had to reef the sails except for the jib, while the wind seemed to come in gusts from every quarter. The waves roared and rose, looming like mountains; how they weathered the storm he never knew. After this, each new voyage added something mysterious and different to the boy's experience, and he would leap on board eagerly, his hat tied under his chin, his dungarees turned up to his ankles and his sleeves rolled to the elbow, the ends of his shirt tied in a knot above his belt-buckle; a bull-fighter enters the arena brave in embroidered satin, carrying sword and cape—there was a touch of the bull-fighter about Severino—he came, after all, of the same blood. Even now, undone by age and sickness, Severino thinks with nostalgia of the old times when he fought the sea.

'Those were good days; good days.' He mutters to himself.

They were off the Long Beach by now and the curving sweep of sand was white with moonlight, sparkling foam broke at the foot of tall black crags standing beyond the stretch of sand and at the end of the beach steep dunes were lost in blue shadows. Between the shores and the 'Fair Weather', Severino saw something—and the short hairs rose at the back of his neck—something which shone with many-coloured lights, a great galleon, Dom Sebastian's galleon, sailing slowly toward the beach. Everywhere there was complete silence, broken only by the murmurs of sea and wind.

Severino is oblivious of sea, wind, sails, tiller. He realizes he is standing on the line that separates life and death, the frontier of the unknowable, and what he feels is awe, not fear. The ship draws silently nearer to the shore, surrounded by a strange calm. Even the waves, rising and falling, are hushed; the 'Fair Weather' holds steady on her course which takes her so close to the enchanted ship that Severino can see the horse and its rider on her deck.

'It's the King!' he exclaims, standing immobile with prickling scalp and staring eyes.

Dom Sebastian leaps his white horse onto the sand and gallops down the reaches of the Long Beach; the moonlight strikes sparks from his gold and silver harness, and the horse and rider move as one. A centaur, a King, a ghost, or a sailor's fancy — at the end of the beach the horseman turns back still at a gallop, riding in a halo of iridescent silver and gold.

Severino clutches the edge of the bench with both hands; he tries to rise but his legs are powerless. He watches, holding his breath and unblinking so as not to lose the sight of the King leaping back aboard the ship. But King and horse and galleon dissolve and vanish; he realizes that he is sitting on the steersman's bench, gripping the tiller, unable to believe that he had dozed and dreamt, as old men do.

The moon seems to have shrunk, and is half-hidden by scudding clouds. There is no coastline to be seen, the 'Fair Weather' is out on the open sea. Quickly, he adjusts the tiller and his figurehead, a green mermaid, veers to starboard, curtsying to the waves that try to reach her, and the timbers groan and shudder in the freshening wind.

Severino can tell by the position of the stars that dawn is not far off; he looks about him, still confused by his experience. Had he really seen the King's galleon, or had he dreamt it? It can't have been a dream, he tells himself, knitting his eyebrows. On the other hand, the King can only be seen during the nights of June — and this is August.

'I saw it all, I know I did,' he affirms, passing his hand over his wet face.

He looks over at Pedro, who is lying curled up on the cotton bale, his hands tucked into his armpits, against the chill of the night. The lamps at the cabin entrance swing to and fro slowly.

Every boatman on these coasts knows that it is unlucky to see the King's galleon. Severino is no exception. He cannot help remembering the poor madman, Chico Nolasco, a fuzz of white hair above his black face, who used to play the *berimbau** on Cathedral Square, and who had lost his wits because of having seen, on a moonlit night of June, Dom Sebastian aboard his ship, just off the Long Beach.

---

* *Berimbau*: A musical instrument played by Negroes in Brazil.

163

# CHAPTER XXV

The breeze is heavy with moisture. The moon has lost its warm flush and seems to be growing paler as it hangs above the dark grey sea; in the sky, the stars are going out one by one in the translucent blue of the hour before dawn. Eastward, a faint glow of pink begins to show above the coastline, deepening to rose flecked with brightness.

Severino looks to starboard, his eyes seeking the Long Beach, and has to acknowledge to himself that it has already been left behind. Far away on his port bow he can see a dark sail, apparently motionless. His body is heavy with fatigue; he leans back, still intent on the marvel he had seen — had he really seen it? The slim figure of the King, all gold and silver, galloping down the moonlit beach.

He had once, while in prison, had another strange experience. One night he had seen Celita standing before him, wearing the dress she had been buried in. Astounded, he sat up in the hammock but before he could get to his feet, the figure blurred and melted, and only the light of the day breaking showed in the window. A dream? A true vision? It had happened long ago, but he could still recall its smallest details: the lines of her figure, the colour of her dress, the subdued halo of light surrounding her.

He rarely dreamed, or if he did, could not remember his dreams nor wished to. But this particular dream or vision intrigued him so much that he thought of consulting Father Dourado; perhaps he ought to have a Mass said for her soul's repose. However the priest was away in São Luis. When he got up from his hammock he had felt the same weight in his limbs as he felt now, leaning with his arms spread out on the back of the bench.

He stood up, trying to shake off the numbness. 'I'd better

not mention it to anyone,' he thought. 'A still tongue's the wisest.'

He went over to where his grandson lay asleep and shook him lightly by the shoulders. Pedro woke reluctantly, stretching his thin body before opening drowsy eyes. The dawn light lay frostily on the sea; the boy yawned, raised himself on his elbows as he put his feet down on the deck, and then tucked his shirt into his trousers.

'Time to wake up,' Severino told him.

The boy took a dipperful of water from the big jar and went to the boat's side to wash his sleepy face; Severino blew out the lamps. The image of the great ship, ablaze with brightness, seemed stamped on his brain; wherever he looked, it was there, calmly riding the dark sea in an aureole of unearthly light. What if it were a warning of his approaching death, Severino frowns, tries to shrug away a twinge of fear. What man is brave enough to face the inexplicable without a tremor? Of death he is not afraid. He had paid for his crime in this world and is certain that when he closes his eyes for good here below, they will open to the sight of Celita's face in that other world where there are no more partings and all are merry together before God.

'There's Pedro, that's the trouble,' he argues silently, watching the boy dry his wet face. 'Antonia can manage without me; he can't. No, I can't die yet. He still needs me.'

A thought occurs to him: one year. Let him have one year, no more. Silently he bargained with death; a year in which to teach Pedro all that he knew of the sea's mysterious ways. Perhaps a little less, the boy, although shy and reluctant of speech, was clever, and had the sea in his blood. Once the boy is freed from Antonia's pampering, he'll turn out all right. Severino looks at his grandson with pride, taking in his height, the eyebrows growing in a thick bar, the bright red hair. He can see him already, master of his own boat, sailing the seas of Maranhão.

'In a year, I'll have taught him,' Severino reassures himself, ready to manoeuvre the boat toward the high sea.

Grasping the tiller with his angular hands, he makes as if to pull it toward him, but delays as if his strength had suddenly failed him. Pedro approaches, stands at his side:

'I'll help you, grandad.'

A while later, with knitted brows, dropping his affectionate tone and shouting so as to be heard above the wind, the old man suddenly cried out, his eyes on Pedro:

'Luff! Luff the flying jib! Just a bit more to starboard, a little more! That's right. Tighten the stay! That's it.'

At such moments Severino's instinct is to shout, impose his will on the wind and the sea with a mouthfull of curses, as is the way with old sailors.

The 'Fair Weather' leaned to starboard, as if she were about to heel over. The jib and the mainsail shudder in a blast of wind, the cables sing, the hull strains and groans. The boat holds steady on her course in the golden morning light.

Severino makes his way back to the steersman's bench. It is a fine clear day with a few scattered clouds in the sky and the sun burns red above the horizon. Its reflection is broken up into dancing lights on the surface of the water. But the heat of the day has not yet begun. Beneath the waters they can see the dark hungry shapes of sharks following in the foam of the wake.

Dona Corina was sitting in her hammock, knitting-needles twinkling in her busy hands; hoarse but undefeated, she had resumed the monologue interrupted by a few hours of sleep.

'It's the sharks I'm afraid of, whenever I make this trip. You'd think they're going to jump right on deck and snap—there goes a mouthful, you, me or anyone! Lord, just to think of it makes me shiver. If you'd seen what I saw once, in São Luis, on Spring Water Beach, you'd feel the same way! A shocking thing, dear! I'll never forget it, if I live to be a hundred! I can see it still, the way you remember a nightmare—for a nightmare it was! Did you ever hear how Lula Flores came by his death? It was all in the newspapers; people talked of nothing else for months! He lived in a little house he owned on the beach there, near my son-in-law's, the one who's married to my Cornelia—do you know her? She's the prettiest. You've never seen her? What a pity! She was invited to enter a beauty contest once; and even today, with five young children to care for, people turn round in the street to look at her. Oh, I'm not saying this just because she's my daughter, she really is a beautiful girl. Well, as I was saying. One Sunday afternoon we all planned to go swimming together. All, that is, except me; such swimming as I do, if you can call it that, I do in my own bathroom, with the door locked. Not that I'm old-fashioned; I keep up with the world, dear, but don't expect me to go peacocking up and down the beach showing off my figure. God forbid! There's a time for everything, my dear. You may well ask, what does the old woman go to the beach for, if she doesn't swim? Well, I'll tell you; I like to sit on the sand and watch people enjoying themselves. But coming back to Lula Flores; well, poor Lula, he was a cheerful soul, fond of company and always ready to help if need be. He'd spend the day in his bathing-trunks, an old straw hat on his head, fishing, swimming, and lying in the sun. Just to show you how kind he was, he nearly always gave away the fish he caught instead of keeping them for himself. Well, there he was fishing one afternoon, quite late it was, with the water up to his breast and his rod in his hand when, all of a sudden, he saw one of those devils in front of him; it wasn't even one of the big sharks, but a shark it was just the same.

'It went straight for him, and before he knew it, its teeth were in his belly. Poor Lula gave a great shout, the shark swam away, and I saw Lula come staggering out of the water, all red with his blood, his hands to his belly to keep his bowels from slipping out! He took a step or two, poor soul, and fell on the sand, and didn't get up again. He died right there, lying in a pool of his own blood. By the time the doctor got there, there wasn't anything he could do. And, do you know, that shark came back and swam up and down, quite close to the shore — the devil! It only made off in its own good time.

'My dear, it was terrible! Never have I seen anything like it. People were fainting with horror, my own daughter among them. Naturally, no one was going in swimming after that. My son-in-law shut up his home for the rest of the holidays and went back to the city. Ever since that day, sharks are the only thing I'm afraid of, sailing. Just think of it! To be eaten alive by a brute like that! Mother of God!'

Jacob, his eyes ringed with purple and his curly hair dishevelled, thrust his head through one of the portholes.

'Good heavens, it's already morning! And me thinking it was the middle of the night! If it hadn't been for you, ma'am, talking right beside me — in my ear, you might say — I'd still be fast asleep. No, Dona Corina, it's no use at all looking at me in that cross way! I'm just a poor young boy, quite harmless, why won't you be kind to me? If you get cross, you'll just have to get un-cross again, that's all. Emotion's dangerous at your age ma'am. It's bad for the heart; and I don't want you to die on my account. Oh, if you could see yourself, your eyes are so big and round and full of sparks! Your nose gets sharper, and the veins in your neck stand out. I'm afraid of you, Dona Corina, you might throw me to a shark! I'd better get out of here quick!'

The old woman struggled to rise from her hammock.

'It'd be no more than you deserve. Insolence! It would put an end to you and your nasty ways. Get out of my sight before I smack the grin off your face, and teach you the proper way of speaking to a respectable woman!'

The wind blew stronger, drowning the sound of her angry voice. Laughing, Jacob went out on deck and started to comb his hair, preening himself before the pocket mirror he held up before his face.

Pedro watched the sea swell and subside, and noticed how the light changed on the moving crystal of the waters. With the money Antonia had given him he would buy drawing paper and crayons in São Luis, and a box of water-colours. But what if his grandfather objected?

'I'm not a child any longer,' he said to himself defiantly.

Instinctively, as he watched, his keen eyes picked out a tint, an outline, a reflexion here and a shadow there, to store in his memory. He waited for the fish to jump, glittering in the sunlight, from the tumbling waves, streaks of live silver that flashed and quivered in the bright morning air. They had come to a patch of wild water; further ahead the sea lay in dead calm as far as the horizon. This contrast between stillness

168

as of a lake and the ruffling of wind-driven waters gave birth to an endless succession of shifting fragmentary colours that changed in range and depth as distances altered and the sun rose higher.

A new world was opening to his eyes; his concentration on its wonders, so fresh, so joyful, made him forget the empty feeling at the pit of his stomach, which had seized him at the beginning of the voyage, when the green mermaid at the prow poised herself and then dived deep, deep, into the watery hollows.

'Well, Beautiful, won't you say good-morning to poor little me?'

Pedro turned and saw Jacob smiling at him, comfortably wedged between a bale of cotton on one side and a coil of rope on the other. His eyes took in the long face beneath the black carefully-combed hair, slick with oil, the slanting eyes, the pointed chin, and the mouth smiling crookedly and showing a flashing gold tooth. The shadows under his eyes seemed painted with charcoal; his red shirt was open at his neck, round which he wore a gold chain with a cross attached. One arm was propped up negligently on the cotton bale; a large watch, with a broad silver band was on his wrist. With his other hand he stroked his face, where a rosy bloom showed on his cheek, too fixed to be natural.

Before Pedro could answer him, he went on:

'I dreamt of you all night long; now I've got a new name for you.'

Pedro was too taken aback to reply; Jacob said quickly:

'Temptation, that's what I call you; because that's what you are to me!'

Just then Clementino Pinto, his eyes swollen with sleep and his book still tucked beneath his arm, drew near Severino. One fat hand held on to the beret that the wind was trying to snatch from his head.

'We'll reach São Luis by afternoon, you think, Skipper?'

'Before sundown, God willing, Sir.'

'Splendid', Clementino smiled approvingly.

'The approach is much safer by day; to tell you the truth, I don't care at all for the Alcantara Reef; a nasty place, much

169

better to navigate it by daylight. At night, quite frankly, it scares me! Two of my friends, very dear friends indeed, lost their lives there, on their way from Curupuru to São Luis. I lost a cousin as well, who was closer to me than a brother. When I was a boy, I used to haunt Coronation Quay, to eat watermelon and listen to the stories the boatmen had to tell; I heard a lot about ships wrecked on the Alcantara Reef. Someone told me that it's a great flat stone in the middle of the sea, just beneath the surface. If a boat's master is ignorant or imprudent, he'll sail right over it, unaware of the danger below. When the tide turns, the waves boil up and lift the boat, and when it comes down again, it crashes on the rock and breaks up. There never are any survivors; even if a man can find a plank to cling to, the sharks are there, waiting for him.'

Severino, his cigarette at the corner of his lips, peers at Clementino through narrowed lids. His face is expressionless, his thoughts far away. Dom Sebastian's galleon, lighted up and dazzling, seems to be constantly before his eyes. He knows, now, that he must make his preparations for a longer voyage than any he has sailed on before. A year is still all he asks. He wonders how Celita is; how will she greet him? Holding his cigarette between his fingers, he says to himself, in a murmur:

'Everything's different in Heaven.'

# CHAPTER XXVI

It was almost noon, and Severino could hear the rustling of the twig broom someone was using to sweep the courtyard with. He was leaning back in his hammock, with his old almanack open on his knees.

The deep-toned bell of the Cathedral sounded once, and the

170

echo spread and died in the air; other single notes followed at intervals, low and full. Without raising his eyes from the page Severino made the sign of the Cross.

'Whoever it may be, may they rest in peace.'

In the cell next to his Lucas Faisca was whiling away his Sunday rest hour tuning his guitar. He hummed a song, plucked at the strings to get the notes right; fell silent, then hummed and plucked again.

The Cathedral bell continued to toll. Severino got up and went over to the window; thinking of Father Dourado, he called out in a loud voice:

'Can you hear the bell, Faisca?'

'I can tell it must be for somebody important. They must have promised the ringer a special tip: his hand's improved. He'd never do as good a job if it were for me!'

At twelve o'clock Faisca called Severino to the window.

'I've got news for you,' he said exultantly. 'Good news, man. The best bit of news we'll hear this year, either of us! Yes, today to me, tomorrow to you, as the saying is. Guess who they're tolling that big bell for? I told you, didn't I, it must be somebody important; so it is. Somebody *very* important, Severino! He died this morning, they must be cheering their heads off down in Hell, that pleased they must be with their new recruit!'

He laughed heartily and spat far and strongly through his yellowed gap-teeth.

'Can you guess, Skipper? Well, I'll tell you: it's the son-of-a-bitch who sent us here.'

Severino thrust his face against the bars of the window.

'Dr. Genesio? The Prosecutor? Dead?' He exclaimed.

'Watch your tongue, Skipper. The swine was a judge already. And a bad judge too, as worthless as his own mother. However, there you are. He's finished now. May the fiend fly away with me if Satan doesn't turn out a grand parade in his honour. Yes, he's for the devil's cauldron today, to try the taste of boiling pitch, curse him. I can finish tuning my guitar, now. It's uncanny, isn't it, Skipper? Over there, the big bell is tolling while I sit here singing.'

171

Severino, at the window, his hands gripping the bars, was as motionless as stone. Minutes passed in a heavy silence. Finally he asked:

'Did he die suddenly?'

'Oh, no! Very slowly. He was riding that flashy chestnut of his, and came to grief, two days ago; it wasn't only the fall, the brute kicked him as well—serve him right! He took a day and a night to die, bawling all the while like a calf that's been taken from its mother!'

Severino turned away from the window, paced up and down his cell, frowning intently; from time to time he stopped, struck his clenched fist into the palm of his hand, and then resumed his monotonous walk.

'He should have died at once—he shouldn't have been given time to repent of all the evil he'd done', he said in fury, 'if he repented, maybe he's not in Hell after all! He may even have had time to get Father Dourado to help him die—the swine!'

He went back to the window and called Faisca's name.

'I'm worried, friend. Do you know whether Father Dourado gave the brute Extreme Unction? It'd ruin everything!'

Faisca pulled at his sparse pointed beard with a nervous hand.

'I doubt it, Skipper, I doubt it. What! Clear a path to Heaven for a rogue Purgatory'd be too good for? The priest's not such a fool, Skipper; I doubt he'd do it. Although it's true enough what they say: you can't trust a man who wears a skirt!'

When his noonday meal came, Severino was unable to eat. To and fro he went, from wall to wall, like a caged wolf. His cell had never seemed so small, so stifling. He would stop at the window, grasp its bars as if he wanted to bend and break them, and stare wildly down into the empty sunny courtyard. No sound broke the Sunday silence except the mournful strokes of the big bell. Now and then the breeze, freshening for a moment, raised a little cloud of dust from the bare ground. Next door, Lucas Faisca plucked the strings of his guitar, cleared his throat with a rasp, and sang in a high cracked voice, alternately bewailing a lost love or threatening vengeance. From the cell beyond the cell beyond him, a deep

172

voice mocked him lazily. 'Don't be a fool; women are all whores at heart.' The police sergeant's dog began to bark. Severino's restless feet kept to their unchanging rhythm. He felt a crazy impulse to hurl himself at the iron door and beat on it with his fists. He wanted to get out, run into the street and up into the Cathedral's bell tower, and force the ringer to stop. Why toll the bell for the repose of a soul who had never deserved God's mercy? Let him go to his appointed place in Hell.

It must have been about four o'clock when he saw Malaquias, one of the prison guards, crossing the courtyard, 'Hey, Malaquias! I want you to do me a favour.'

'All right, Skipper, what is it?'

'Please get Father Dourado to come. It's a matter of life or death', he said urgently, 'go now, at once, I'll make it worth your while.'

Malaquias took off his cap, scratched his white head thoughtfully.

'I'll not deny I could do with any little you can spare me. But I don't see how I can bring the priest in such a hurry. They're burying the Judge in a little while, Father Dourado must be on his way over already. There're the last prayers to be said over the corpse, and then they'll close the coffin — and that'll take time. And then the funeral itself — the sacristan going ahead carrying the Crucifix, then the priest, then the hearse (and you know how they keep the horses at a walk), and then all the people following on foot. Say an hour, from the deceased's house to the Cemetery. At the Cemetery there'll be speeches made before they lower the coffin into the grave. I'm willing to bet there'll be at least four speakers: the Mayor, the Public Prosecutor, the Headmistress of the Municipal School and the President of the Town Council. Now just think it over, Skipper, and tell me whether Father Dourado'll be home before seven o'clock, at the earliest. And once he's home, he'll want his dinner; once he's had his dinner, he'll want his hammock, and a bit of rest, I shouldn't be surprised.'

Severino cut short Malaquias' long-drawn-out speech.

'I'll give you double what I usually do if you can get the

173

Father to come today. Any time he likes, but this very day, Malaquias, tell him I need him badly, it's life or death to me, let him come for the love of God! You know I'm no liar. If I say it's life or death, you may be sure it's so!'

Malaquias put his cap back on his head.

'Well, I haven't much hope, but I'll do my best; it won't hurt me to try, but I can only get hold of him at the Cemetery.'

Less than half-an-hour later, Severino, still at the window, saw Malaquias come slowly into the courtyard, dragging his lame foot.

'No luck, Skipper,' he called from the end of the courtyard.

'I ran all the way from here to the Judge's house', he said as he stood at last beneath the window, 'and I met Father Dourado just as he was cleaning his boots on the doormat. He wouldn't let me finish giving him your message. He can't come before tomorrow. Tonight, when he leaves the Cemetery, he's got to go straight to the Cathedral for Saint Anthony's Novena. After that he's going home, he says, too worn out to go out again. He was up until two o'clock of the morning, giving the Judge Extreme Unction, and hasn't had a minute's rest since. He's worn out, only fit for his hammock, that's what he says. You're to be patient, Skipper, he'll be here early tomorrow morning, as soon as he's said his first Mass.'

Alone in his cell Severino fell into a fever of frustrated rage. He had been cheated. His enemy, the creature he hated most on earth, the man who was to blame for Celita's death, had managed to escape after all; instead of the endless torments of Hell, so richly deserved, Father Dourado had helped him to find his way eventually to Heaven! To Heaven, where Celita was—Severino writhed at the thought—Celita, too pretty, too vain, to resist the blandishments of an experienced seducer! And he, Severino, not there to protect her from her own folly.

Impossible to fold his arms and do nothing; but what could he do? He racked his brains trying to think of something before it was too late. Horrid visions filled his head, of Dr Genesio arriving in Heaven, tall, handsome, his thick hair shining with hair-oil, and Celita coming to meet him in a glow of content, her large eyes full of challenge and desire.

'Father Dourado—I've got to speak to Father Dourado', he

174

muttered in an agony, flinging out his arms in despair as he continued to walk the narrow space from wall to wall.

Only the priest with his knowledge of God's mysterious ways could tell him for certain what might be happening up there, this same moment, between Dr Genesio and Celita. Only he, wise in experience, cool-headed and shrewd, could tell him what to do to save his wife again — and again? How often would she need him to rescue her frailty, her poor, pretty weakness? He felt giddy, his thoughts in a whirl. Tomorrow night might be too late. He clasped his aching head in both hands.

The sun was sinking, the shrill cry of cicadas came from the trees in the street outside. Suddenly the answer came to him: he, too, would die. Freed from his body, his spirit would reach Heaven and meet Dr Genesio face to face. This time Celita would be safe from him; it was the Judge that should be himself judged, before the face of God. He looked feverishly round him until he caught sight of the hook from which he slung his hammock. Measuring its distance from the floor, he decided that it would do; that night he would hang himself.

Now that his mind was made up he felt calmer; he was able to sit quietly in the chair next to the chest of drawers and wait in the gathering shadows for the black stillness of night. Next door, Faisca's guitar was silent at last and the bell had ceased to toll. Presently they would bring his supper, before the daylight had quite faded. Severino sat without moving, his legs crossed and his hands folded on his chest.

During the long years in prison, shut out from sun and wind, his face had lost its tan; beneath the deep furrows and criss-cross of wrinkles the skin showed pale and lifeless, the sunken eyes seemed darker. His fiery hair had turned rusty, patched with white at the temples. His Adam's apple stood out in his thin neck, where the skin was darker than his face, and his half-grown beard made him look like a man recovering from some severe illness, with his big bony hands and his skinny legs on which the wide trousers hung in folds.

When the jailer brought his supper, Severino did not bother to go and fetch it from the window-sill where the man had left

175

it. He felt no hunger, only thirst, a queer, bitter-tasting thirst that dried his mouth and constricted his throat. He drank a glass of water, and then a second glass, and went back to his chair. Before sitting down, however, he took the rope that held up the hammock, made a noose on it, and hung it up on the hook in the wall. In imagination he went over his moves one by one: he would stand up on the chair, put the noose round his throat and kick the chair away. Would the rope take his weight without breaking? Yes—of course it would, it held up his hammock when he lay down. The window darkened; Malaquias was peering in through the bars, his head blotting out the light.

'I was in Cathedral Square when the funeral procession crossed it,' he said. 'You never saw such a crowd! It was the finest funeral that's ever been seen in this town! And in perfect order, too. Yes, Skipper, they certainly gave him a good send-off—all the big people were there, everyone you can name. A whopper of a funeral! Even fat old Nunes, the notary, who never leaves his house, was there in his wheel-chair. Yes, there's no doubt about it, the Judge was a popular man, very popular.'

He put his hand in front of his mouth to hide the gaps in his teeth.

'They say he left three widows: his wife and two girl-friends, each with her own house, too, paid for by him. Not to mention the others, just casual, once-in-a-while, girls, and everyone knows there were plenty of them, Lord forgive me—he wasn't a man but a stallion!'

Severino sprang up in fury.

'A bastard, you mean! A miserable, worthless, shameless scoundrel, who should neve have been born!'

Malaquias would not agree.

'A lot of people thought the world of him, Skipper.'

'A scoundrel,' Severino shouted as he went towards the window.

Malaquias was already walking away.

'A scoundrel! A cursed scoundrel!' He yelled at the old man's retreating back.

He fell to pacing up and down again, alternately wringing

his hands and clenching them into fists, thrusting his fingers through his hair. It was already dark within the cell. A firefly hovered in the opening of the window, and the night breeze blew chilly from off the sea. Outside a bat swooped low across the courtyard. Severino pulled the chair into place beneath the hook in the wall and poured himself a glass of water. He watched the water rising in the glass and a thought struck him.

'If I kill myself, isn't it a mortal sin? Then how can I go to Heaven? It'll be Hell for me, dying in a state of sin! Then I can't kill myself!'

His trembling hand spilled the water over the window-sill. Madness! It had been madness to think of killing himself. He stood there, clutching the glass and water jug, his thoughts in confusion, conscious only that he had been within an inch of doing something that would have cut him off from Celita forever. And lost his own soul as well.

'Christ!'

Quickly, with shaking hands, he took the rope from the hook, undid the noose and slung his hammock. The lamp in the courtyard shone feebly into the cell. Unsteadily he lit his own small lamp. The rest of the night he spent rocking wide-eyed in the hammock, the creaking of the rope in the hooks a background to his restless thoughts. Dr Genesio and Celita, Celita and Dr Genesio. Together in God's Heaven, while he, Severino, ate his heart out, walled in, alone, helpless. He bowed his head, pressed his hands to his throbbing temples. Then he looked up, saw through the window a sliver of sky bright with stars. He left the hammock and began his weary walk again. Halting by the window he watched the darkness lighten and the first gleams of dawn appear. Sunlight blazed down on the courtyard when he saw the thin figure of Father Dourado following Malaquias towards the prison entrance.

'Well, he couldn't come yesterday, but here he is now,' the man said, as he let the priest into the cell. He left the door half-open and went away. Severino brought forward the chair and motioned for the priest to sit.

'Oh, Father! Ever since I heard of that man's death yesterday I've had no peace! I never closed my eyes all night. I need you, Father. I need you — I need you!'

177

Father Dourado stood by the chair, resting one hand on its back. He looked attentively at Severino, who was twisting a handkerchief in his uneasy fingers. The priest took in the pallor and haggardness of the man and tried to comfort him.

'Whatever you've got to tell me will remain between us two, Severino. Speak out; remember I'm more than a friend — I'm a priest doing God's work among men. You've got nothing to fear; whatever's troubling you, share it with me.'

Severino bent his head for a moment and then looked up,

'Father, answer me truly: did you give Dr Genesio the last sacraments — Extreme Unction?'

'Yes, of course I did.'

'You forgave him his sins?'

'I did so in God's name.' The priest confirmed, puzzled by the question.

Severino took a step forward, his eyes wide, his chin thrust out.

'And he can go to Heaven now — just like that?'

'Why shouldn't he find God's peace, Severino?'

They stood for a moment, eyes locked, faces close together, hardly breathing.

Severino broke the deadlock.

'Father, you know what a son of a bitch he was! A rogue, a filthy swine, a scoundrel, Father! And evil; why he was meaner than a snake! A devil, Father, a wicked, heartless devil! And you forgave him his sins and put him on the way to Heaven, to God's own Heaven! And where's Celita now, just tell me that, Father Dourado! She's in Heaven, isn't she? Now tell me: who can swear that that beast, once he finds himself there, free to do as he likes, isn't going to try to lead her astray? Eh? Answer me, Father!'

The priest bit his lips trying to contain a smile; it was too much for him, however, and he threw his head back with a mighty peal of laughter, while his thin fingers spread over his faded cassock as he held his belly.

'Father,' shouted Severino, the veins standing out on his neck, 'this is serious, terribly serious! How can you laugh? Stop it, for God's sake!'

The priest looked at him warily; Severino seemed capable of anything in his wildness. He put his handkerchief to his lips, leaning against the wall of the cell. He waited a moment and then said incisively:

'Get that foolishness out of your head, Severino. The sins and miseries of this world have no place in the next. Make yourself easy. Everything is different in Heaven.'

# CHAPTER XXVII

Antonia was surprised to see sunshine flooding the room when she opened her eyes. Her body ached as though bruised; it took an effort to lift her head and prop herself up on her thin outstretched arms, and feel along the floor with her bare feet, searching for her old slippers. Narrowing her eyes against the brilliant sunlight she thought vaguely that she had never slept so late before. Was it ten o'clock already? Noon? It was hard to tell, the light was so intense.

'It can't be twelve already,' she murmurs, with a half-smile. Once on her feet she felt dizzy, and held on to the end of the hammock, waiting for the feeling to pass. An ox-cart went by in the street outside, the wheels turning ponderously, rattling and squeaking; a window slammed in the breeze, the *corrupião* sang loudly on the verandah. As she took an uncertain step forward, clinging still to the hammock, the old woman said aloud:

'Pedro'll come back; I know he will.'

Yes, by the grace of God, through the intercession of Our Lady, Help of Sailors and blessed Saint Lucy, Pedro will come back. Aunt Noca had seen it in the cards last night, on the dining room table; the cards had foretold the 'Fair Weather's'

179

return. That's what Aunt Noca saw, and why should Antonia doubt her? God is merciful, Antonia, He will not leave your prayers unheard. Aunt Noca's cards are old, greasy, worn at the edges, but they always tell the truth, when the old woman mutters a prayer to Saint Cyprian and lays them out on the table. That's why you were able to sleep after all, having smoked your pipe in the swaying hammock. All the same you walk about the room and your voice, as you say, 'Pedro'll come back,' is low and full of fear. How should you not fear for him, a boy and his grandfather, weak and sick old man that he is, in a small boat somewhere on the sea out there?

'He's in God's hands.'

Before she reaches her bedroom door Antonia pauses, frowning. Surely she is being ungrateful.

'I only think about Pedro, pray for Pedro. What about Severino? He's my man, after all, I've spent almost my whole life with him—no, I don't want to lose my old man, not yet! Oh, dear Lord, when I pray for Pedro's safety I mean Severino's as well, You know it!'

Dragging her feet, she goes out into the passage and toward the sitting room. She has a vague memory of having gotten up in the middle of the night to lock the front door. Had she really done it? And what about Aunt Noca? Had she stayed in the house overnight or had she gone home?

'Poor old Father Dourado, his memory's gone and he hardly makes sense these days—maybe I'm getting to be the same way. God forbid! It's bad enough to be old, I don't want to be addled in my wits as well!'

She looks in at the sitting room door; the front door is closed and so are the windows; above the shutters there are fan-shaped insets of clear glass through which shafts of sunlight stream into the room, gay with dancing motes of dust. In its shabby frame Celita's photograph looks down from the wall.

'God rest her soul,' the old woman sighs.

There is the settee with its cane seat and one arm broken, she must have it mended. Only one chair has survived of the two that matched the settee, and the yellow of the straw is dark with age. Opposite the settee, between the two windows, the long mirror hung in a tarnished gold frame, bought by

Severino to gratify one of Celita's last whims. The glass was dull and blotched with age; light sank into it and was lost. The ornaments Severino used to bring back after each voyage had all been lost or broken, including the little boat made of glass that looked so like the 'Fair Weather'.

Antonia looks around her wistfully, opens one of the windows and goes back into the passage. She stops short and feels in her pocket for matches. Had she left them on the straw mat on the floor by the hammock, beside the pipe? No, they aren't there—where could they be? Then she remembers that before going to sleep she had lighted a candle in front of the picture of Saint Lucy. There was the box of matches beside the copper candlestick down which the melting wax had run. She picks it up, her eyes on the picture; she had been about to start the day without her usual morning prayers.

'I've never forgotten before,' she thinks, annoyed. Then her eyes wander to the square mirror above the chest of drawers, and what she sees there makes her shiver: a thin face, the dry papery skin scored by deep wrinkles, high cheekbones and a sunken mouth that moves as hers moves. She stares at her reflection, the living face staring at the face in the mirror. Could that really be her? So worn, so wrinkled, with swollen eyes and grey hair covering her ears. Yes, it is herself. A small painful smile tilts her lips sideways, and her reflection faces her with the same crooked smile.

'Yes; an old wreck, that's what I am,' she says to herself.

She puts an unsteady hand to her hollowed cheeks, covered by a fine net of wrinkles, touches the furrows that run from beside each nostril to the corners of her mouth, and remembers the young Antonia of days gone by, whose long loose hair smelt of jasmine, firm-bodied and plump, smooth and fine of skin; the girl who gave herself soul and body to Severino, leaving parents, sisters and friends to live with him among strangers in a place unknown to her. Her memories are so vivid, it might have happened yesterday; Pedro is forgotten and the picture of Saint Lucy, and the radiance of the morning sun pouring into her room. It was night when she came to this house for the first time, and she can still recall the flowered dress she wore to steal away from her home, the red

181

paper flower in her hair—whatever had become of the silver bangle she wore, on that night so long past? And the gold ring Severino brought her from Sao Luis? The morning breeze is heavy with the scent of jasmine, hanging in wreaths over the fence. The ox-cart has gone on down the street. Above the rustle of the palms in the yard she can hear the bird singing. Antonia leans her elbow on the chest of drawers and gazes into the mirror, suspended between past and present; how swiftly, how strongly, life had spun its web of days and nights, joy and tears.

Yesterday's world is gone, finished, dead, for everyone except Antonia; she alone can evoke its realities, for a little while; however it soon sinks back into the shadows of the years, and all that is left is a withered old woman peering into a mirror.

'That's the way life is.'

She murmurs a Salve Regina, quickly crosses herself and walks out of the room; the full skirt hangs limply, the lace ruffle hides her shrunken bosom. She fights against the recurrent dizziness and weakness; her swollen feet seem to drag lead weights after them. She goes slowly out to the verandah, open to the sea and steeped in sunshine.

She is not hungry; the well-chewed bit of tobacco in her mouth has taken away her appetite for breakfast. Standing by one of the verandah posts, she looks along the beach and sees the pier, whose end is almost submerged by the rising tide. Tears sting her eyelids, but she will not cry.

'He's far away by now; where shall I meet him when they come back? Down at the pier's end, or here on the verandah? Oh, he knows I'm an old woman now; my boy won't mind if I wait for him here instead of going all that way.'

But perhaps it would please him to see her sitting on the pier ready to greet him. After all, it's not more than she can manage; the slope'll be difficult but she can borrow Severino's cane, the one he's never used.

Her wrinkled face broke into a smile.

'A sight I'll look, hobbling along with a cane!'

She continues to look at the pier where the waves are rising higher. The surface of the sea glitters in the morning light. Far away a boat spreads its sails, making for the open sea; two gulls are flying low above the water. She thinks of Mercedes, slim and dark, waiting for Vicente. It does no good to beg her to come back to the house; not until nightfall will she return, climbing wearily up the slope, the child heavy in her belly. Mercedes is sure that her husband will come back—at any moment she may sight his boat's dark sails. And when he lets go the anchor, just beyond the pier, she will be there to welcome him.

Antonia, who secretly has lost all hope, encourages her.

'There's been many a boatman come home again after not having been heard of for more than a year. Yes, and found his wife dressed in mourning and praying for his soul!'

'I'll be praying too, Aunt Tonia; when Vicente comes back I'm going to spend the whole day on my knees, before the picture of Our Lady, Help of Sailors, in thanksgiving!'

It's your turn now, Antonia. Year after year you waited for Severino on this verandah, never doubting that he would return. Even if he delayed a day or two, you were so sure he would come back that the long hours passed without troubling you. It's true that, once, he stayed in Sao Luis longer than usual and when he finally came, he brought Celita. After that you waited in silence, shut in your room, but still confident, trusting in what Aunt Noca's cards said. The impossible happened, Celita died, you took your place again, with the other woman's baby in your arms, and Severino depending on you for the things a man needs from the woman in his house when he's in trouble himself. You brought the baby up better than her own mother would have done, loved her dearly, found her a husband.

When your man came home, thinner, paler, graver, the house was full of flowers and friends, Vicente in a new suit, waiting to ask her father for permission to marry Mercedes. After being shut up for so long Severino had grown awkward; he shouted for you to come and tell him what all the fuss was about. You were sitting in your room in your Sunday dress, a flower in your hair, uncertain, embarrassed. And everything was your doing, even to the girl's dress, rich with embroidery and lace, and the lace tablecloth, almost hidden by dishes full

183

of good things you had cooked. How people fingered the lace and admired it, Antonia!

The cage swung in the breeze, the bird pouring out its song; the long fern fronds quivered and swayed.

'Hush! Save your song for when Pedro gets back.'

One week, maybe two, and the 'Fair Weather' will show up on the skyline at the entrance to the bay, the limpid sky above and sunlight all around, just like today; Severino sitting on the steersman's bench and Pedro busy with the mainsail. The green mermaid rises and sinks; the boat glides gently to rest at the end of the pier.

'God has always been good to me; when things go wrong, He stretches out His hand and sets them right.'

To wait is also to hope; but waiting is weary work, Antonia, especially at your age, bent, deaf, full of aches and pains. You look older than Severino, and yet you are the one who looks after him and worries about his health. And once he's back, you'll want him to go to sea again. A man in the house, with nothing to do, gets out of temper, Antonia; querulous, touchy, grumbling at every little thing. It's the pain that worries you, that claw that grips him relentlessly, shutting off the air from his lungs. Once he's cured, let him go back down the pier and sail out to sea, at the helm of his boat. That's the way a man is. And stubborn, every mother's son. Will Pedro be like his grandfather or take after Vicente? He was with you for so short a time, Vicente, living in this house with Mercedes; all you can remember is a young man who laughed and strode easily, and was kind to everybody. Perhaps the sea doesn't like people who are gay and kind. Maybe Pedro had better be like the old man, proud, obdurate and reserved.

Antonia goes into the kitchen, blows on the cinders, sets a lighted match to the kindling and waits for the flame to rise beneath the iron pot; it will be a while before the water boils. She goes into the yard carrying a sharp little knife and makes for the rose bushes growing near the house.

'I've nothing to do all day, I might as well go to the Cemetery and take Mercedes some flowers. Poor little one! She always loved roses, red roses especially!'

It is a long way to the Cemetery, the street twists and turns,

184

better go early, before the sun gets too strong. The walk cheers the old woman; suddenly the thought occurs to her: had she locked the door? She is already quite far from the house. She shrugs and smiles.

'There's nothing to steal, only an old woman's odds and ends, who would want them?'

At the Cemetery gates she stops to rest and get her breath back, holding the roses to her breast. Neco Torres comes forward, taking off his hat.

'You haven't been here for a long time, Dona Antonia', the man says.

'Too busy, Seu Neco. I've never a moment to myself! But Mercedes knows I don't forget her.'

She draws a deep breath and makes her way down the narrow path paved with jagged uneven stones, that wanders among the graves, the clean white new graves, and the shabby ones, in need of a coat of whitewash. Turning off to the right side she sees the stone cross and patch of flowers beneath which Mercedes lies. As long as she lives Antonia will remember the cold afternoon, wet and windy, when she watched them lower the coffin into the grave and had to turn away and leave Mercedes there. Today is warm and bright, a gentle wind stirring the leaves and making the casurarinas shiver. It is a place of peace as palpable as the living silence of an empty church: blessed be God, who gives to those He loves — peace. Antonia sits on a corner of the marble slab and puts the roses down carefully. A bird darts by on flickering wings; a butterfly hovers just beyond; there are glints of sun from the chipped granite of a nearby headstone. Her lips move in a soundless gabble of prayers as she thinks of Mercedes the child, Mercedes the girl, slim and dark and loving.

'Pedro's gone on a journey', she says finally, 'He ought to reach São Luis this afternoon, God willing. Saint Lucy and Our Lady, Help of Sailors, will look after him. Don't worry, child.'

One rose lies forgotten in her folded hands. She lowers her eyes so as to pray undistracted, repeats in a murmur the prayers she has already said, crosses herself and rises.

'Until next time, my darling.'

185

Instead of taking the way home she walks down another path, holding her sunshade at an angle to protect herself from the bright heat; at the end of a row of graves she pauses, waits to make sure that no one is near, and lays the rose on the black marble of Celita's grave.

'May Our Lord give you His Light,' she says quickly.

It would not look right to be seen lingering by the grave of Severino's other woman, so she walks away indifferently, slowly enough to be able to say an Our Father and Hail Mary for Celita's soul before reaching the Cemetery gates and passing out into the long street lying in the glare of mid-morning.

## CHAPTER XXVIII

Jacob said confidentially:

'I'll come and fetch you and show you the town, would you like that? Don't say no! I'd be so disappointed I might jump overboard! I mean it, you know; I always mean what I say. If I tell you that I'll jump into the sea if you refuse me, you can be sure I'll do it! It's a shame they've taken away the trams, it used to be so amusing, one could see most of the city without getting off the tram. All you had to do was stay on it until it got back to where you'd started from. It's not a big town, though, we can do it on foot and I'll show you all the sights. Or I might get a car. I'm sure I could get a car — I've got a way of getting what I want, you know! Yes, I'll get hold of a car, don't you worry. Afterwards, I'll take you to my place and give you a drink; what do you say to lovely, iced grape juice, eh? Now, don't laugh, though you're even handsomer when you laugh! Aren't you, poppet?'

He raised his arm, pointing.

'See, there's São Luis! Over there.'

Pedro could only see the coastline, green in the misty afternoon light, and drawing nearer. They were no longer alone on the sea; around them boats rocked at anchor, becoming more numerous as they approached the city. Piercing the mist, spears of sunlight seemed to cleave the water, breaking it up into scintillating reflections, so that Pedro was obliged to narrow his eyes against the dazzle.

Jacob shaded his own eyes with his hand. 'See? There's the Alcantara Reef. We'll have to sail right round it, quite a long way.'

Turning to Pedro, he saw the boy was no longer beside him but was going toward the poop, staggering on the heaving deck. Reaching Severino, he sat down beside him, on the steersman's bench and handed him a battered tin mug, which the old man put avidly to his lips. 'What a devoted grandson,' Jacob said ironically.

Going into the cabin, he stopped in front of Neco Torres' daughter, limp and pale in her hammock.

'When do you expect it? This month? Good God! I'm glad you didn't tell me before, I'd have been terrified it might be born during the crossing! And so you're glad you're going to have a baby all of your own! And a husband all of your own, too! That's right! Doesn't the Bible tell us to grow and multiply? And do tell me, is it a boy or a girl you're wishing for? A boy? Of course! Well, I'll bring you luck, and it'll be a boy, you can be sure! Have you chosen a name for him? Why not call him Everaldo? I'm mad about the name Everaldo! Or you could call him Roberto, that's a beautiful name, too.'

He leaned down to look at Dona Corina's knitting.

'How lovely! Why, Dona Corina, I had no idea what an artist you were. I saw how busy you were, those great big needles never stopped, but, really, I had no idea! Let me congratulate you!'

Severino had felt the first stab of pain just as he was beginning the manoeuvre that would take the boat away from the Alcantara Reef. His right hand stiffened on the tiller while the other went to his breast; stooped and tense, it seemed to him that if he tried to breathe, the pain would lance through his heart like lightning, and he would faint. Nonetheless, he kept his eyes on the mainsail and said to himself in dry-mouthed defiance, 'It's nothing, it'll pass!'

His dark face, tense with the struggle to contain his pain, might have been carved from wood. The sun shone full on the rigid muscles of the jaw and the nose grown suddenly sharp. In the shadow of his hatbrim, the eyes were two black holes. The wind whipped at the worn felt brim, and he pulled it lower; his pain was a private thing. No one must see it.

A sudden flaw caught the sails, and the boat heeled steeply to port, while the waves dashed at the hull. Severino leapt for the cable of the mainsail and hauled on it with both hands, although his chest seemed to be torn apart. The mainmast swayed back to vertical again, and he sank down on the bench while Pedro stumbled along the deck in his direction, the mug of herb tea in his hand.

'Here's your tea, Grandad,' the boy said anxiously, his eyes on the old man's drawn face, livid and gleaming with sweat, the breeze puffing out his shirt above the thin shoulder-blades.

Severino nodded, unable to speak, his hand on the tiller, watching the 'Fair Weather' 's prow beginning the long curve of the course she must take to round the Reef. Minutes went by in an endless half-hour as the old man fought his illness, grim and unyielding: this was the one spot in all the sea where no one but he could sail the boat to safety. Not even Faisca could have taken his place. The claw of pain held him, cruelly relentless; he fought back in mute determination, eyes wide and jaws contracted. At times, he felt himself weaken, exhaustion loosening his limbs, and he would react savagely, clenching his fists and digging his teeth into his lower lip. There flashed through his mind the memory of the white horse galloping down the moonlit beach. Was this the meaning of it? No. And no. He *would* not die now, he would go to São Luis and return, as he had sworn to do. Even if this time should be the last.

Pedro brought him his mug refilled; he put out his hand to take it, and the lightning struck again, cleaving his breast. He took two gulps and gave the mug back to the boy, in a daze of agony, body and mind. If he lost consciousness who would take the boat into Coronation Quay? He stared fixedly at his grandson and saw how the boy watched him closely, flinching at every sign of pain.

The sky was clearing, with only a few tufted white clouds driven north by the wind. Against the skyline a crowd of masts became visible, but as yet no gulls flew, dipping and swooping, above the sea's surface. The crumbling houses of Alcantara were dark against the bright horizon.

High up on the prow, Jacob began clapping his hands. 'There! There's Sandy Point!' he cried.

He skipped down the deck towards the cabin.

'Dona Dulce, Dona Corina, Seu Clementino, come and see! We've sighted Sandy Point already! Sao Luis isn't far off! Come along, Pedro! Hurry up, my friends—it's such a beautiful sight, you musn't miss it!'

In spite of the radiance of the afternoon the long spit of land pointing out to sea was still indistinct.

Dona Corina Soares stood in the cabin door clutching her long bone needles and ball of wool. She looked toward the coast and then peered at Jacob, who was hopping about the deck, one arm dramatically pointing. She shrugged, turned to Neco Torres' daughter and said wrily: 'What a fuss! The hen's clucking already before the egg's been laid! I think he's hysterical as well as—well, you know what he is!' She smiled scornfully, showing large, uneven teeth. 'It'll be an hour or so before we get to São Luis; you'd better lie down in your hammock, child. There'll still be time for me to finish your baby's jacket!'

She sat down in her hammock and cleared her throat, coughed once, and began casting off the stitches at the end of a sleeve. She talked on while she worked, with the smug malice of a woman whose favourite occupation lies in discussing the faults of her acquaintances, and their mistakes.

'Yes, dear, if I'd known Jacob was going to be aboard I'd have come by another boat. See, as soon as I set eyes on him I hid my handbag—here it is! And do you know why? He might just take a fancy to it; that's why! Yes, child. A pansy, as you call it, and a thief as well. Mark my words; a thief, that's what he is! But he won't get any change out of *me*. I'm sitting on my handbag, my money and my jewelry, and he'll have to reach

189

underneath my behind before he can get at them, and that won't be easy, I promise you!'

She showed her teeth again in a smile that spread whitely below her thin hooked nose. The needles clicked; clack-clack went her busy tongue.

'Do you remember Rufino the choirboy? A thin fair boy, always well-dressed, and such nice manners! Haven't you heard what Jacob did to him, during that week or so he spent at home? My dear, he ruined the boy, dragged him down to perdition! It's quite true—there was a terrible scandal! I know all about it because I'm Abdalla's neighbour, you see. They caught the two of them, Jacob and Rufino, naked, my dear! in a house of ill-fame! With two black men! Two black men! Oh, it's too dreadful, just like Sodom and Gomorrah! Nothing like that had ever happened before, not in our town! What times, child; what times! I do believe it's the end of the world.'

Pedro kept close to his grandfather, looking with curiosity at the crowd of houses standing out against the skyline; they bulked larger as the boat sailed on in the violet haze of twilight shot through with sunset gleams.

'Are you better, Grandad?'

Severino nodded; but the truth was that he still breathed in painful gulps. His left hand was still pressed to his chest and his tense body trembled with fatigue. He wanted badly to let go, lie down on the bench and give way to the vertigo that made his head reel; as tough as he was dour, however, his inflexible will kept him in this place, head erect.

'No. And no. I won't die on this crossing.' He repeated to himself, hand steady on the tiller, eyes intent on the waves the prow slid through. Silent, unmoving, he might have been carved from the same block of wood as the bench on which he sat. A long time passed before he let his left arm fall into his lap and breathed in deeply, his lungs freed once more from the tight bands of pain.

He mopped his wet face with his handkerchief; the attack was over and he was still alive, but he felt that this was the last time that he would sail into Coronation Quay as skipper of his own boat. Never again would he battle his way past the

Alcantara Reef on his way to São Luis. Once he sailed again for home he would be leaving all that behind him for good: a world now closed for him, a life's work done. He felt an unaccustomed moisture beneath his lids. This was goodbye.

There was Sandy Point on one side and the Bonfim headland on the other, clasping the bay in their long embrace. The Bulwark, lined with age-old palms, guarded the Governor's Palace. Below it, jostling the boats that crowded the water, the rising tide flung its foam against the stone wall of Coronation Quay. Memories stirred in Severino's mind.

'There it is, as I've always known it.'

Dona Corina, Clementino, Neco Torres' daughter crowded aft, Pedro among them, gazing open-mouthed. The city seemed to float toward the boat, the blue and white tiles of the housefronts lining the steeply climbing streets. Only Jacob moved about restlessly, stretching up on tiptoe and craning his neck, exclaiming in delight, now rubbing his hands in glee, now pointing to the town with his thin arm outstretched, the gold bracelet with his name engraved on its plaque shining on his wrist.

'Just look at it! Isn't it wonderful? Oh, there's no place like São Luis! Wonderful! Prettier than ever by twilight, with the stars coming out above the roofs—look at the bridge, the bridge of Saint Francis!'

Fortunately the wind, blowing towards the land, carried his words away together with his affected cries of joy. On the poop, lost in his own thoughts while he kept watch on the sails, Severino could not hear him. It was just as well; his São Luis was a different place, seen by his eyes alone.

191

# CHAPTER XXIX

Once the passengers had landed (Jacob was the last to go, complaining bitterly because he could not find a porter to carry his huge trunk), Pedro walked slowly round the deck, and then jumped up on the flat roof of the cabin, drinking in the sights and sounds of evening.

His first vision of São Luis, its gentle hills lying between two files of tall palms in the light of a blazing sunset, had filled him with excitement. The wild seas that boiled over the Alcantara Reef and reached almost to the foot of Sandy Point had been left behind and the 'Fair Weather' was gliding gently through the calm evening waters. Astern of them the dead city of Alcantara was ghostly in the mist. The streets and steeples of São Luis drew nearer, becoming more distinct; he could see clearly the row of two-storied houses just beyond the quay.

Sailing by Sandy Point Pedro looked curiously at the ruins of the Fort of Santo Antonio, but soon he had eyes only for the great ship lying at anchor in the port. A launch passed by them, small as a beetle on the swelling tide and he turned to watch it; a man standing on the poop waved a greeting and the boy waved back. Looking around him, he saw his grandfather at the tiller, sitting stiffly on his bench, his face haggard, his jaw set. In his excitement, the thought of going to help him never entered the boy's head; all he could think of was the city before his eyes, many-layered, rank on rank of dark roofs rising above the tiled housefronts, bathed in a lingering glow of dying light. What was that moving so quickly down the street? A bus! And there was another one, and a third behind it. He drank in the new colours and unfamiliar outlines as the boat sailed swiftly toward the worn stones of Coronation Quay, lying between the weathered bastions, beneath the Bulwark Wall; a stone ramp led down into the water, off which two boats lay at anchor. To one side the lazy waters of the Anil River, on the other the serene flow of the Bacanga, while the port itself was crowded with boats of every kind, from ponderous ferries and swift launches to the *alvarengas\** and winged *igarités*; seagulls hovered above them and urubus flying heavily on slow black wings. The new bridge arched grandly over ˙the water, linking the town to the headland of São Francisco. It was thick with traffic, a steady stream of cars and buses; beneath it a boat slipped over the water, all sails set.

A while before, Jacob had turned back before leaving for a last word with Pedro. His black hair glistened, his red shirt lay open on his breast. He pointed toward the heights of the town.

'I'll come to fetch you early tomorrow,' he whispered, conscious of Severino's eyes on him, 'I'll be there, on the quay. Do come, now! You really will? I'd be so disappointed if you didn't — I might kill myself! You know I *always* mean what I say, so be sure to come!'

The last light died out, a pale transparent veil of blue fell over the city, sea and sky, through which roofs and steeples showed black against the horizon. Lamps were lit all around the quay, shining with a reddish tinge; an evening wind blew fresh from off the sea.

Standing in the prow Pedro watched as the 'Fair Weather' turned to starboard, smoothly following the line of the quay and slipped past the Bulwark Wall, as though it were going to turn into the Anil River. He was still gazing up in admiration at the wall, marvelling that he was forced to crane his neck to do so, as Severino began to haul down the mainsail with sure, swift movements, at the same time gauging the boat's speed and the strength of the tide. It was the old man who let go the anchor as they came to the ramp, while Pedro stood gazing at the city, and pulled the bar of the tiller against his bony chest to prevent the hull from scraping against the stone wall of the quay. He saw his passengers safely ashore, helping each one to jump the narrow gap between deck and ramp. When the last one had gone, he let himself sink down on a coil of rope and

* *alvarengas*: barges for carrying freight.

leaned against the cabin's structure, and exhausted, panting, knowing that any moment his old enemy would grip his heart and squeeze his lungs, he watched his grandson take another slow turn round the deck and felt an unreasoning desire to laugh.

Pedro went up to the poop so as to look at the city from a different angle. It lay beneath a sky powdered with stars; in the east a growing light was diffused above the housetops. Hearing the sound of a car going by in the street by the quay, Pedro leapt again to the cabin roof and looked eagerly, taking in the maze of streets and squares, narrowing his eyes as he tried to distinguish a particular stretch of street, fascinated by the headlights of a car driving up a sloping road, the street lamps like a string of shining beads. He felt as if he were taking part in some festival.

The vague dream that from time to time had troubled his imagination returned, but this time with a definite shape and flavour, and he swore he would make it come true. He would stay in São Luis forever: this was his place.

As a child, turning over the pages of Celita's old magazines that Antonia had given him, he had studied the pictures of paved streets and many-storied houses whose walls were gay with coloured tiles, the wide avenues filled with bustling crowds. That was when his dream first began to haunt him. Later, he had longed to go to São Luis to study for the priesthood in the Seminary there, but his grandfather had violently denied him. Other magazines found their way to his enquiring hands, lent by Father Dourado, and the old longing came back; some day, when he was grown-up, he would go to São Luis to live, and perhaps to study painting. Dona Hilda, his teacher, impressed by his talent, had told him that that was what he ought to do. 'It would be wrong to leave you here, there's nothing for you', she said.

After that, whenever he saw the 'Fair Weather' leave the pier on her way to the city, he had followed the boat with wistful eyes.

Dona Hilda offered to speak to his grandfather, but the boy knew only too well what the old man's reaction would be.

194

'No', he said hastily, 'better not say anything.' He nearly added 'I'll go when I'm ready, and no one can stop me then!' He thought better of it, however, and held his tongue while he rolled up the drawings that Antonia would hide later on.

And now, here he was in São Luis! How different from his little town. Everything was a marvel to him; instead of dark streets, with an oil lamp's feeble glow at the corners, tall posts followed each other up the streets and narrow alleys, each crowned with a bright cone of light, tinged with red. They lined the Bulwark Wall and the edge of the quay. The headlights of passing cars shone like great red eyes as they moved up and down the sloping roads. From the windows rectangles of light fell on the pavements. Was it always like this, the boy wondered, or was it a feast-day, a celebration? He listened for the peal of church bells sounding in the night, he looked up at the sky searching for the green, blue, yellow, crimson of fireworks. Listening intently, he could hear no music, only the light breath of the night wind and the hollow sound of the waves breaking on the sand dunes.

'It must be this way always!' he thought joyfully.

He wondered who the parish priest was. In which direction lay the Cathedral? And the jail? The Governor's Palace, surrounded by palms, loomed above the Bulwark Wall. He decided it was too big to be the jail. There were so few dogs barking! Were the trees he could see growing in the empty street full of nests of owls and *bacuraus*?* Did the *saracuras* sing at daybreak?

He noticed that the sky above the black roofs was clear of clouds, and that the stars had dimmed; a yellow radiance was growing in the east. In a little while the moon sailed above the roofs, a great full moon, round and golden, slowly climbing the heights of the sky. The city, bathed in transparent moonlight, looked unreal, the tiled walls of the houses at the back of the quay gleamed like porcelain. The moonlight ran like water down the steep ways, poured over the roofs, trickled down the leaves of the trees, and flooded the scarred Bulwark Wall, half-hidden by creepers.

* *bacurau*: night bird belonging to the *caprimulgida* family, of which there are at least twenty five (25) kinds in Brazil.

It made Severino's face, already pale, look livid as he leaned against the cabin structure, paralyzed by pain. Beneath his hand his heart leapt and shuddered. Bad as the attack was, he knew he would not die, not this time. He had enough strength left to beat Death once again; he still had to sail the 'Fair Weather' home. Rigid, unblinking, he waited patiently for it to pass. Slowly, cautiously, he began to breathe again. His face relaxed, and he looked up at his grandson who was standing in front of him.

'Why didn't you call me?' Pedro asked reproachfully.

The old man let his hand fall on his lap.

'It didn't last and didn't hurt much. I'd have called you otherwise. It's over now.'

Silence fell between them tinged with shyness; they looked at the city lying before them in the night, each busy with his own thoughts, Severino rose with an effort, put a hand on the deck rail to steady himself, and walked slowly aft; then he walked back again and sat down, this time on a bollard, facing the town.

'I could have anchored at Campos Mello Ramp, or opposite the Desterro', he said slowly, without looking at the boy whose eyes were on his face, 'but I wanted to come here, although few boats do. It's where my father anchored when I sailed with him for the first time. I wanted to bring you here as he brought me.'

Without meaning to he sighed deeply, and put his cigarette to his lips quickly, to hide his feeling.

'Some day, you'll bring your son here in your turn. You'll remember your grandfather then, just as I remember my father now.'

He lifted his head, let his glance wander over the silent quay as he drew slowly on his cigarette.

'When I was your age Coronation Quay was a very different place. It was full of people, coming and going, noise, life! To tell the truth, the only things that have lasted my time are the quay itself, the sea beneath us and the Bulwark Wall. They've done away with the old market and the fishsellers' stalls on Caju Beach, down there. Pity. Everyone goes by the bridge—the quay's a dull place now.'

196

The moon, rising, had dwindled in size; it seemed to hang between the twin towers of the Cathedral.

Severino went on, breathing short and shallow.

'There were times, when the fruit had ripened, cashews, mangoes, watermelons, the place used to look like a fair, all day and all night! They used to stack the watermelons in piles as high as houses. A man could choose the one he wanted and sit down and eat it on the spot. The rich people hadn't started building over there yet, there were just some old houses with iron balconies. When you saw a lantern hanging over a door you knew that it was a place where they sold fried fish. There were little boys everywhere, shouting at the tops of their voices, selling lengths of sugar-cane and *pamonhas\**. And there used to be gas lamps instead of these electric lights that hurt one's eyes. Time goes by, and things change for the worse, that's the trouble.'

Pedro who was sitting on the planks of the deck, stretched out yawning, his hands behind his head.

'Wouldn't you rather sleep in the cabin? You'd be sheltered there.'

There was no answer, and Severino, looking at the boy, saw that he had fallen asleep. In spite of the old man's age, he still liked to sleep in the open himself, the breeze soft on his face; he smiled, looking at the boy's tranquil features and red hair steeped in moonlight. Wearily he made his way to the cabin entrance and lit the lamps. A feeling of sadness came over him suddenly; he walked back up the deck towards his bench, his heart heavy with the certainty that he would never again return to Coronation Quay.

He let himself slump down on the bench and half shut his eyes; his lean body swayed back and forth, keeping time to the rocking of the boat; memory after memory came to him—there was Celita standing on the stones of the quay, while dawn gradually lightened the night sky; once again he sailed toward the cove where they had spent the day together, locked in love. The old houses, the trams drawn by donkeys, the carriages and the clatter of horseshoes on stone, boatmen,

---

* *pamonha*: A sweetmeat made from green maize.

street sellers, the blind Portuguese who played the guitar, the black man in a long-tailed coat with a monocle in his eye, the crazy blonde woman who cursed the sea, the visions came and went in his head and wiped out the present, jostling each other beneath the hissing gas lamps. Some came unsought, others he summoned deliberately, taking his leave of them and the things of which they had become symbols. One by one, they came, brought by the light of other days, as though time had gone into reverse bringing back each moment of fleeting emotion; no sooner remembered than lost again. Strangest of all, these crowding memories that faded so swiftly, forced unaccustomed tears to his eyes and brought him a dull longing for death; as though death might restore to him his lost world.

Suddenly a woman's voice called from the quay wall.

'Hey, Redhead, have you got a cigarette?'

He looked up and saw her, small, dark, her face thick with make-up; her hair was drawn back in a knot and long earrings dangled from her ears, while her ample breasts threatened to spill over her low-cut blouse. He recognized her: it was Lila, who came each night to the quayside to pick up men; she only slept with sea-going men, be they boatmen or fishermen. He went up the steps two by two, the packet of cigarettes in his hand. When he got to the top, she laughed, throwing back her thin shoulders.

'I've got a cigarette already! I wanted you to come up on the quay; I've slept with your father and I want to sleep with you. Come, give me your arm, Redhead.'

It had happened sixty years ago, but Severino can still feel her firm breast brushing his arm, and they walk side by side down the narrow pavement, round the old market place and up the dark slope. He can see the small crowded sitting room with its cane settee, the open door into the bedroom, where the iron bed rattles as though it were going to fall apart. The lamp in the sitting room sends its weak rays through the open door and he can see himself in the oval mirror, in shirt-sleeves dungarees and leather sandals. Somewhere Lila is singing a lullaby as the water from the shower runs off her body. Still wet, the towel wrapped around her waist, she comes to the door and calls his name.

An hour later she said to him as he dressed, stretching her naked body lazily in the creaking bed.

'What's the hurry, Redhead? Your father knows you're with me. And you needn't pay me, he's paid me already. Paid me very well, too.'

Going back at dawn, he goes down the stone ramp and feels the water lapping gently about his ankles. His body feels astonishingly light; he knows that this night has made a man of him. He can no longer show fear when the gale blows savagely and the figurehead at the prow dives into the hollow of the waves; he must stay on deck, steady, unflinching, ready to face whatever comes, prompt to handle canvas and tiller with the same ease that his father and grandfather showed.

Before going into the cabin to spend the night sitting in his hammock, Severino covers Pedro with an old rug, and draws an empty cotton sack about his head, to protect it from the dew. Looking at the boy, he notices he is nearly full-grown already, and wonders whether he will find, nearby, another Lila who will sleep only with sea-going men.

# CHAPTER XXX

The first thing he saw through drowsy startled eyes were the lights of the city, the bright lamps crowning tall narrow posts. He jumped to his feet, took a couple of steps forward, felt the deck steady beneath him; the 'Fair Weather' lay at anchor, and he was not dreaming. It was all real — the stone wall of the quay rising in front of him, the line of trees in the middle of the avenue, the row of old houses opposite the quay.

A breeze from off the sea blew chilly between his shivering shoulders and he tucked his hands into his armpits to warm them. From the edge of the deck he looked up, with a thrill of joy, to the sky above the roofs, where the uncertain light of dawn was beginning to show behind the Cathedral's twin towers. He stayed motionless, listening. He heard a distant cock-crow followed by others as the roosters in the neighbourhood gradually awoke. And the sea no longer beat against the boat's hull. He walked round the cabin to the other side of the deck.

The wind was colder there, but the sky was clear and the dawn light lay palely on the water, so that Pedro was able to see that the falling tide had uncovered wide strips of sand, as though the waters of the bay were emptying. The boat's prow lay on one of the sandbanks.

He wondered what he ought to do; perhaps he should wake his grandfather. Going into the cabin he saw the old man sleeping, his legs hanging over the side of the hammock and his head resting on a rolled-up sheet; he was sitting, not lying, his mouth half-open and his breathing coming quick and short in an uneasy doze. Pedro stood beside him in the light of the storm-lantern, hesitating. Finally he went back on deck. What good would it do to disturb his grandfather? They couldn't get the boat off the sandbank, not at low tide. He leaned on the taffrail, looking toward the gap between Bonfim Point and Sandy Point that was the entrance to the bay. Somewhere in the same direction a lighthouse blinked in the dark haze, while over the town the light was growing stronger. He could make out a growing number of sandy strips and crests so that he thought it would be possible to cross the entire length of the port, jumping from one patch of sand to the other.

'You'll come swimming with me off Sandy Point, sweetie. Some people like Springwater Beach better, but not me. I like Sandy Point, it's less crowded. Whenever I go, I spend the whole day there and only come back at night. Now that they've got the bridge, you don't have to cross by boat any more, it's only ten minutes away. I'll have a lovely tan all year round!'

Looking to his right toward São Francisco Point, Pedro could see the headland jutting above the strips of sand, and remembered Jacob standing beside him, the wind blowing

200

through his hair and tugging at his red shirt.

'You'll get a tan too, sweetie, your skin'll go a beautiful brown, just like mine! Oh, how good-looking you'll be! Don't tell me you won't come, I can't bear it! Just think, a whole day in the sun together! It makes me feel all funny just to think of it!'

The lanterns of the boats anchored in the port were gradually being extinguished, and as though in answer to a signal, the daylight brightened; a flood of light washed over the town and the sea. Along the waterways that threaded the sandbanks moved canoes and *igarités* propelled by oars; soon, however, their coloured sails filled with wind.

If they had been home Antonia would already have been busy, opening the windows to air the house, laying the table for breakfast, putting fresh birdseed in the *corrupião*'s cage and would now be in the kitchen waiting for the water to boil. After breakfast, he would be able to see her thin stooped figure wandering about the yard and stooping over the vegetable plot to examine the plants that shone with dew, chewing absently on her bit of tobacco.

The thought of her made Pedro uneasy; he could guess now how anxious she must be, thinking only of their return. Not a doubt but that when the time came she would prepare their favourite desserts, cover the dining room table with her best embroidered cloth, and then sit down in the rocking chair, looking out to sea with her bright eyes framed in wrinkles. When the 'Fair Weather' 's sails appeared at the entrance to the bay heading for the pier, she might even go down to the beach, waiting to meet him with a smile full of love and joy, eager to put her arms around him. How would she feel when she learnt that he had stayed in São Luis? Pedro leans his elbows on the deck rail, and forgets to look at the scenes around him. Streets and squares, hills and headlands are beginning to glow with colour in the morning light but his eyes are fixed on the ripples than run hissing on to the sand and there sink and disappear.

He grew afraid of weakening; drawing himself up, he walked to the prow and looked at the town, full of challenge and promise, steeped in the gold of morning.

'Just as soon as I can I'll bring her over to live with me', the boy decided.

The trees on the avenue were loud with the cries of swallows and *bem-te-vis**. The old houses, their windows flung open to the street, looked wide awake. Buses sped by the quay and came and went over the bridge.

Yesterday's excitement returned; Pedro's eyes roamed over the town, trying to see into its furthest corners. Up the slopes went his searching glance, taking in the gleaming tiles of the housefronts, lingering over church steeples, sorting and storing the variety of colours that gave an added gaiety to the sparkling morning. He wondered what the streets were like that wound about the top of the hills. How large was Carmo Square? On what side of the town would he find the Ribeirao Fountain? Remedios Square must be there on the left, the one with green palm trees and a little church at one end. He knew that Broad Street, lined with shops on either side, began at Carmo Square and went on and on, apparently endless. Why had they named one of the streets after the Sun? They all lay equally drenched in sunlight! Father Dourado had told him that the Seminary was beside the church of Santo Antonio—was it that one, lifting its two rectangular towers above the huddle of roofs? If so, the Seminary must be one of the tall houses next to it, probably the bigger one, on his left. He already knew where the Cathedral was, and the Archbishop's Palace stood beside it. Eyes narrowed against the blazing light, Pedro took in every detail, even to the black shapes of the urubus, sailing high, two by two, above the multitude of buildings.

He was so absorbed by what he saw that when his grandfather called to him from the cabin, he gave a start of surprise. Going in, he took the mug from the old man's outstretched hand. It was time for their coffee.

'I thought you were still asleep, Grandad,' he said, alarmed by the old man's haggard pallor. Sleep had done him little good; his swollen eyelids, jutting cheekbones and unshaven chin made him look much older than his real age.

* *bem-te-vi*: Literally: 'I see you clearly'. 'Pithangus Sulphuratus', a bird very common in Brazil.

'Did you feel ill at night?' the boy asked.

'Nothing much, it was soon over. God tempers the wind to our weakness, son. I'd like to get better, but if I don't, it's no matter. I came as far as this, and don't feel any worse. Now I've got to think about getting back tomorrow or the day after, while the moon's still full.'

They were sitting opposite each other in a patch of shade near the mainmast, Severino perched on a bale of cotton and Pedro on a coil of rope, drinking their coffee in silence and taking bites out of the slice of fluffy cake that each of them held.

The old man spoke first.

'Now you know there's nothing out of the ordinary to sailing a boat. All you need is the taste for it, time and patience. In a few days you'll know how to handle the 'Fair Weather' as well as your grandfather. Another two or three crossings and you'll be fit to steer. I don't have to *show* you, all you have to do is watch me. The rest'll come. The knowledge's there, inside you; you've got the sea in your blood.'

He looked keenly at his grandson and noticed how the boy dropped his eyes. Sadness came over him suddenly, and his eyes became vague. It was hard to step aside. In spite of all that he had suffered, he still loved his work at sea and did it with enjoyment. It was a good thing to be the skipper of your boat and your own master. However, he knew, quite clearly, that his life was nearing its end. He took comfort from the thought of Celita, waiting for him at his journey's end.

'Nobody lives forever. Everything must end some day for each of us, there's no dodging that. I thank God that I've lasted this long and can hand over the 'Fair Weather' to you', he said.

His throat felt tight, he cleared it raspingly to hide his emotion, turned away from his grandson and went into the cabin, a cigarette held loosely in his fingers. He was still inside, hanging his mug upon its hook, when he heard someone on the quay calling his name. He recognized the voice; it was one of the men who had come to unload his boat. He shouted to them to come aboard.

A while later he came on deck wearing over his shirt an old black coat that Pedro had never seen before.

'I've got to go to Long Beach to see to some things,' he said, moving clumsily in the coat which was too big for him and bore the marks of having lain folded in his trunk.

'Then I'll drop in at the Harbourmaster's, and be back around twelve-thirty.'

While the men unloaded the cargo, Pedro sat down on a bollard; he was beginning to feel impatient at Jacob's delay. Every few minutes he looked up at the summit of the ramp. Hadn't Jacob said that he would come early?

A wooden plank had been placed, leading from the deck to the foot of the ramp. Along this plank the cotton bales were being shifted by the three men unloading; their black glistening backs swung rhythmically as they pushed each bale along, and then with a concerted heave, sent it smoothly up the ramp to the level of the quay. E-o! They cried at each heave.

Pedro watched with interest, looking forward to the moment when the three bent and swung together with their cry of e-o! The sun shone dazzling on their bodies, making the swelling muscles glisten on the torsos, smooth and black as ebony. Watching the strong, supple bodies, he felt a disturbing desire to touch their backs, slick and shining, and feel their rounded muscles. He was amused by his own absurdity, and went on watching until the last bale reached the top of the ramp and the men went away.

The town was now fully alive, windows wide to the sun and the streets full of noise and motion. The tide had reached its lowest ebb; many boats were aground on the strips of sand between the shrinking waterways. It was beginning to turn, with a ripple of waves beneath the gull's outstretched wings.

Pedro struck his fist into his open palm. It was too bad of Jacob! Why had he promised to come if he didn't mean it? He paced up and down the deck, without losing sight of the pavement at the top of the ramp. Finally he made up his mind. Why should he go on waiting? He would go by himself. He stopped to think for a minute. 'I can always ask my way. After all, I'm not a child anymore, I know very well what I'm about.'

He felt the boat move beneath him, rocked by the rising

tide. The waves had covered the sandbanks and were breaking gently at the foot of the quay's stone wall. Looking at the bay, he saw that some boats had already spread their sals and were gliding out to sea. The brilliant light sparkled from the crests of the waves and lit the blue depths of the moving waters; on either side the headlands stood out in their beauty. A thick plume of dark smoke lifted from the stack of a ship that hid the end of Bonfim Point.

He stared at the boats that slipped away into the distance. Frowning, he imagined what his life would be if he took his grandfather's place on board the 'Fair Weather', sitting on the poop bench grasping the tiller, all his life, year after year, sailing from the pier of his home to Coronation Quay and back again and perhaps being lost at sea like his father. No, not for him. He was no boatman. And he had to free himself now — or never.

He seized the boathook, waited for a wave to lift the hull, and succeeded in hooking one of the iron rings attached to the ramp. Carefully he pulled, until the boat's side was nearly scraping the stone. He slipped a rope's end through the ring, brought it back on deck and made fast. Before he knew it, he was standing on the quay, looking down the avenue, first one way and then the other, not knowing which way to take.

# CHAPTER XXXI

The old houses bordering the Long Beach, built of stone and whitewashed, many of them having their walls faced with ancient Portuguese tiles; with their sculptured stone doorways, projecting eaves and belvederes looking towards São Marcos bay — these old houses, Severino, are beginning to die.

It takes only a glance at a quiet corner of the sunny streets, to see that, for all of them, their dying has begun, and the heart knows a pang of sadness. Memory evokes a past still recent, but how different from the present! An oppressive sense of doom and dissolution hangs over them, in spite of the countless windows wide open to the street, with here and there a figure leaning on the delicate tracery of a wrought-iron balcony, eyes on the pavement, or peering down the steep cobbled way. Grandly they stand, the big doors thrown open in their frame of Portuguese stone, showing· a spacious corridor with the stair at the end, ample shallow steps and finely turned balusters carved in hardwood, leading invitingly to the two upper floors. Nonetheless, they will die as old trees die, crowned with a last brief burst of life, wasted by age but still erect.

The streets through which the old man walks, his worn black coat hanging loosely on his thin shoulder-blades, are full of morning sun and bustle. From sunrise to sunset the streets are full of people. The pavements empty only when the shadows of the ancient houses slant darkly across them. Then silence falls and an aching loneliness; the steps of a solitary passer-by have a hollow sound, like those of a mourner walking among graves.

Severino pauses at a street corner and looks nostalgically along the stone paving walled in by the looming housefronts of another century. He remembers the heavy carts that used to rumble over the cobbles, drawn by slow-moving donkeys, their hides flicked now and then by the carrier's whip. The narrow pavements would be · crowded: street-sellers, dockers, shipowners, boatmen, gipsies and sailors, who thronged the streets all day, the whole week long. Only on Sundays, doors and windows closed, a guard lounging in front of the Treasury, another guard by the Customs House, were the streets quiet, as they were today, steeped in lazy golden peace.

Along the broad stone flags of the pavement Catarina Mina had once walked in high-heeled silk sandals, a black woman so well-known that the alley whose narrow flights of stone steps led from Nazareth Street to Pier Street was named after her, and here too, the black man Mandail had strolled, in frock-coat and monocle, stately and handsome even in madness, a book beneath his arm, his raised forefinger saying Hush! as he murmured that the Bacanga River nearby slept at night as a man sleeps.

Built by black slaves, the fine houses of Long Beach had been old when Severino was a boy; they had endured as though they had been raised to last forever, beautiful, deep-rooted, indestructible, their gleaming fronts looking majestically down upon the streets, solid as the walls of a fortress, and it was true that they had outlasted the rich merchants responsible for their building.

The ground floors, opening directly on to the pavements with their large iron rings where men tied their horses, were crowded with shops, offices, banks, greengrocers, bars and warehouses, doors wide open above sills of stone worn smooth by use. Upstairs were the bedrooms and saloons of their owners; hung with painted wallpaper, furnished with jacaranda, silver handles to chests and cupboards. Often, during the late afternoon, the notes of a waltz or polka would float from the drawing-room windows into the street. During the heat of the day, when the street noises died down awhile, the rooms resounded with the creak of swaying hammocks, while the sea breeze blew gently on the sleepers' faces.

All that is finished. Inside the large rooms, once bright with sun, the shadows gather, behind the rows of sad shuttered windows. If a gust of wind blows one of them open, the shutter will be left to swing and clatter, there is no one to close it again. The belvederes from which a man could see the ships far away in the open sea, are like rooms where a corpse has been waked. Silence hangs heavily inside the houses and over the street outside. Urubus perch on the rooftrees, dismal and black, with curved beaks and cruel eyes. At night, bats circle and squeak; during the day, rats scurry through the empty rooms barred with sunlight.

What will happen to them, these grand old houses, before they crumble under the sledgehammer's blows? Perhaps the same fate that overtook the lovely tiled houses of Chalk Street, with their eaves of porcelain tiles and balconies of iron worked as fine as filigree, turned into brothels now, crowding round the old Convent of Divine Mercy, become today's Police Barracks.

Even when the last throb of life, the last remnant of splendour, has died away, something of legend, of poetry, that flowers best among ruins, will cling to some of Long Beach's old houses. The moans of slaves, the dragging of chains, the idle slam of a door, wandering steps troubling the midnight hush, somebody running up a dark stairway, the sudden crash of falling plates and a muffled rumour of angry voices — such sounds will be heard for years inside the old houses whose emptiness draws the ghosts that love to linger in ruins and abandoned dwellings.

Long Beach may keep its secrets to itself; but one generation will hand down to the next tales of violence and despair: the beautiful girl raped by a slave and murdered, hanged by him from her own hammock hook; the merchant who jumped from the highest window and now goes back every night to his long-closed shop on Pier Street to meet his creditors and beg for time in which to meet his debts; the old woman who killed herself because she forgot where she had hidden her store of gold doubloons; the Negro lad who was whipped to death for stealing, although he had earned the money doing odd jobs, money that was to buy his freedom, and who, each year, is seen joining the procession in honour of Saint Benedict the Black, patron of slaves, just as the litter bearing the Saint's image enters the church to the peal of bells and bursting of rockets.

Perhaps the ghost of Dom Diogo de Souza, in cocked hat, knee-breeches and silver-buckled shoes, still haunts the silent maze of streets, looking for the promenade he caused to be built over filled-in swamps, when he was Governor of the *Capitania**.

Severino goes his way, his mind full of memories; as he goes down one of the steep alleys leading to the sea, he lifts his eyes for a moment, looking for the gas lamp on its iron bracket that used to hang there, but it has gone.

* *Capitania:* Brazilian territory was formerly divided into large areas known as Capitanias; later, these were sub-divided into provinces and the name Capitania was discarded.

'That's where it used to be.' he says to himself in disappointment.

No longer are red lanterns hanging over the doors of the places that used to sell fried fish; only one or two are left in the little streets off Coronation Quay.

In Andrade's big warehouse, by the empty shelves, two grey-headed employees are yawning behind the counter, and he looks about him with discouragement, while old Andrade comes forward to shake his hand.

'Long Beach is almost finished', Severino says to him.

Andrade is in his shirt sleeves, a gold watch chain across the front of his white waistcoat, his black tie held in place by a jewelled pin. He frowns, the wrinkles of his forehead deepening.

'You notice it too?' he answers. 'I keep saying the same thing; Long Beach is dying. You remember how it used to be? I can hardly believe it; living here as long as I have, sometimes I think I'm dreaming! They say it's because of the new port of Itaqui, that's being built; once that's ready, it'll be the end of Long Beach. A shame, I call it; it grieves me to think of it. They're in such a hurry to get Itaqui ready, money's being spent like water. At first, it looked as if they'd never get it done but now, spending like drunken sailors, it's going ahead in bounds. And what for, sir, can you tell me that? What for? The sea's just the same, over there or over here. I don't understand it. It's all for nothing, just a whim. We had Long Beach, right here in the town, everything in its place, just as it should be, what do they need another port for, all that distance away? If this place was too small, they could have made it bigger; there's plenty of sea and plenty of land. But no; oh no! It's old, it's out of fashion, let it go. You can see what's happened; even during the rush hour you can stand in the middle of the street to read your paper, there isn't traffic enough to bother you. You can see the men idling by the Treasury Building, beside Campos Mello Ramp, sunning themselves like lizards, there's no work for them to do. Here on Coronation Quay, that you know better than I do, you can count the boats, these days. This warehouse, that used to be always crowded from morning to night, as you well know, is so empty and silent it makes one uncomfortable. To think we've known Long Beach at its best, full of carts and trucks, the pavements blocked with piles of freight, goods being loaded and unloaded, customers waiting their turn, everyone talking their heads off!'

He let his arms hang hopelessly and sighed, closing his wrinkled eyelids. Then he opened his green eyes again.

'Well, we must be patient; it's a law of life after all, decay comes after ripeness. It'll be my turn some day; I've lived quite long enough!'

The two employees smile; the old man stretches out his thin arms, palms upwards, towards a chair standing by the counter.

'Please sit down, Skipper.'

'Well, Seu Andrade, God allots each man his time, and only He knows when it runs out. For my part, I'm getting ready to leave, too. I can't do it yet because I've still some things to see to. But I've begun to put my house in order. I've been a boatman for sixty years, time to be handing over.'

Old Andrade moved back a step and leaned his elbows on the counter.

'Are you selling the 'Fair Weather', Skipper?'

'No, I'd never sell her. I'd rather do what I did with the other boat, let her rot away at the end of my pier, as you know. I'm handing her on to my grandson; he's almost a man grown. God didn't give me a son but He did send me a grandson to take over from me.'

'You're quite right, Skipper. You've worked hard and earned your rest. Unluckily, I can't do the same. I'm the prop of this place—no, I'm more than that, call me its foundation, take me away and it'll collapse! When that happens, people'll know what kind of man I was, they'll be fair to me at last. God knows, they criticize me enough! It's true I've no patience any longer, I lose my temper over any little thing! Well, whose fault is that? Not mine, I'll be bound! I haven't changed but the world has, Skipper; it's changed greatly.'

'It's wise of you to get out of it all, I only wish I could do the

210

same. But I can't, so I just have to hang on, as you can see. I can tell you one thing, though: if anybody wants to move out to Itaqui, let them go. Just don't count on my doing it. Here I'll stay as long as God wills. Let them all go. I'll come down to Long Beach every day and open my warehouse doors, as I've always done. Even if I have to do it all alone.

That's gospel truth, I mean what I'm saying, I'm ready to take my oath on it, Skipper!'

Having vented his anger, he fell silent, let his shoulders sag, stroked the end of his moustache.

'Bring your grandson here', he said at last. 'Any time you choose, I'd like to know the boy. I'll make a point of being as good a friend to him as I am to his grandfather. He'll have credit here, just as you have always had, Skipper; at least while I, Filomeno Andrade, am alive, and very much your servant!'

The pain was diminishing; Severino waited for it to pass off before answering. As soon as he could speak, he drew a careful breath and wiped his pale moist face, then raised his eyes to the old man's face.

'I'll bring him here later this afternoon, or perhaps tomorrow morning. I'm not saying it just because he's my grandson, but he's a fine looking boy, with the same red hair that I had at his age, but taller than me, and not one for talking. He keeps to himself, doesn't make friends lightly, which is as it should be, if he's going to follow the sea.'

When Severino went out into the street, the sun was high overhead. He crossed to the opposite pavement, drew a deep breath and walked slowly away. Would he ever sail the 'Fair Weather' back to São Luis?. Could this be his last journey? To reach the Harbourmaster's, he had to go up Pier Street and then turn down Palace Ramp. But suddenly he turned about and went down Pier Street in the opposite direction, turning into Chalk Street as if to take leave of the old houses he would never see again. They stood in rows on either side of him, proud old witnesses of Long Beach in its heyday, and offered him, in the glittering sunshine of the empty street, the refuge of their shade.

# CHAPTER XXXIII

He stood on the quay, feeling beneath his feet the stones of São Luis; here was a dream come true, and he was shaken by joy and fear. This first experience of new and unknown territories sharpened his senses to vivid awareness of possibilities he could not as yet imagine. The physical sensation of treading unfamiliar ground was at first stronger than any other.

Looking at the town from the 'Fair Weather' 's deck, his feelings had been different; in a way, he was still on home soil, and the city he looked at seemed not quite real; it might have been a pictured city, something imagined rather than experienced through his own flesh, nerves and blood. Now, however, he felt its solidity beneath the soles of his sandals and the sun that illumined its streets lay warm on his skin. He could touch it, resting his hands on the parapet of the quay and feeling the texture of the sunbaked stones; he could smell it, and breathed in deeply, trying to draw into himself, through quivering nostrils, the odour of a different dust, of the trees along the avenue, of the freshness of a morning unlike any other morning he had known. The little town of his birth, with its sandy streets, the modest façade of the old Cathedral, the low houses that seemed to cling timidly to the earth beneath them, the old pier at the bottom of the yard, the shuffle of bare feet on the dusty ground, the mournful groaning of the ox-carts going slowly by — all this had been left behind. About him now there was space and clear-cut form and a shining cleanness; even the trees looked different, with their massive trunks and tossing green branches ruffled by the breeze.

It was a world quite new to him, and his exhilaration was mixed with uncertainty. Buses came and went and cars full of people who took no notice of him, any more than the busy passers-by, too intent on their own affairs to spare him a glance. They neither knew nor cared who he was. They were strangers to him likewise as he stood watching; some walked down the street and disappeared round the corner, others crossed over and went up the steep ways leading from the quay, busy, purposeful, not bothering to exchange greetings. Each person seemed intent on his or her own business, incurious of the others, cut off by indifference.

Were they always like that in São Luis? He felt disappointed; timidly he started walking in the direction of Palace Ramp. As he advanced deeper into the town, the feeling of physical ownership returned; from time to time he put out a hand to touch a branch that overhung the street, or one of the tall electric light posts. He picked up a crumpled ball of paper from the ground, caught at a falling leaf, and a few steps later discarded them in favour of a pebble, smoothly rounded, which lay sparkling in the sun. This he put into his trouser pocket and went on his way, smiling.

Coming to the semi-circular bastion that was all that remained of the old Fort of São Damiao, he stopped to look at the white marble memorial framed by two ancient cannon. He read the inscription carefully and realized it was the Remembrance Stone, as it is known, put up to commemorate the crowning of the Emperor Dom Pedro II; he stroked the plinth lightly, and then went to inspect one of the guns, a smile of absorbed happiness still on his lips.

Coming to the bottom of the steps leading to Palace Hill, he hesitated, unsure whether he ought to follow the avenue bordering the quay. He stood there for a minute, looking at the dockers who were sitting or standing on the steps in the shade thrown by a high wall; some of them were lying back and laughing, while a man, dark, respectable-looking and middle-aged, holding a book with a black cover, announced that the end of the world would take place on the following Saturday. It would come, he said solemnly, bringing a plague: a rain of fleas.

'Watch out', he warned, 'anyone with blood in his veins will be sucked dry, drained to death. Then God will come down

213

and do *this* (and he clicked one thumbnail against the other) and that's the end of the fleas! There'll be a terrible crack like an explosion! Even God will disappear!'

Pedro joined in the laughter, turned his back on the madman, and went slowly up the Hill, feeling the blood beating in his temples. He knew that on the heights above him, to his left, he would see the Governor's Palace; facing him would be the Cathedral with the Archbishop's Palace next door. When he got to the top his excitement was such that he stood, open-mouthed and eyes wide beneath raised brows. He leaned against the parapet in a daze. Turning left, he walked on for a short distance and stopped. The view that lay before him took his breath away. At the end of the avenue one of the Cathedral towers stood out boldly, completing the façade where three doors stood beneath a double row of windows. He looked toward the Governor's Palace, recognized the two bronze lions on either side of the entrance, and spied a sentry carrying a rifle. He looked from one side of the street to the other, admiring the size and beauty of the buildings; the trees had recently been pruned, so that the sun shone brilliantly on the avenue sweeping into the distance in a broad straight line. Pedro could see no flaw, as he stood looking, his chin resting on his hand; then he walked to the bridge that spanned the avenue and crossed over to the right-hand pavement.

He could hear Dona Hilda's pleasant voice in his memory, as it had sounded in the little schoolroom of his boyhood.

'The Governor's Palace is on Maranhão Avenue, which leads to Benedito Leite Square and the Central Hotel. From there it's easy to get to Carmo Square.'

He remembered the shadow of sadness in her hazel eyes, that made him ask:

'Why don't you go back to São Luis, ma'am?'

'If only it were possible! But I can't go yet; I married here, my children were born here, my home is here. Perhaps later, when my children are grown-up and I retire, I might go back.'

He walked leisurely along the pavement. The number of cars going by, which seemed to increase every minute, left him confused and uncertain. How was he ever going to cross the street? Perhaps he should go back to the bridge. Then he noticed that groups of people came and went calmly, in spite of the speeding cars. He would wait until he was more accustomed to his surroundings.

The decision to stay in São Luis had crystallized; there could be no going back on it. He could not return to his home, so small, so far away, even though the thought of Antonia's grieving face hurt him.

'But it'll come all right in the end', he reassured himself.

He began to plan what he would do. He had enough money (in the back pocket of his trousers, secured by a safety pin, was the money Antonia had given him) to pay his expenses during the first few days. But after that, what? Well, God willing, he would find something — he had some schooling, knew how to draw, had picked up a little Latin from Father Dourado, it shouldn't be too difficult to find a job, even though he had to work in a shop.

'Getting here was the problem; that's all right now,' he thought.

He would have to find a cheap hotel or boarding-house; but how? Where could he enquire? He thought of Jacob, and hated him for letting him down. Why hadn't he come? He began to scrutinize the persons who passed by him, hoping to see Clementino or even Dona Corina Soares. But no, that wouldn't do at all; of all the 'Fair Weather''s passengers, only Jacob could help him. The others would surely tell his grandfather; as it was, he must find a place to hide where the old man wouldn't be able to find him, or else his plan would come to nothing. He was beginning to get worried, and stared about him with troubled eyes, at the houses, the cars, the people in the street.

Someone behind him seized his arms so that he couldn't move. He struggled, aware that people turned their heads to stare. He gathered his strength so as to shake off the stranger's grip, but the pressure fell away and suddenly Jacob was before him, his thin face shining with sweat, slanted sleepy eyes laughing, wearing a flowered shirt over bright red trousers.

'Sweetie, I don't know what to say! When I saw how late I was, I could have jumped out of the window!'

215

He poured out a flood of words, stopping at intervals for breath, laughing one moment and serious the next, holding Pedro's hands in his and moving his body incessantly back and forth.

'Just imagine, my dear, I forgot to set my alarm clock! I got to sleep pretty late, well after midnight, and only woke up when the sun was shining on my face! I jumped out of the hammock and looked at my wristwatch; almost ten o'clock! I threw my clothes on anyhow, rushed down the street and kept on running till I got to the quay; there was the boat, I called your name a dozen times, no answer! So I sneaked down on deck, had a look to see if your cross old grandfather was about; I called out to him, went round the deck and into the cabin, but there was no one there. So I went over to the quay again, ran down toward Long Beach and saw the Skipper in the distance. I turned back of course; it struck me that you might have gone to Carmo Square—so I ran and ran, and now I've found you, sweetie! Isn't it wonderful!'

He slipped his arm through Pedro's.

'Come along, we've got a long day ahead! But first we'll slip into the church and thank Our Lady for letting us meet!'

They turned to cross the street, but at the edge of the pavement Pedro drew back, terrified by the speeding traffic. Jacob pulled him forward, and he followed him, too confused to resist, staring about him with frightened eyes. They entered the main door of the church and the wide nave stretched before him towards the baroque altar, sumptuously carved and gilt. He walked forward slowly, staring about him at the white and gold, the cherubs and scrolls of foliage, and the life-sized images of saints standing in niches on either side. Oh, if he could only stay there for as long as he pleased, perhaps forever. His childhood dream of the Seminary returned. Perhaps he could still become a priest. And a priest could be a painter as well, surely.

'Isn't it beautiful?' Jacob whispered, leading him to the row of benches directly before the altar rails. 'It's like a jewel; just look at the roof—delicious!' His voice changed and his mouth lost its smile. 'Kneel down and give thanks!'

216

He knelt himself, clasped his hands and bent his head, with exaggerated piety; his lowered eyelids glistened with make-up. Pedro paused for a moment and then knelt down also.

As they left the church, the street seemed fuller. The strong morning sunshine sparkled on the tiled walls, gleamed on the black asphalt, and flung ripples of light on the water of a fountain in the middle of the square in front of the church. Light and heat blended with noise and movement, while a mild breeze blew steadily. On the terrace of the Central Hotel opposite, the little iron tables were beginning to fill up as people sat down to rest in the area of shade round the hotel.

'This way', said Jacob, turning left down the narrow pavement in front of the church. Then, changing his mind, he took Pedro's hand and led him across the street to another square with a statue in its centre and bordered on one side by a stone parapet. Still holding Pedro by the hand, he leaned over the parapet, pointing to a long street, divided by flights of stone steps and flanked by ancient houses, that led downhill.

'This is the street where I live. That's my home, that little belvedere looking out to sea, there on the left. We'll have a look at the town, and then I'll take you there. I do so want you to see my little nest. Although I shouldn't say so myself, I've made it look quite lovely—everybody says I could be an interior decorator, you know! They may be right; I'm longing to know what you'll think of it, my dear!'

He turned to face the square.

'It was much prettier before, with flowers everywhere! I used to love coming here, in the late afternoon, when the flowers' scent was stronger, but now I almost never come. That old man there, with his arms crossed, made of bronze—he has to stand there, in the blazing sun, looking at the clock!' Jacob giggled. 'You see that house on the corner, at the beginning of my street? It used to be a whore-house. As the old bronze gentleman, who was Governor here at one time, was a very serious type—a prig, in fact—they stood him up there with his back to the brothel where the girls were raising hell!'

He laughed again, shrilly, pressed Pedro's arm against his chest and broke into a run, only to slacken speed again. 'Now

217

I'm going to show you the most dangerous place in all Sao Luis', he announced. 'You'll have to be careful, sweetie! Very careful indeed! Move a little further from me. I come here knowing it's the same as stepping into a snakepit. This place really frightens me!'

Pedro looked doubtfully at his friend, wondering whether he was joking or speaking seriously. Then he looked at the square in front of him, surrounded by houses; a church showed its imposing front, further along, on a corner, stood a large four-storied house, its walls faced with Portuguese tiles, the overhanging eaves edged with porcelain plaques. In the middle, another statue: this time the bronze figure was seated and reading a newspaper. Everywhere people stood in groups, sat together on the benches, or hurried along the pavements; at the crossings little crowds gathered, waiting for the traffic policeman's whistle. One very fat man, his umbrella open against the sun, shared its protection with a thin mulatto who whispered in his ear, his hands moving in emphatic gestures.

Of all this only the cars and buses coming and going, with a clamour of shrieking brakes, sounding horns and snorting exhausts, made Pedro feel uneasy, if not frightened. The noise and rush made him raise his eyebrows and open his eyes wide, and then frown above narrowed lids as he hung back from the edge of the pavement when Jacob tried to get him to cross.

'If you ask me, this place should be called Gossip Square', Jacob said, taking Pedro's arm. 'Don't laugh, my dear, I mean it! Nothing can happen in São Luis that isn't known and talked about here. That bench over there, in front of the Post Office, is famous; it's a meeting-place for the spitefullest tongues in the whole of Maranhão. I know they say dreadful things about me—tomorrow, they'll probably be saying the same of you, you might as well know it! Yes, they make us pay for our sins beforehand here!'

He threw back his head defiantly.

'The hell with them. How a man lives is his own business, isn't it, love? If God made us different, why should we try to go against Him? It's *my* life, I'll live it as I please.'

He laughed, putting up a hand to the side of his mouth to hide the place where a tooth was missing.

'São Luis is the only town in the world that has a street called Envy. Envy Street! It's true, my dear, I swear! You needn't look at me in that mischievous way! After all, gossip comes from envy, doesn't it? Well, let them talk; we'll get out of here quick, and don't forget to make the sign against the Evil Eye!' His own fingers curled in the gesture; as they passed in front of the Cathedral, he crossed himself, from forehead to navel, with an assumed· air of contrition, his left arm still linked in Pedro's.

'It's too hot to walk, let's take a car.'

Jacob signalled to a taxi, opened the door and made Pedro get in.

'Saladino', he said to the driver, 'take us to Remedios Square, I want my friend to see a little of São Luis. But drive slowly — there've been a lot of crashes lately, and I don't want to die — life's too much fun!'

The taxi drove off and Pedro clung with both hands to the edge of the seat. His stomach felt queer and a chill raced up his spine. The unaccustomed speed made him dizzy, but with the breeze from the open window blowing on his face, he soon felt better, and was able to look out at the houses, the shops, and the passing crowds. There was something dreamlike about it all. Was this really happening to him? Jacob slipped his hand between Pedro's and then took off his gold bracelet and fastened it on the boy's wrist, whispering:

'No, don't refuse it. It's yours, all yours. I want you to have it as a sign of our friendship. For we *are* friends, aren't we? Friends for ever!'

Pedro, his mind in a whirl of new sights, sounds and smells, did not refuse. And as they got out of the car in front of the small white chapel with pointed windows that was the most noticeable feature of the palm-lined square, Pedro smiled gratefully at his friend and dropped his eyes to admire the bracelet on his wrist from which the sun struck quivering sparks of light.

Jacob drew him nearer.

'Do you like it, my sweet?'

'Very much!'

'I thought the cat had your tongue! It's real gold, you know.'

Jacob's arm was round the boy's waist; linked as close as a courting couple they walked slowly by the marble pedestal of the statue of Gonçalves Dias\* and over to the parapet of stone and cement. They stood nestling against each other in silence, looking with delight at the noonday landscape before them; over there the waters of the Anil River flowed into the sea, beneath them ran the railway track, further on a tunnel opened a round black mouth. In the distance they could see *Jenipapeiro*\* Beach on one side and on the other, where a few boats moved slowly beneath their spread sails while others swung gently at anchor, Coronation Quay drowsed in a haze of heat. Far away, beyond Sandy Point, the ghost of Alcantara showed grey against the farthest horizon.

Their hands rested entwined on the parapet as they watched a canoe navigate the river mouth. Pedro told his friend how he planned to stay in São Luis.

'This is the place for me, I know it, and I'm not going back. But I've got to find somewhere to hide, or my grandfather'll come and take me away. Can you find me a boarding-house, a cheap one? I haven't got very much money.'

Jacob said nothing for a little while; then he made Pedro turn round until the boy could see his face flushed with emotion. Tears were running slowly down his cheeks.

'Just see what you've done to me, love! I'm crying for joy! Oh, this is one of the happiest days of my life. I didn't want you to leave, I'd have done anything to keep you with me! And now you're staying, you'll come and live in my little place! You won't have to spend a penny, my sweet; two can live as cheaply as one!'

He took Pedro in his arms and covered his face with kisses, clasping him tightly in an embrace that seemed to last forever.

---

\* *Gonçalves Dias*: 1823–1864, a romantic poet from in the state of Maranhão. .

\* *Jenipapeiro*: 'Genipa Americana', tree belonging to the '*rumiaceae*' family, very common in the North of Brazil.

# CHAPTER XXXIII

At the Harbourmaster's Severino had to wait a long time.
Several times he got up to leave, and then, reaching the
window or the door, he would compose himself to patience
and light another cigarette; blowing the smoke out in light
puffs, he would walk back to his chair for another spell of
waiting. It must have been nearly noon before he left, the 'Fair
Weather''s clearance papers in his hand, and walked down
Palace Ramp, his thoughts on his grandson. If he had waited
for his cargo to be unloaded, Pedro might have come with
him; however, he thought, there wouldn't have been time that
morning to do all the things he had planned to do with the
boy: introduce him to clients and suppliers, show him the
Treasury, the Customs House and the Harbourmaster's
Office, stroll round the town with him so that the boy could
see for himself Carmo Square, Maranhão Avenue, Formosa
Street, the Little Port, the corner where the Central Hotel
stood, Broadway Street . . .

'We'll go this afternoon, when the sun isn't so strong', he
decided.

Going down the last flight of steps he saw a barrel-chested,
broad-shouldered, narrow-hipped figure approaching; the
man's left cheek bore a knife-scar, he hopped along on one
leg, the crutch in his right armpit pushing up his shoulder.
Severino stopped to wait for him, and asked, his stern face
softening into a smile:

'Well, Sebastian! How's everything?'

'Things are as you see, my friend, I drag along as usual,
with my crutch and my rheumatism. I'm more than eighty
years old, time to have made room for a younger man! But
since I didn't die at sea, I've got to wait and die in my
hammock, like other people.'

221

He went on his way to the click of his crutch on the stones. Before Severino's eyes, a knife-blade flashed suddenly in the warm glow of a storm-lantern, but he seized the man's arm and tripped him up. Chico Brito fell heavily on the floor of the bar, ghastly pale, with staring, terrified eyes.

'You're the one who's going to die, you bastard!'

But before his calloused seaman's hands could close round the neck of the man writhing helplessly beneath his weight, Severino feels himself pulled forcibly away and turns to meet Sebastian, who holds him with one arm, the other arm hugging his crutch.

'You're not going to ruin your life on account of this scum, Severino? A man like you has no time for this kind of shit — you've given him a good scare, now forget him!'

Vainly, Severino tries to remember why Chico Brito, who sold kites in a corner of Coronation Quay, and stayed apart, silent and sullen, had wanted to kill him. There must have been a woman in it. Or had some trouble-maker been at work? He did his best to remember, looking toward the building where the fight had taken place. the doors of the bar are closed, a black man is sleeping on the doorstep, naked from the waist up, his bald head tipped back, the heavy muscles showing beneath the skin. On the pavement beside him a shaggy-coated drop-eared dog is curled up head on paws; the dog's eyes are alert, he knows that he is there to guard his sleeping master.

Severino looks back up the Ramp and sees Sebastian, clop-clopping along the strip of shade cast by the Bulwark Wall, a ragged straw hat on his big head.

In the glare of midday the avenue seems longer. No breath of wind stirs the trees. The high tide laps soundlessly at the stone wall of the quay. A sleepy peace has descended on the houses along the quay and the narrow twisting streets leading off it, on the boats riding at anchor, on Palace Ramp and the Treasury Building. The heat beating down seems to have immobilized the city, lying hushed in brilliant sunlight. The flight of a single gull across the sky seems like an interruption, almost as startling as the sudden appearance of a cart coming noisily down Pier Street, the carter's whip cracking against the donkey's grey hide.

Long Beach was deserted; there was no one to be seen on Coronation Quay; nothing but silence and emptiness, a foretaste of their long-drawn-out death in the sun.

Severino began to say over to himself, one by one, the names of the boatmen he had known, like a charm against solitude. What had become of Jeronimo and Januario? Where were Casimiro and Jovino? And Alonso and Turibio, whatever had happened to them? It was years since he had seen them; they must all be dead by now. Perhaps only Sebastian and he were left: he, with the pain in his chest, Sebastian with his rheumatism and his wooden crutch.

Rejecting his thoughts of death, Severino's imagination began to call up visions of life, peopling the empty quay with figures of men and women, craning out of this window, going up that ramp, leaning on the parapet: men intent on their card game, sitting in a circle at the top of Campos Mello Ramp, or testing their strength, hands locked and forearms straining, elbows resting on the wall; himself stopping to buy one of the crudely-rhymed stories, illustrated by naive woodcuts, that Neco Maneta used to sell at his stall near the Treasury; Lila Soledade, Spanish Rosa, Maria of the Virgins. The faces danced before him like specks of dust caught in a shaft of light, and their voices sounded in his ear. Suddenly it was dark, with gas lamps burning here and there. Severino is sitting on the wall of the quay, waiting for dawn. Celita stands near him in her red dress, a flower in her hair, holding her shoe in her hand and laughing wildly as she asks him, 'Are there no trams around here?' Before he can answer, she leans against the lampost and slides gently to the ground, laughing louder than ever, as the bluish light of the lamp falls on her face.

Can it be that the extraordinary vividness of his memories is a sign that his end is near? How much time has he got? A week? A month? He is content to leave it to God. His only need is for time enough to hand the boat over to Pedro. Then he can die in peace.

Severino crossed over to the opposite pavement, walking quietly so as not to interrupt the flow of memory. The heat felt like a solid weight on his head, and he pulled his hat further down and walked a little quicker, skirting the quay wall; he could see the 'Fair Weather' 's mast, the sail neatly clewed up, swaying lightly as the boat was rocked by the tide.

Before he reached the ramp, he had a clear vision of the death of Coronation Quay, natural conclusion to the final silence that had fallen on Long Beach. Oh, the houses would still be there, and the avenue with its trees, the stone-and-cement parapet; but boats would no longer cross the ocean to anchor in that bay. Caju Beach, that had once linked the quay to the ruins of Victory Grange, with the noise and colour of its market stalls and fried-fish stands, had already disappeared. It was the bridge spanning the distance from São Luis to the headland of São Francisco that had done it. It was a long time since the port had been dredged, so that, at low tide, the multitude of sandbanks seemed to hint that the bay would soon be silted up. Pedro would drop his anchor at Itaqui, on the other side of São Luis; but this port by the Anil River would always be Severino's. As it was, Coronation Quay was almost finished; most boats preferred to anchor off Campos Mello Ramp, or at the Little Port. Only the 'Fair Weather', faithful to her past, kept on coming back to Coronation Quay, as she used to do when carriages still clattered along the streets of São Luis, drawn by matched horses, with a coachman in livery to drive them.

Standing on the platform at the top of the ramp he called to Pedro. Below, the 'Fair Weather' swung to the tide at the end of its cable. Each succeeding wave tried to bring it nearer to the quay but, held back by its anchor, it rode the water placidly, still six feet away. Severino went down the ramp, pausing when he felt the seawater wet his soles; putting his hands to his mouth he called to his grandson again, louder, but there was still no answer. He went back upon the quay, leaned on the parapet and shouted. Was the boy asleep in the cabin? Descending the ramp once more, he was able to see into the cabin as the boat shifted its position. The hammock was

224

empty. He went on down until the water came to his waist; on a sudden impulse he plunged into the sea, fully-dressed as he was, his hat still on his head. A couple of strokes brought him to the boat's side, and seized the gunwale with both hands he hauled himself on board.

The effort had worn.him out; but although his breath came in short gasps, he did not stop to rest but went round the deck, into the cabin and the hold, frowning, with set jaws, on edge with irritation. Where could the wretched boy be? Probably he had gone off to town, without stopping to ask for leave.

'Who told him to go?' Severino grumbled, his pale face set in grim lines, the Adam's apple jerking up and down in his throat. 'He had no business going anywhere! I told him to wait for me here, and that's what he should have done!'

It occurred to him that unless he restrained his anger, his illness might return. He almost wished that it would. If his own grandson wouldn't obey him, he had no longer any part in this world. He sat down heavily on the coil of rope, his hand on his breast. But the pain never came; gradually he relaxed and his hands lay quietly on his knees as he remembered the wondering curiosity of his own boyhood, the first time he came to São Luis. He, too, had gone up to the quay alone and strolled down the street that led to Long Beach and ended by getting lost. He had trudged for more than three hours, looking for the way back to the quay, and finally had found himself in the square before the gates of the Cemetery, at nightfall. Eventually, he had asked a passer-by, and the man, laughing, had exclaimed that Coronation Quay was much too far to reach on foot, he'd better take a tram. But he was determined to walk; so the man gave in and told him how to get there. Severino crossed his legs and put his cigarette to his lips; his face softened as he recalled the long walk back, in the dark of night, that brought him at length to a sloping street at the end of which he could hear the muffled beat of the tide against the stones of the quay wall.

'He can ask the way, like I did', he thought, drawing a deep breath. 'It'll be good for him, teach him to look after himself.'

The afternoon wore on; Severino tried to thrust down a

growing feeling of anxiety. From time to time he would rise from the poop bench, walk up the deck and look toward the platform at the top of the ramp,

The sun sank, an evening breeze sprang up salty and fresh, making the branches sway and loose shutters rattle. The old man's annoyance returned. After all this time the boy had surely been able to find his way back! He had probably skipped his midday meal, too. He must be standing gaping at a church, a shop-window, the entrance to some alley, forgetting that his grandfather was waiting for him and worrying.

Beneath their widespread sails the fishing *igarités* were triangular silhouettes somewhere between Bonfim Point and Sandy Point. Although they seemed motionless they were slipping home. A freighter, smoke pouring from its funnel, let go its anchor chain, heavy and clanging. The streets of Long Beach had grown lively again with cars and carts, and hurrying men; boats were anchoring off Campos Mello Ramp and the little Customs launch was preparing to leave.

Severino grabbed his hat and put it on again impatiently; he had made up his mind to search for his grandson. He would find the boy, wherever he was, and bring him back, with a good box on the ear to teach him not to play such a silly trick again.

The tide was falling, and a lather of foam ringed the sandbanks that had begun to show, and on which gulls perched awkwardly; other gulls flew low above the sea or plunged in, fishing. The light in the sky had turned from gold to pink.

Severino walked off towards Long Beach, he was sure that the boy was somewhere in the net of narrow streets and alleys that turned and twisted between the old houses. He went along them scowling, with neither greeting nor question, looking at the houses and the faces that passed by him. He had forgotten all about his illness.

Coming back by Pier Street he stopped near a dock worker who was standing at the foot of the steps of Palace Hill.

'Tall, red-haired, wearing his shirt outside his pants, and sandals? No, sir, I haven't seen anyone like that around here.'

There was a scream of brakes, tyres rasped against the pavement; a fat man in a white suit was hurled across the street, his straw hat flying. Severino grew pale—what if the boy had been run over like the fat man in white—his hat flying—

'The Ambulance! Get the Ambulance!' Someone shouted.

A crowd gathered round the fallen man, all traffic stopped. Severino found himself going up the steps on legs that shook. He did not know what to do, where to go. There was a bar just ahead, he went in and asked for a glass of water. His hands were trembling so, he had to use both of them to lift the glass to his lips.

Back in the street he said to himself:

'I'd better go to the City Hospital and enquire, right now.'

# *CHAPTER XXXIV*

Going up the stairs Pedro stepped as lightly as he could, shifting his weight so as to get maximum support from the banister clutched by his tense hand; however, the creaking wooden steps sounded as loud as gunfire, so that everybody in the house must hear. On the landing above him Jacob's thin figure standing beneath the skylight gave him an encouraging wave, as he picked his way carefully from step to step, afraid that at any moment an indignant woman's voice would shout at him to go back.

'Dona Ana doesn't allow me to have visitors,' Jacob said as Pedro reached the landing. 'Let's be as quiet as we can; I'll lead the way. Tomorrow, when you've made yourself at home, I'll go down and sweeten her up. It'll be all right, you'll see.'

As he started up the last flight, Pedro heard voices and

stopped. He flattened himself against the wall out of range of the skylight, holding his breath in the dimness; it was no use, he would be found and sent away. But where could he go? Not back to the boat, that was sure. The voices died away, swallowed by the street noises. Jacob was standing by the door of the belvedere, doubled over in silent laughter.

'What a fright they gave me, love! I swear I turned cold all over — see, my hand's like ice!' Jacob whispered, turning the key in the lock.

The door opened, and the first thing Pedro noticed was the big rectangular window, whose panes let in the last of daylight, already veiled with dusk. As he stood blinking, the light overhead was switched on; it hung in the centre of the ceiling, adorned by a green shade with scalloped edges. The whole room was so neat and elaborately arranged, it might have belonged to a fastidious girl. The curtains had embroidered borders, two red rugs covered the floor; there were cushions on the little cane settee and the leather trunk that stood in a corner had a cover of blue velvet, as did the flowered hammock hanging limply from its hook. A pair of dainty slippers were by the bed. On the walls hung an oval mirror and two large pictures in gilt frames; one showed Romeo climbing up a rope ladder to embrace Juliet, in the other a troubadour playing his mandolin beneath a closed window. A statuette of Saint Anthony stood on a little pedestal, a stub of candle burning before it, stuck in a saucer by its own wax.

'Well, what do you think of it?' asked Jacob proudly, admiration. 'You like it? I did it all myself. Dona Ana's always trying to meddle, but I don't let her. This is *my* place, I don't want anyone interfering. Do you know who embroidered the swans on that carpet? Me, dear! It took me over two months to get them just right, and I'm not ashamed of my work! Not a bit! People are envious, you know, I've already earned quite a bit of money doing this sort of thing. I let them talk, and keep my fingers crossed.'

He put his hand to his mouth.

'God, I'm speaking so loudly, somebody may have heard.'

He opened the door a crack and stood listening, one hand on his hip, the other on the handle, looking from the staircase to Pedro, eyebrows lifted in irony.

'No,' he murmured at last, 'no, it's all right. They didn't hear me.' He shut the door again cautiously, so as to make no noise.

Pedro looked about him lost in admiration. Between the pictures a guitar hung from a gilt hook. A bookshelf stood beside the window, its shelves filled with books protected by tissue-paper covers, each with a label written in red ink attached to its spine. Beside it stood a magazine rack with a china dog, a greyhound, adorning its top. There was a sewing machine in one corner, protected by a felt cover on which the initials J.A. were embroidered, in an elaborate monogram, and a refrigerator stood in the other corner, with a basket containing bread on top of it.

The room was quite long, the roof sloping down on either side, its uncovered tiles resting on varnished rafters. The angle was so steep that it was impossible to stand upright there; one of these spaces was curtained off to serve as a wardrobe, the hangers placed on a pole running between two of the rafters. The other space, also curtained, contained a washstand and a chamber-pot.

'Dona Ana simply adores me,' said Jacob as he stood by the window. 'She treats me like a son — you'd never think I was only a boarder, she spoils me so! But she's jealous, terribly jealous! If she had her way, she'd lock me up in a monastery somewhere, and be my only visitor. But she's a saint, that woman; a real saint. It won't be easy to get her to let you live here with me, but we'll work it, I'm sure we will. From now on, nothing can separate us, isn't it so, dear?'

He twisted the latch of the window and threw back the shutter. Before them, the river flowed into the sea, the fading crimsons of sunset playing on the waters. Above the old roofs the same tints died away in the blue-grey sky. A breath of wind set the lamp swaying.

Pedro had sat down on the edge of the bed, his legs stretched out before him. He needed time and quiet in which

229

to accept that everything about him existed, was in fact reality. All the new impressions of the day crowded his mind like so many blissful dreams in a tangle of sights, smells and sensations that had to be sorted out, examined singly and savoured at leisure. There was the discovery of the new part of the town, the lunch at the restaurant, the wandering through the steep twisting ancient streets with their tiled houses, the shapes of things; their colours, lights and shades. And, finally, that interval of silence by the mossy little wall of a fountain, watching the water tumble from the open mouths of baroque stone heads.

The room in which he sat was half his own. Everything had been easier than he could have hoped! He felt a twinge of distress, like the prick of a thorn, when he remembered his grandfather. The old man must have searched for him up and down the town. He was probably back on the boat by now, but next day he would search again, hurrying through the squares and the streets.

Eventually he would understand that his grandson had gone for good, wanting no part of the hard boatman's life. Then he would go back to the 'Fair Weather', wrapped in a stern and silent pride, and hoist the sails and make for the open sea, taciturn, frowning, his cigarette at the corner of his lips. Who would care for him if the illness struck him down?

Well, he was in God's hands, as all men are.

Jacob came toward him unbuttoning his shirt.

'Don't you want to take yours off, too? You'd better; it's so hot.'

He folded his arms across his breast, coyly, and scampered about the room, 'Don't you dare look at me!' he exclaimed. Half-dressed, his mincing and bridling was like a caricature of a girl's behaviour. The gold medal shone on his thin chest, covered by a mat of black hair growing up over his shoulders. He stopped in front of the mirror, patted the hair by his temples and wetting his fingertips with his tongue, smoothed his eyelashes, emphasizing their curve, his eyes on Pedro's reflected smile.

'One has to take care of one's looks,' he said, running a

small comb over his eyebrows. 'I certainly look after mine; I've made up my mind that I'm never going to be old and ugly. Age and ugliness—Ugh—I'll keep them locked out of my room, out of my life!'

The thought made him laugh, he whirled lightly on his heels.

'Dona Ana says I'm the Devil himself. Me! You couldn't find anyone else as fond of fun, light-hearted and kind. And Roman, Apostolic, Catholic, into the bargain, devoted to Saint Anthony, who looks after me and gives me everything I ask, thank God. Whatever would become of me without Saint Anthony? The world's full of nasty, envious people, love!'

He went into the curtained wardrobe corner and came back with an armful of clothes which he threw on the bed. There were shirts printed in bright patterns, a pair of striped pyjamas, T-shirts, underpants, socks; the bed looked like a shop-counter.

'They're all yours, love! Did you think I was going to let you go on owning nothing but the clothes on your back? We'll have to buy pants because you're taller than me, but as for shirts, socks and underpants, I think they'll fit.'

Pedro blushed, and felt tears prick his eyelids as he looked at the profusion of clothes spread out before him. What a gift! He felt so grateful that he longed to hug Jacob with both arms and bury his face on his shoulder to hide his wet eyes.

'And I'm going to give you a gold chain just like mine; I've got two, see?'

A thin gold chain lay in his hollowed hand; he fastened it round Pedro's neck.

The daylight had gone, and the window framed an oblong of darkness. Far beyond the rooftops, a lighthouse winked its red eye. The sounds of steps reached them, going up and down the stairs. From the ground-floor came the clink of plates, and the rhythmic hammer-blows of a shoemaker, working late, with the music of his transistor radio to keep him company. The cries of children playing drifted up from the street.

Pedro stood quietly watching their reflections in the mirror, while Jacob clasped the chain round his neck. He felt an impulse, never before experienced, compounded of sensuality and fear, that might at any moment throw him into Jacob's arms. He fought it, clenching his fists and standing motionless, while Jacob, stepping back, looked admiringly at the medal hanging on Pedro's smooth chest.

'Oh, you look wonderful, lover, absolutely wonderful!'

Jacob clapped his hands and jumped for joy; beneath his feet the planks creaked loudly and he put his hand to his ear, listening intently, his eyes wide above his gleeful smile. Then he straightened his shoulders and approached Pedro, using his hands in a complicated pantomime. He ran on tiptoe toward the boy and taking his face in his hands, began dropping little kisses by the corners of mouth. Then, with one of his sudden changes of mood, he went to the refrigerator, opening the door with exaggerated caution, his finger to his lip. Without a word, using only gestures, he gave Pedro to know that they would have their supper now. Light as a dancer he skipped about the room on tiptoe, in a kind of comical ballet. He set the table, paper plates, a dish of sliced ham, bread, glasses, a bottle of some sweet fizzy drink, not forgetting the paper napkins. Finally he draped a folded towel over his arm and bowed ceremoniously to Pedro, inviting him to sit down.

'Dinner is served; will the gentleman please take his seat?'

They were still eating and enjoying the spacious cool serenity of the night about them, when the stairs creaked beneath heavy feet. Startled, they both looked towards the door, Jacob about to bite into a sandwich, Pedro holding the bottle with which he was going to refill his glass. The door opened brusquely and they came to their feet, their faces white with terror, too frightened to move; Severino, his head almost touching the lintel, stood before them.

Jacob's face had gone bloodless, his lips were mauve. He moved back a step, instinctively protecting his face with his hands, but the blow caught him on the side of the head and flung him across the room, to fall with a crash in the corner where the washstand and chamber-pot were half-hidden by the curtain. There he stayed, peering out from behind the curtain, while Severino, grinding his teeth with rage, seized

232

Pedro by the shoulders, shaking him brutally back and forth, and drove him against the wall pinning him there, one hand lifted to strike. His jaw shook, he could not speak for rage. He wrenched the bracelet from his grandson's wrist and tore the chain from his neck snapping it in half. Then he seized him by the arm with iron fingers and pushed him towards the door, like a policeman propelling a criminal. They stumbled down the stairs and met Dona Ana panting her way up, a wet dishcloth in her hand. At the sight of Severino's face, her mouth fell open, but no words came and she shrank back against the wall to let them pass, her pasty face rigid with shock, her eyes wide with amazement and terror.

Down in the street Severino gave Pedro another savage push so that the boy went staggering ahead of him along the narrow pavement. With a shaking hand, Severino put a cigarette to his lips, and stopped to strike a match; a lamp shone down, and, it seemed to him that Pedro's shoulders had the same droop, his waist the same pliancy, his walk the same girlish delicacy, as that double-damned whore, that cursed seducer, that creature, neither man nor woman, Jacob.

# CHAPTER XXXV

It had been a morning of rain and sudden cold winds, and there was still a chill in the air, while ragged dark clouds drifted across the sun. Antonia put on a long-sleeved blouse and wrapped herself in an old black shawl before going down to the pier. In the afternoon light the lazy water of low tide was as smooth as oil; she sat down on the edge of the planks with her feet hanging down out of reach of the water.

She reckoned that Severino would stay in São Luis for one or two days only, just the time needed to unload his freight. The 'Fair Weather' would be back that very afternoon, if her prayers to Our Lady, Help of Sailors, had been heard.

'God willing, they'll sleep safe at home tonight', she said to herself as she sat down.

That morning, after the rain, she had gone down to her garden to see whether her vegetables had taken any harm. Then somebody clapped hands loudly at the street door. She went to see who it was, brushing the earth from her hands and from half-way down the passage saw Father Dourado at the open front door, a cap covering his white hair.

'Is Severino back yet?' he asked, scraping the soles of his shoes on the square iron grillwork in front of the entrance. 'I want to have a word with him, Dona Antonia. It's something important, concerning the church.'

'He's still away, Father, but he ought to get back this evening, please God. They should be home by then, he and Pedro.'

The old priest went on cleaning his shoes as he looked at her over his spectacles with an expression of surprise.

'What, isn't he back from São Luis yet? Has anything gone wrong, Dona Antonia? If I'd known he was going to take all this time I'd have sent for what I need by some other boat. It's two months since I asked him to buy me a whip, a good strong whip. Two months, Dona Antonia, and neither Severino nor the whip have turned up. And I need it; I need it urgently, Dona Antonia! Well, is he coming or isn't he?'

'Oh yes, Father, he's coming, by God's favour. He only left on Tuesday, he couldn't possibly be back before today.'

Father Dourado drew his spectacles down and peered at Antonia through the lenses.

'Tuesday? Last Tuesday, this week, you mean! It can't be, Dona Antonia! One of us must be a little gone in the wits, I'm afraid! Are you sure he only left on Tuesday? No, no, it isn't possible. Why, it was two months ago that he came to say goodbye to me, and asked me whether I wanted anything brought back from São Luis. He told me he was leaving next day: Am I in my dotage, Dona Antonia? You must be wrong.'

Antonia put her hand in front of her mouth to hide her smile and the gaps in her teeth.

'He left here on Tuesday, Father,' she said again.

The priest tucked his umbrella under his arm.

'Well, when will he be back?'

'This very day, please God, towards evening.'

'In that case, tell him to bring me the whip as soon as he gets here. I'll be awake till ten o'clock, he can knock and I'll hear.'

He turned as if to leave. 'Thank you, Dona Antonia.'

'Won't you come in and have a cup of Coffee?' the old woman asked gently.

Father Dourado leaned on the handle of his umbrella.

'Is there anyone else in the house?'

'No, Father; just me.'

'In that case, Dona Antonia, you must excuse me, but I can't accept your invitiation. If you and I should be known to be alone together in the house, there'll be gossip. Don't laugh! It's quite true, I know what evil tongues people have. Oh, they're bad people in this town! Poisonous, 'my child, worse than rattlesnakes. One has to watch one's step, you may be sure!'

Antonia could not help but laugh.

'Now, Father! I'm an old wreck, and so, forgive me for saying it, are you! What could they say about us, at our age?'

The priest shook his head gravely.

'Dona Antonia, you don't know anything about evil — how deep its roots, how tenacious its grip of human nature! I've had daily experience of it, hearing confessions for fifty years! I know it well, believe me! Take calumny now; *no one* is safe from it, *nothing* is sacred. The horrors I've heard, Dona Antonia, horrors to make your hair stand on end; it's what turned my head white so early! I've never seen such a place for wicked tongues; they'll say anything about anybody, with reason or without. If they see me leaving your house, knowing that Severino is away and you're all alone, neither your wrinkles nor my cassock will stop them talking, we'd end up disgraced, Dona Antonia, and Severino, you know what he is, he'll want to kill me. And the Archbishop will suspend me!

And all for what? For the sake of drinking a cup of coffee with you! No, Dona Antonia, you really must excuse me.'

He straightened his cap, tucked the umbrella under his arm again.

'The coffee'll keep until Severino gets back. Please don't be offended, but it's better to stay clear of trouble. I know the wickedness human beings are capable of like the palm of my own hand. Goodbye, Dona Antonia, keep well. Blessed be Our Lord Jesus Christ, who cleanses us from sin!'

'May He be forever blessed!' she answered.

Down the street he went, taking short, uncertain steps and threatening stray dogs with his umbrella, his shabby figure stooped by age. Standing in the passage Antonia laughed softly, full of pity for the old man. Poor Father Dourado! She went back to weeding her vegetable bed, picked a lettuce leaf to put in the *corrupião's* cage and chased away the hens that were pecking around the pumpkin vine. On her way back to the house she gathered the ripe guavas to save them from the birds; she looked up at the flowering mango tree and stopped to feel a fat jackfruit. In spite of her age, her beginning rheumatism and the damp of the overcast morning, she felt well and active. Before going in she cast a glance at the black sky, that gave no hint of the weather improving.

'Pray God it gets better.'

She went into the little room next to the kitchen, opened the tin trunk in which Pedro's drawings were kept, and taking them into the dining room, admired them one by one, as she had done so often before.

'Who'd believe he thought of all this by himself? He even learnt to draw all alone; all Dona Hilda did was to put the pencil in his hand. It's all his own doing. God bless you, child, and may Our Lady and Saint Lucy add their blessing to His!'

Sometime before dawn hearing the rain beating against the window, she had turned up the lamp. Suddenly she was sure that Severino had left São Luis that night on his way home. She prayed to Saint Peter to keep the rain away from the boat that was bringing her boy back to her.

'Remember his name is Pedro, too. And look after Severino; he's a sick man.'

She gave the hammock a push to set it swinging and began to say her prayers. Of a sudden she found herself in the dining room, in bright daylight; she could see the 'Fair Weather' at the end of the pier and Severino and Pedro coming up the ramp. Her joy was such that she jumped to her feet — and found herself standing in her own room, the oil lamp burning and the rain drumming on the roof. Then she really did go into the dining room and spent the rest of the night in the rocking chair, the black shawl about her shoulders.

By mid-morning she was in the kitchen surrounded by bowls and saucepans, preparing the roasted sucking-pig that was Severino's favourite dish; Pedro would have a chicken with *molho pardo**. Before going to inspect her vegetable garden she put a big saucepan to simmer, full of jackfruit and sugar, seasoned with cinnamon and cloves, for their dessert.

Later, she laid the table, not forgetting the lace table-cloth, and got everything ready, she was so sure that the 'Fair Weather' would arrive before night, with Severino at the tiller and Pedro handling the sails. Then she went down to the pier to wait.

It was a misty day with hanging clouds, and she could hardly make out the shapes of the returning boats. She would sight a dark sail far out to sea and wave in her excitement as if it were Pedro standing in the prow behind the figurehead. But before she had time to rise the sail drew nearer and Antonia, with a shrug of her skinny shoulders would see that it was a strange boat, and lose interest.

'Old people's eyes always let them down!'

Another sail appeared against the cloudy horizon. This time it had to be the 'Fair Weather', with its high prow and tall mast, the sail was the right colour — she straightened, eyes sparkling — but no; the boat sailed nearer and her whole figure drooped in disappointment.

The wind freshened and daylight began to fade. Huddled in the folds of her shawl, the old woman scanned the sky with aching eyes; dusk came down about her and still the 'Fair

* *molho pardo*: (brown sauce) — A sauce using the blood of the chicken as one of its ingredients, like the French 'canard au ang'. An excellent dish, much appreciated in Brazil. .

237

Weather' had not come. Her legs that dangled over the side of the pier were cramped and painful, and the cold wind made her rheumatism worse; sharp twinges of pain flashed through her knees, the knotted fingers of her right hand, and the calf of her right leg. It would be dark in a little while, she ought to climb the slope and go home before night shut down but she lingered until the distant lighthouse opened its round red eye and the oil lamps were lit in the twilight which swept like a dark wing over the beach.

Antonia walked slowly back along the planks of the pier, hoping that she would not slip and fall; sometimes she would stop and turn to look out to sea again through bright narrowed eyes, stubbornly hoping. She went up the sandy slope and stopped to rest by the fence, her legs trembling with weariness; Disappointment lay heavy on her heart and she had to fight back tears. A gust of wind blew sharply upon her, big drops of rain fell on her face, and she hurried through the yard into the house, picking her way through the puddles that glinted as the lightning flashed in the sky.

Antonia lit the candle and looked sadly at the table laid for three on the fine web of lace, the glass dish of jackfruit sweet, the bowl full of ripe guavas. She stood for a moment leaning on the edge of the table, her throat constricted, about to weep. Then straightening herself defiantly she said aloud:

'There's no reason why they shouldn't arrive later on! Severino knows the way just as well by night; God has taken them in His hand, He'll bring them home in His own time!'

She sank into the rocking chair, trying to remember her dream of last night. Overhead, the sullen skies broke into torrents of rain. She left the door unlocked and the lamp alight and stayed rocking in her chair, alert for the sound of steps on the pavement, and listening to the voices of rain that mingled with the high-pitched moan of the gale that swept the sea.

# CHAPTER XXXVI

The long hands, their backs corded with veins seemed unable to rest; they turned the old hat round and round, twisting its worn brim. Severino's face showed the same strain. Preoccupied, not knowing how to begin, he avoided the eyes of the woman sitting opposite, composed and attentive, her feet thrust into flowered slippers, the hem of her dress drawn modestly over her knees.

It was she who finally broke the silence.

'I'll be glad to help you, Seu Severino; what would you like me to do?'

He cleared his throat, shifted his legs uneasily and gave the brim of his hat an extra twist, lowering his head.

'Excuse me, please, if I don't know how to say it properly. If it was for me I'd know how to ask for it without trouble; but when it comes to asking on behalf of other people — I'll ask you again to excuse me and not take offence where there's none meant.'

'That's all right, Seu Severino', the woman answered, folding her hands in her lap. 'Make yourself easy. We're alone here, with no one to overhear. Don't be embarrassed, just tell me what it is you want.'

She got up to close the window and went back to the chair.

'Go ahead, Seu Severino.'

The room was small and narrow, its only furniture a cane settee and two matching chairs. A lace curtain hung crookedly over the window with its two shutters. No breath of air stirred its folds.

Severino made up his mind to speak.

'If it were for me I'd already have asked you. But it's for my grandson, he's practically a man already, old enough to be with a woman, but he hasn't done it yet.'

The woman lowered her lids and smiled, traced an invisible
line on her skirt with a fingernail. It was a relief to hear the
reason for the old man's embarrassment. She continued to look
down as if in shyness; then turned turning her head sideways,
she glanced at him out of slanting eyes.

'How old is your grandson?'

She was no longer young and had never been pretty—her
round face was marked by acne, there were lines at the corners
of her mouth. But she had a good body, her legs, especially,
were plump and shapely. She must have been nearing forty;
her hair was drawn back smoothly into a plain knot, there was
a streak of white above her temple. The tight skirt showed her
full thighs, and through the wide armholes of her sleeveless
blouse he could see her breasts hanging free.

'He's fourteen,' replied Severino, letting go his hatbrim.
'But he looks all of eighteen, a good-looking boy, taller than
me, and red-haired. Thin, I grant you, but pretty strong just
the same. I think, ma'am, that you'll enjoy sleeping with him.
Might I know your name?'

'Duda.'

'Well, Dona Duda, as I said, you'll like him.' The old man
was no longer nervous and his voice was firmer.

'I brought him with me to São Luis for the first time, and
thought we might as well take the opportunity, you might say.
There's a right time for everything in this life, as you know.
We live in a small town—a village really—it'd be difficult to
find a clean woman, free of sickness. And then you know it's
the first time; it's got to be with a person who—who knows
about it and is patient. And I've only got to look at you to see
you're the right one.'

Duda dropped her eyelids again.

'You're too kind, Seu Severino! I do what the others do,
that's all. If this is the way my life was meant to be, well, it's
God's will and I accept it. I don't complain; the Lord will
make it up to me after I die.'

A constrained silence fell between them. Severino hitched
his trousers up over his knees; the chair creaked sharply
beneath the weight of his body.

Duda stirred and sighed.

'Are you going to bring him here yourself?'

'Indeed I am,' said the old man, with a resolute look in his keen eyes. 'He doesn't know his way about the town yet. I'm coming with him to make sure he doesn't go to the wrong place.'

'Afternoon's the best time for me. I'm always alone then. You'd better just knock on the shutter so as to let me know. Don't come in the evening. I'm always busy at night.'

Severino stood up.

'I'll bring the boy tomorrow afternoon.'

'Don't bother to knock on the shutter, then. I'll have the door on the latch, just walk straight in.'

As he was leaving, Severino stopped at the door, turning his hat in his hands.

'Please — be patient with the boy — do your best, ma'am! He's shy, it mightn't work the first time, give him all you've got! A lot of boys of his age fail when the time comes, you know. Everything depends on the woman. I don't care what it costs me, I'll pay whatever you say, twice the usual price if need be.'

The woman smiled, her large eyes brightened and softened.

'Don't worry, Seu Severino. Bring me your grandson tomorrow and everything'll be fine, you'll see!'

'God willing.' the old man said gravely.

'God willing.' she echoed.

'There's something else I want to ask you,' Severino added. 'Tomorrow afternoon, while the boy's with you, I'll be waiting on the pavement here outside. When it's all over, will you open the window and tell me — well, tell me the score?'

As she smiled and nodded, he pulled out his crammed wallet from his hind pocket and began to peel off note after note from the thick wad before the woman's astonished eyes, ceasing only when she gestured him to stop.

'That's plenty!'

The old man added another note to the little pile and held it out to her.

'I've only got this grandson. There's nothing I wouldn't do for him. Grandfathers, well you understand. The boy means more to me than anyone can ever know.'

He took Duda's cold hand in both of his, shook it in silence,

241

blinking a little; then he turned away and went quickly down the street, for fear that she might see his tears.

Oh, Boatmen's Alley, how changed you are! What has happened to the old paving stones left over from Colonial days, that used to be so sharp underfoot? Up from Coronation Quay all the way to Egypt Street you turned and twisted between the narrow bounds of ancient houses, breathlessly climbing the steep sunny hill. Some essense of the old city seemed to cling to your stones, your irregular strips of pavement, walls that had seen the stumbling passage of the Jesuit priests, expelled from their convent by order of the Marquis of Pombal, Minister and royal favourite. How grievous the sound the church bells! Shocked faces peer from the chinks in the shutters, watching the old priests go by in their rusty cassocks, their leather sandals slipping and tripping on the rough stones, driven like criminals along that same Boatmen's Alley that Severino is descending with bent head and wet eyes.

Reaching the foot of the slope he spreads his hands wide, in anguished enquiry.

'My God! Can it be possible?'

The lamp in Chalk Street shines down on Pedro, Severino gazes in horror as the boy walks ahead of him: it is Jacob's own tripping pliant gait, his languid nonchalance, his gold chain, the bracelet—Severino hides his face in his hands; then dropping his arms hopelessly, he walks along Coronation Quay. He had spent the night sitting awake in his hammock, his thoughts in confusion. Little by little, while the moonlight crept across the floor of the cabin, they grew clearer, took shape. If the boy was really a homosexual he would have to kill him. There was no other way out. Severino would rather see him lying dead than watch him turn into another Jacob. However, he would test him first, give him a chance to prove his manhood with a woman.

'I can't throw him overboard unless I'm sure. It all depends on her.'

It is late afternoon; gulls hover on lazy wings above the sea and the *igarités* are making for home. A cool breeze springs

242

up, ruffling the branches of the trees along the avenue, scattering the fallen leaves and raising puffs of dust. In the distance, the 'Fair Weather' 's bare mainmast draws short arcs across the sky, beyond the stone wall lapped by the rising tide.

Severino's steps are slower. Head bent, he is conscious only of the struggle going in his mind and heart; he has lived through it once before, when he made up his mind to kill Celita, the same sick horror, the same dread of life's impossible demands, the same distrust of himself.

'Can it be possible? My God!'

That morning he had tried not to look at his grandson, afraid of seeing that in his face, his walk, his gestures, that would confirm his suspicions. Finally, he could not bear it any longer, glanced quickly at the boy, and was plunged into gloom. Even Pedro's voice sounded different, shriller, somehow artificial, like Jacob's. Severino's brows drew together, he withdrew into himself, caught up in the struggle to accept the hideous necessity forced on him by fate. Out in the open sea, beyond the Alcantara Reef, his own hands must force his grandson overboard.

From the top of the ramp he saw Pedro sitting on the steersman's bench with crossed legs, looking dreamily into the distance. The thought came to him in a flash: why not take Pedro to the woman this very afternoon—this moment? He shouted hoarsely:

'Come up!'

The boy, surprised, jumped down onto the ramp and the old man said curtly, 'Follow me.'

He strode ahead of his grandson till they reached the foot of Boatmen's Alley where he stopped to draw breath. It was only for a moment; he breasted the slope and forced himself up the steeply curving street; he felt his weary body as a dead weight, dragged ahead by sheer will power. Pedro walked beside him silent and puzzled.

When Duda opened the door, surprised to see him there again, he smiled at her and taking the boy by the arm pushed him into the passage.

'Here's the young man, Dona Duda. Why leave it till tomorrow?-

243

Pedro looked from his grandfather to the woman wondering what it all meant. He moved as if to go back into the street. The old man seemed to tower above him suddenly, his face convulsed.

'You're staying here. I'll be back to fetch you.'

Severino went out and slammed the door. Pain stabbed through his chest and he pressed his hand to it. He took two unsteady steps forward, his wracked body hugging the wall for support. Somehow he managed to get over to the pavement opposite, where a high wall, its top bristling with fragments of broken glass, protected somebody's yard from inquisitive eyes. He let himself sag until he was sitting on the door sill. The moments that followed were charged with an agony worse than he had ever known. Bent over, unable to breathe, he wished passionately that God would let him die on the instant, before he knew for certain that his grandson was that wretched thing, a—he could not bring himself to say the word. Yes, death would come as a proof of God's mercy: he was old, he had suffered overmuch already, he was no longer needed in this world. He waited, motionless, for death to come. After a while he bent his head lower yet, covering his pale face with his hands. A long sigh escaped him, full of bitterness and crushing grief. The air expanded his lungs, the pain grew less. He realized that he could breathe again. 'God doesn't want me yet', he thought wearily.

Severino stayed where he was, quiet except for his panting breath; sweat trickled icily down his temples. Desolately he went over the suspicions he had never before acknowledged: the boy's love of solitude, his skill in drawing, the dolls he had played with as a small child. Even his boyish love of the Church, the wish to exchange the trousers he wore for the skirts of a cassock (as it seemed to Severino) the old man saw as proof of Pedro's unmanliness. Tears sprang into his eyes and he wiped them away with the back of his hand; it was useless to rebel, but fate had been hard and bitter to him and he could not accept it. All too soon he would have to repeat, in every detail, the far-off tragedy of Celita's death. He must tell Antonia of his crime, make his confession to Father Dourado, and finally give himself up to the Police Commissioner. Back to jail he would go for the rest of his life, misunderstood, hated by everyone, his only comfort the knowledge that he had done his duty.

'What, me, Severino, accept a homosexual in my family! My own grandson, who was going to take over my boat! Never! I'll serve my sentence to the end, and trust in God's pardon.'

The breeze of early evening swept up the street, a tree thrust its green bough above the wall, with a rustle of dancing leaves. There was a feel of moisture in the air and shadows were beginning to fall already.

Severino raised his face from his hands and looked about him, then up at the colourless sky and finally stared dully at the row of houses across the street. From a first-floor window, a curious eye peeped down at him through a half-open shutter. Further down the street a bald, middle-aged man stood in his shirt-sleeves at the door of his house, his eyes on the old man. Severino looked back at him defiantly; taking his hat off, he passed a tired hand over his wet brow. How long had Pedro been in the woman's house? An hour, an hour and a half? Longer? Severino felt certain that enough time had passed, and he fastened his eyes to the woman's closed window, his heart thumping hurriedly in his chest.

'I won't wait for the freight old Andrade promised me', he thought gloomily, 'I'll leave tonight as soon as the moon's up. What must be, will be, if it's God's will.'

Shadows lengthened on the cobbles of the steep little street, lights already showed in some of the houses. Occasionally steps echoed in the silence.

In spite of the chill of the breeze, sweat continued to trickle down Severino's face; he did not know what to do with his hands, nervously clenching and unclenching. He watched the window in growing agitation. A light went on in the cramped little sitting room, and he sat up tensely, gripping his knees. Then he heard someone at the latch of the shutter, and it opened, just a crack. Duda smiled at him with long slanting eyes, buttoning her blouse over her breast.
Severino wrenched at the shutter, opening it wide.

'Well?'

'Everything's fine, Seu Severino,' she said contentedly, her hands still busy with her buttons.

'He did it twice, never gave me a moment's rest. He's quite a boy, your grandson!'

# CHAPTER XXXVII

The city lies tranquil in the moonlight; its porcelain façades reflect the silver light in broken gleams. Severino sits on the deck of his boat waiting for the dawn; he is changed, and the new Severino is a man full of serenity and renewed hope. The double file of tall palms stretches down the avenue, and the breeze, whispering through the crooked streets of the quay, is heavy with brine. It brings him occasional faint sounds, the plaintive chords of a distant guitar, a whistle sounding from the deck, the groan and creak of the old boats swinging at anchor. These mournful night voices blend with other, inner voices, private to each man and part of his essential being, childhood echoes, memories of youth and maturity; as the years pass, enclosing us in thickening walls of silence, only these secret voices are left to us, and when we die, they also die. Once more at peace, reconciled to his fate, Severino listens quietly to the tale of his life, as many a man has told it to himself, alone and late at night.

The moist air blows softly on his face and bare arms.

'When all's said and done, God has been good to me,' he thinks with a smile, watching the sky lighten above the roofs.

Severino will remember, as long as he lives, walking down Boatmen's Alley that evening. A sudden wind sprang up, and he wanted to whirl with the wind, join in the dance of the spinning leaves that blew down the hill toward Egypt Street. His right hand clasped Pedro's arm; they hurried down the street breasting the gusts that swept towards them. The old man's coat blew out on either side, like black wings, and Pedro's shirt filled with wind like a balloon, making them laugh. They fought the wind, heads down against the dust; a stronger blast snatched Severino's hat away and sent it flying, but Pedro leaped after it and brought it back to his grandfather, his face bright with laughter.

The moon had not yet risen and the sea was invisible in the darkness, broken only by the intermittent flashing of the lighthouses of Saint Mark and Sandy Point, and the weak glow of storm lanterns from boats at anchor; as Severino and Pedro came to the ramp, the moon showed its red rim above the roofs and began to sail slowly up the sky, surrounded by a halo tinged with rose and lilac. Its cold light grew stronger and flooded the bay, falling on the sandbanks threaded by the ebbing waters of low tide and here and there on a boat, its keel lying high and crooked on the sand. Severino lay down on the steersman's bench, with a couple of rolled-up sacks for a pillow; the tide began to fill again, with a quiver of moonlight on the quiet water. On Sandy Point the ruins of the fort, all black and silver, recalled old legends, half history and half myth.

Severino had made the boy take the hammock in the cabin, saying that he preferred to sleep on deck in the cool. Pedro hung back, but the old man, with an imperious tenderness new to him, took his grandson by the shoulders and made him lie down. Now he also lay back on the bench, too short for his long legs, one arm hanging over the edge, aware of discomfort but too happy to care, going over in his mind the promises of the boy's early virility he now remembered: the firmness of his walk, his clear laugh, his way of taking decisions without hesitating, just as earlier he had sat in wretchedness, recalling quite different traits. How mistaken he had been! The dolls, the drawings, were pure childishness, and harmless. Now his grandson was a man. He thought of Pedro and glowed with pride, easing his cramped limbs. He had lived longer than most of the men of his family, he had borne sorrows that none of them had known, but this had been granted him, to see his daughter's son become a man fit to take over the 'Fair Weather' and master the ocean, as the men of his blood had always done. Yes; Severino hadn't lived in vain. His life had form and meaning, and neither would be lost even when he was laid in the earth. Through his grandson, he would continue to sail the sea, to enjoy women, to listen to tales of love, of ghosts, of storms and miracles, such as seafaring men love to tell, at evening, when the last light fades from the quiet bay.

It was nearly midnight when Severino sank at last into sleep. peaceful and dreamless, his face caressed by the breeze, his body rocked by the rhythm of the tide. He woke before dawn, refreshed and strengthened, and went into the cabin to steal a look at his grandson, sound asleep in the hammock, his face calm in the slanting moonlight. Back on deck he sat down to wait for daybreak, a smile deepening his wrinkles and narrowing his eyes.

The fading moonlight gives place to a streak of dark grey on the eastern horizon. At almost the same moment arrows of rosy light spring up into the sky and suddenly the sun is there, drenching the houses and the bay with brightness and sparkling on the crests of the waves.

Severino, a cigarette in his mouth, leans his arms on the deck rail and steeps himself in the sun's warmth. Had he been home, he would soon be on his way to the Cemetery to tell Celita the good news — Celita who had come once more to meet him, laughing, a flower in her hair — he knew it was a trick of memory, of nostalgia, but all the same he had felt her presence vividly, just as he used to feel it in the old days in jail. He had neither moved nor spoken, cherishing the vision, aware of its briefness — it had lasted no longer than the fugitive moment of dawn.

He knows that death holds his heart in its hand and he is not afraid, but desires it, only not now, not yet — he needs a few more days, a week or so, to teach Pedro how to handle the boat. Again he realizes that death is an act of will; it can be fought and resisted. Otherwise he would never have reached São Luis. Thinking of Dr Estefanio's fat body encased in his white tunic, the man's swollen eyelids and double chin, the plump hairy hands resting on the table, he smiles in secret triumph and decides to visit the doctor's consulting-room when he gets back. Here I am, he will tell him, the living proof that all your medical science is just nonsense! Well, perhaps he wouldn't do it; after all, why bother?

'Everybody makes mistakes, only God is never wrong.'

He walks softly into the cabin where his grandson is sleeping and goes below to prepare breakfast. While he waits for the water to boil he opens the enamelled tin box, takes out a *beiju*, nibbles it, listening to the crunch of flour between his strong teeth. The water in the pot starts to simmer and Severino whistles a tune Celita used to sing. He takes his grandson a strong mug of coffee. He calls the boy's name and gives the hammock a shake, then ruffles the red hair saying jovially.

'Time to wake up, Sleepyhead. We've got a lot to do today, if we want to get away tomorrow morning. Up with you now!'

How changed he is, Severino the boatman, lord of the coasts of Maranhão. It seems as though his heart has only now become aware of the deep tenderness he feels for his grandson; he follows Pedro's every movement as the boy sits up, yawning and stretching, his bare feet feeling for his sandals, his lids narrowed against the brilliant sunlight streaming into the cabin. Old man and boy look at each other and smile. Pedro sips his coffee rocking gently in the hammock, quite at ease, looking at his grandfather who, standing with his back to the porthole, smiles down at the boy.

Later that morning, Severino and Pedro sat together on the steersman's bench, watching sweating dockers stow away the cargo in the 'Fair Weather' 's hold. Severino crossed his legs and clasped his hands around his knees, looking at the planks beneath his feet.

'I don't know that I'll be coming with you on the next trip', he said, without raising his eyes or turning his head towards the boy. 'Probably not; this crossing's tired me; the truth is, I

249

need a rest. I'm not a young man any more, I'm getting on for eighty, God'll be calling me home one of these days. And this thing in my chest, you've seen it for yourself, won't let me go. One fine day it'll be stronger than me, and that'll be the end.'

His calloused hands untwisted, then fastened round his knees again.

'However, it's no matter; Faisca ought to be over his fever by then, he'll sail with you. He's got a nasty temper, it's true, but he's a good shipmate for all that; if you know how to handle him, there's none better. You can rely on him all the way, and he knows just how to manage the boat; I've never seen his like when it comes to handling the canvas.'

Pedro heard him in silence, his legs outstretched before him, his feet rubbing against one another, a frown between his brows.

'You won't have anything to worry about. The sea's in your blood, you'll know what to do. You'll see that in a couple of days you'll have learnt all there is to it, it'll come as naturally to you as if you've been doing it all your life. That's the way it was with me. At first I was scared, but that's to be expected. Once I'd faced my first storm and come through safely, well, then one finds out one's strength, you see, and doesn't want any other kind of life. One gets a taste for the sea, you might say, and there you are—nothing else'll do for you.'

At ten o'clock Severino led Pedro into Andrade's warehouse. The old man was there, in white trousers and shirt and a white waistcoat, a pencil behind his ear. He looked at them over the rims of his spectacles and waited for them to draw nearer.

'I was thinking of you, Skipper. There's no need to tell me who the boy is. Your grandson of course—congratulations!'

He reached over the counter, shook Pedro's hand warmly and looked keenly at him.

'Well, my boy. I'm your grandfather's friend and glad to be yours, too. You can count on me—except when they move the port to Itaqui. I belong here on Long Beach where I've always traded, and this is where I'm staying!'

He turned his eyes on Severino and went on without pausing.

'They're ruining our town, Skipper! All they talk about is the new city, the new houses, the new streets, the new port, the new Maranhão! I've had it up to here! I'm thinking of giving up reading the papers, that's all they talk about. Why a new Maranhão? There's nothing wrong with the old one, the real one, the Maranhão of our day! Yesterday, a friend offered to sell me some land over at Itaqui; I lost my temper, told him what I thought of it all and sent him packing. New Maranhão—Itaqui—Rubbish!'

When they left an hour later, the old man was still complaining excitedly. He went out on to the pavement with them, and peered down the street from under his hand, up and down.

'Everything's so quiet it seems like Sunday! And it's Friday, one of our busiest times! Dreadful! It's enough to make one weep. Some day I'm going up to the Palace and tell the Governor to his face just how wrong he is. And if he's not there I'll tell his secretary, or his aide, or the soldier on guard! I've got to get it off my mind, somehow. Long Beach may be dying, Skipper, but I won't hold my tongue and just let it die, you may be sure!'

The brilliant sunlight struck dazzling reflections from the porcelain tiles, the chipped cobbles, the pitted flagstones. It was so bright it hurt their eyes. In front of the houses on one side ran a strip of shade, hardly wide enough for one person, but the see-breeze brought some relief from the heat.

Pedro was walking in the shade and tried to get his grandfather to change places with him; but the old man refused, saying that his hat was protection enough, while Pedro was bare-headed.

They passed a shop-window with a display of watches, the old man stopped and made his grandson stop also.

'I was thinking of giving you my own watch, but it's a pocket-watch, too old-fashioned for you, besides it doesn't keep good time any more. You need a good watch; you can't sail without one.'

Leaning over the counter Pedro chose a watch with a metal like bracelet that looked like silver. Severino, however, picked out another one, more expensive.

'It's bigger, and the sea air won't rust it. Never mind the price. I want you to have a proper watch, fit for a boatman to wear.'

With his own hands he slipped it on the boy's wrist.

'See? It's better than the one you chose, better-looking and stronger, too.'

He took his grandson to lunch at the restaurant he had always gone to, in an alley by the sea, frequented only by boatmen, fishermen and bargemen; he ordered the dish he had given them the recipe for many years ago. When they finished their meal Severino glanced round at the cramped space, the stained and peeling walls and said with a queer wistfulness: 'I used to come here a lot when I was young.'

And throughout the long afternoon, Severino, talking and laughing, at ease as never before, showed his grandson the twisting streets and alleyways of Long Beach, teaching him the ways of his new world. Later they strolled up Dragarse Hill (so named for its steepness and rough cobbles) all the way to Carmo Square, where the old man bought Pedro a new outfit, tough and durable clothes that would stand up to the weather. Back on Long Beach he searched for the whip Father Dourado had ordered, and stepping out onto the pavement, cracked it two or three times, the thin lash cutting through the air with a hiss.

'It's fine, just fine, just what the Father wants,' he said, 'there isn't a sinner who won't be glad to repent after a taste of it!'

The clerk wrapped it up while Severino praised it, joking. Pedro, already burdened with parcels, offered to carry it, but the old man said no, this he would carry himself.

The breeze died away, it grew hotter than ever. People stood about in doorways, fanning themselves with folded newspapers, or walked along looking for patches of shade. Overhead, the sky was white and glaring; it was too hot — a storm must be brewing.

But not even the heat and glare could stop Severino. From time to time he would pause at a street corner and draw a deep breath, then return to the old streets he knew so well. This was farewell; he would not see the tall ancient houses ever again, their glittering tiles and lovely stone doorways. No matter; his life would go on, mysteriously contained in his grandson's, the next of the long line of men who followed the sea.

He turned off Pier Street into a tiny alley that wound down to the sea. Taking Pedro's arm, he pointed to a door across the street.

'You see that door with the metal plaque? More than sixty years ago my father took me there, to have this design tattooed on my arm. It was an old man named Adam who did the tattooing; now his son's taken over.'

He drew the boy across the street.

'We've plenty of time to get you done.'

Pedro stopped short, his face set, looking up at his grandfather.

'Have me tattooed?'

'Yes, an anchor on your forearm, like me', the old man said, raising his eyebrows as he faced his grandson. The street lay empty about them.

The boy lowered his eyes and was silent. Minutes passed; finally he said:

'I don't want an anchor on my arm.'

Severino dropped the whip and seized Pedro by the shoulders.

'Why not?'

The boy was dumb, his eyes on the ground. The old man shook him, fingers digging into the thin shoulders.

'Answer me!'

Pedro raised his head and met his grandfather's eyes squarely.

'I've got to tell you the truth, Grandad. I don't want to be a boatman.'

'You don't want to be a boatman?' Severino repeated, hoarse-voiced, his face suddenly white, the veins standing out on his neck.

'No, sir.' Pedro said firmly.

'What do you want to be then? A vagabond? A whore like

253

Jacob? Is that it? You're ashamed of me because I'm a boatman, are you? What about your father, wasn't he one too? And my father? All our family, who've always been proud of being boatmen! And you're ashamed, is that it?'

Mad with rage he snatched the parcels Pedro was carrying and flung them away, far down the street. Then he tore the watch from the boy's wrist and hurled it to the ground. Stooping, he picked up the whip, holding it by the handle through the paper wrapper, his face distorted, snapping eyes fixed on his grandson, who backed away until he was stopped by the wall of the house behind him. The old man glared at him, jaws rigid and brows twisted in a scowl; then something happened to change his mind, he turned paler than ever, his shaking lips became blue, and his arm sank slowly to his side.

# CHAPTER XXXVIII

As he went aboard the 'Fair Weather' Severino knew already what he would do. While still in the grip of rage, an idea flashed into his mind and he had seized it with a kind of desperate resolution. Mute and sombre, his wrinkled face set in grim lines, only the muscles of his lower jaw contracted now and then, chewing the bitter cud of rage and disappointment.

Up in the prow Pedro stood leaning against a couple of bales lashed together, his linked hands dangling listlessly in front of him, his head bent; furtively he watched his grandfather as the old man came and went without pausing but without haste, like a man carrying out a plan fixed on beforehand.

Severino let go the mainsail so that it hung free; he checked the stays, tightened a knot or two, his hands strangely steady, a frown knitting his brows. Next, he hoisted the jib; seeing it hang slackly, he turned toward the opening of the bay and looked up at the sky with searching eyes.

The breeze blew faint and fitfully, sometimes dying away altogether; there was scarcely enough to flutter the pennant at the main-masthead. It was a day of concentrated heat. The waters of the bay moved in smooth dark-grey swells as the tide rose lazily. Although it lacked an hour to sundown, the light was dull, as though twilight had already fallen. Thin mists rose from the bay and floated over the Cathedral towers, the Bulwark Wall, and the roofs crowding the hilltops. Towards Alcantara, a swathe of cloud, as black as oil-smoke, darkened the horizon. The gulls had all vanished.

A man came to the top of the ramp, short, stocky and middle-aged, wearing a wide-brimmed hat that seemed somehow to flatten him; he leaned down in the direction of the boat and called to Severino. The old man came up from the hold onto the deck.

'Are you leaving now, Skipper?'

'Yes.'

'May I come with you?'

'I'm not carrying passengers on this trip', the old man replied sourly, disappearing behind the cabin's structure.

The fact was, that on his way back to Long Beach hours ago, Severino recognized the signs of a storm in the making. The flat, breathless heat, the colourless sky, the dying breeze, all pointed to a change in the weather. He had thought of anchoring his boat further along the quay, in the lee of the wall so as to protect it from the coming gale. But now he was sailing to meet the storm. There was no longer any point to living. He knew that he carried death within him and resolved to fight it no more. He could only have hoped for a few weeks at most. Better to die now, die at sea, and take the boy with him, his grandson who had refused the 'Fair Weather' and all that it stood for. How could he allow the boy to live, without a profession or a goal, guided only by his changing whims? To turn into a trifler or worse?

'I'd rather he died.' Severino muttered beneath his breath.

What if God were to punish him for leading the boy to his death? He thought of Hell and a tremor of fear shook him. But no, it would be unjust to sentence him to the fire that never ends; God was merciful, surely He would see that Severino could not do otherwise. Some years of Purgatory he must endure, no doubt, but he accepted the necessity, bowing his head. He thought of Celita; she had waited for him for so long, she could wait a little longer, why not?

'I served my time in jail without making trouble; no one had any reason for complaint. I'll do the same in Purgatory and maybe, through Our Lady's intercession, I won't have to be there for very long.'

He was certain in his heart that God would forgive an act to which he was driven by despair. He was tired to the marrow and there was nothing left for him to do in this world any longer. After all, he was not about to kill himself deliberately, he was only meeting death half-way, and would fight it hand-to-hand as an honourable man should, when the meeting took place. And he would die the way he wanted, not huddled in a hammock but in his own place, the sea, he and his boat together.

When Pedro heard that they were about to leave he lifted his head and looked first at his grandfather and then at the sky, lowering and dark. The sea about them was smooth as milk but he felt an instinctive fear of what might happen later out on the open sea. His heart grew heavy with a premonition of disaster. He saw his grandfather at the capstan, about to reel in the anchor chain, and asked timidly:

'Are we really sailing, Grandad, in this weather?'

Severino, his back to the boy, made no answer and crouched lower, as the thick iron links came rattling over the side; another turn or two and the anchor rose slowly clear of the water.

Favoured by the tide and the current setting toward the mouth of the bay, the 'Fair Weather' slipped along parallel to the quay wall and then headed for the centre of the bay on the course that would take her out to the ocean. Severino lashed down the tiller, ran to hoist the mainsail, and went back to sit

256

on the steersman's bench. A breath of wind filled the sails and the boat's speed increased. Pedro stood at the entrance to the cabin watching the city, half-hidden by mist, fall behind them; a few lights twinkled through the haze although night had not yet fallen on São Luis.

Severino took the tiller again, steering the boat from wave to wave expertly, so as to obtain the maximum amount of speed. The bank of cloud above Alcantara had spread and darkened, letting streaks of sky show through, opaque and milky. At times a flash of lightning split the cloud and there would be a growl of thunder.

'Well, we're in God's hands,' the old man said.

He looked over at his grandson who stood nervously biting his nails. Never would he be able to understand the boy's indifference to the sea. Even now, conscious of the mortal battle ahead, he felt a leap of the heart, a tautening of the will; mortal it might well prove, but at least it would be fought out at sea. He realized now why Pedro had seemed so inattentive on the way to São Luis, scarcely listening to what Severino told him about the direction of the changing winds, the position of sun, moon and stars, the height and breadth of the seas, the handling of sails and tiller, the compass, the coastline he must always keep in sight.

'No wonder he didn't listen, with a head full of the devil knows what!'

He saw the boy go into the cabin and return, carrying the lighted storm-lanterns which he hung up in their accustomed places.

They sailed past Sandy Point; the mist was so thick that Severino could not make out the ruins of the fort. Looking back, he found that the city was no longer visible; only a luminous haze showed where the lamps stood in a row along Coronation Quay. As he looked, he felt the boat quiver as a wave rose sharply beneath its keel; the 'Fair Weather' hung for a minute, then thrust her prow upward, sliced through the water and sailed steadily onwards. He shifted his position, took a firmer grip of the tiller. They were about to enter the main current that swept between São Luis and his home.

257

Of a sudden night enclosed them in compact darkness torn by livid flashes of lightning, thunder rolled and boomed; a blast of wind shook the boat from stern to stern.

The mainsail flapped like a throbbing wing, then filled and swung forward, making the taut stays groan and the timbers creak. They sped forward, checking now and then at a bigger wave, recovering and plunging ahead beneath the straining sails.

About an hour later, Severino sensed rather than saw a patch of blackness that seemed more solid than the surrounding night. He recognized Fear Island; the Alcantara Reef must be near. His seaman's instinct fought disappointment and despair and won. Sails and tiller responded to his deft handling, a life-time's experience took over as he moved about the boat, guiding his eye and hand, lending fleetness and surety to his feet.

A fine rain began to fall, cold, slanting, now from this quarter, now from that. Suddenly a blast of wind pounced on the sail, and then another, blowing from the port side. The 'Fair Weather' heeled over dangerously, recovered and swept on quivering beneath her canvas, now savagely lashed by the rain.

Severino knew very well that it was a matter of staying power; his strength had to outlast the storm. He tried to spare himself and the boat as much as possible and not lose sight of the coastline on his left, where the Alcantara lighthouse showed as a pale blur in the darkness.

When the boat staggered beneath the blows of the abruptly shifting wind, he had leapt to take in the mainsail, and was nearly blown overboard. Pedro, watching his grandfather from the cabin, ran to help him and together they loosened the stays and fought to haul down the sail that the gale was trying to tear from their hands. Together beneath the driving rain they struggled with the weight of wet canvas, constantly wrenched at by the wind, until they had made it fast.

The seas were coming crossways, plunging down over the poop, sweeping over the deck now from starboard, now from the opposite quarter. Water washed over the entrance to the

258

cabin and poured into the hold.

As he saw Pedro's skilful handling of the sail, Severino was reminded of Lucas Faisca. The boy showed the same fearlessness, the same instinctive knowledge of what to do in the chaos and darkness of the storm. It was uncanny how he had known how to prevent the sail from being whipped away, and how to keep his balance on a deck that tilted crazily, changing its angle every minute. Pedro was like a dancer who has at last found a stage worthy of him, or an acrobat, swinging through the air, secure in the knowledge that he cannot miss his hold. Severino remembered that Faisca had said to him, after experiencing his first storm:

'Once you've fought it and won, Skipper, you never want to leave the sea again. It's the only life fit for a man!'

Pedro clung to the mast, tightening the lines that secured the sails; Severino tried to get back to the tiller but his strength suddenly failed, and he sank to the soaked deck, panting, one hand pressed to his chest, his eyes closing on the sight of his grandson's cool dexterity, his true grandson at last, bone of his bone and seaman to the core.

It was some time before Pedro looked for him on the steersman's bench; seeing it empty, a shock of fear went through him: had his grandfather been swept overboard? The glare of lightning showed him Severino lying inert on the deck. Swiftly he ran to him and dragged him into the cabin, settling the heavy body in the hammock. Before he ran back on deck he thought that, for a moment, the pinched nostrils quivered on an imperceptible breath.

# CHAPTER XXXIX

The storm-lanterns at the cabin entrance swung in wide arcs with the rolling of the boat. Protected by thick glass shades each reddish flame sank, wavered and shot up again, as if keeping watch over the man who lay unconscious in the hammock while in the howling darkness outside Pedro fought the storm single-handed.

When Severino at last opened his eyes the glimmering lamps were the first things he saw. The rain was still falling heavily, and lightning streaked through the dark at intervals; the wind, however, had slackened, although the 'Fair Weather' was still pitching furiously. He could hear the crash of the waves against the hull, and through the clamour and chaotic motion of the storm, feel his grandson's steady handling of the tiller.

As his mind grew clearer and he realized the danger they were in, he tried desperately to rise, but fell back strengthless. A strange heaviness weighted his limbs and hung on his eyelids. He had a vague memory of a sudden unendurable pain in his breast, of losing his balance on the heaving deck, and then all was a blank. How had he reached the hammock?

He looked out through the entrance, searching for Pedro, and thought he could make him out sitting on the steersman's bench. Severino tried again to rise but was forced to sink back into the hammock, hazily watching the swaying storm-lanterns. He yielded to weakness in the same way as an exhausted swimmer ceases to struggle and lets himself drift. At times the thought of his grandson passed across his brain, and he would try to rouse himself, visions of Pedro at the tiller flitting before his weary eyes; the boy was handling the boat as well as any experienced boatman, but he still needed help.

'Our Lady's surely watching over him!'

Some time later the darkness gave way to a milky radiance,

260

as if the moon had succeeded in breaking through the clouds, and Severino thought that he saw Pedro hoisting the mainsail. He raised his head for a minute and although he was forced to let it fall back, his heart was full of joy. He was neither dreaming nor delirious: the mainsail spread overhead as taut as a wing in full flight, the stays sang and the boat sailed before the wind beneath a watery moon drifting among ragged clouds. The old man's tense features relaxed, he closed his eyes, smiled, and sank back into sleep.

A little before dawn he awoke; Pedro, who was leaning over the hammock, asked:

'Well, Grandad! Are you feeling better?'

Severino was too tired to speak; he nodded and stretched out a hand through the embroidered hammock fringes the boy had drawn over him to protect him from the chilly damp.

Pedro took the cold hand in his.

'We're all right now, the storm's behind us. The weather's clear and I can see the coastline; there's nothing for you to worry about now, Grandad.'

God and Our Lady knew he wasn't worrying. He could die at peace now, sure of having done his work. He smiled at his grandson, clasped his hand firmly, then shut his eyes and went back to sleep. The next time he awoke the sun was high and the deck flooded with light.

By mid-afternoon he felt so much better, he was able to sit up in the hammock, his feet resting on the ground. He did not try to get up; his shaky legs would not have supported the worn old body. Pedro brought him a plate of *maria-isabel*, but he was able to swallow only two mouthfuls. Resting his head against the rolled-up sheet that served him as a pillow, he looked toward the deck and beyond, and saw, to his left, the low green coastline of his home.

'We'll get there before dark,' he thought.

The 'Fair Weather' sailed on smoothly; Severino's eyes dwelt long on the familiar landmarks; each wooded inlet and hill, the coves of white sand, the dark headlands, seemed rich with memories as never before; he seemed to recall the details of each departure and recurring landfall in a long life of voyages;

a sign, surely, confirming that his end was near. Well, if this was God's warning to him, he welcomed it. He had nothing else to ask of Him except forgiveness for his unimportant sins. The others—he would not deny that he had sinned greatly— his other sins had been paid for by sufferings that had been as great.

'I want to have a good talk with Father Dourado, though, before I go.'

Severino knew that after so much trouble and grief, Celita would be waiting for him, cleansed from the stains of the world and purified by God's grace. He remembered Antonia, faithfullest of friends, so old, poor woman, surely she had not long to wait either. Would they be together, all three, rejoicing in God's blessed peace? Why not? Hadn't they managed to live beneath the same roof here below?

'They're not strangers, after all!'

He remembered Antonia's hostile silence.

'In His good time, God will make them be friends.'

The woods along the coastline grew denser, they were crossing the entrance to the bay. He straightened his body and tried to rise. He had to show Pedro how to find the channel into the bay. Giddiness overcame him, he felt a twinge of pain in his breast, and sat quite still for a moment. Then he got to his feet and unsteadily went out on deck.

Pedro saw him stagger, ran to support him, and made him sit down on the steersman's bench. Severino swept his eyes over the ocean, measured the distance that separated them from land at a glance, and changed course slightly; the sails filled with wind.

'We can stay on this tack all the way in.'

Before the houses of the town began to show, Severino looked fixedly at a green tongue of land surrounded by a wide sweep of white sand, that advanced into the sea. Once again, in the blazing sunlight he was crossing Cathedral Square with Celita by his side.

As soon as they reached the square he had said to her:

'We'll go by the church, so that you can go to Father Dourado for Confession. You haven't been to Confession since we got married. Go along; I'll wait for you here.'

She began to laugh, putting her hand to her mouth.

'What on earth for, Severino? What do you mean? You asked me to come for a walk on the beach, not to go to Confession! Who told you I've got sins to confess, anyway?'

Severino's face was sombre; he stopped beside the stone cross in the middle of the square and said again:

'We'll go to the beach later. First, you've got to go to Confession.'

She shook her head still laughing.

'I don't feel like going to Confession, Severino! I can go by myself, you know, there's no need for you to take me!'

Her smile became uncertain as she saw the look in his hard eyes.

'Whatever's the matter with you? Why are you so angry?'

He took her by the arm, forcing her toward the church and said harshly:

'I've already told you I want you to go and make your Confession. I want you to do it. I want you to do it and that's all there is to it, you hear? Do as you're told.'

Celita's laughter ceased altogether, there was fear in her eyes. She began to walk in the direction of the church, her head bowed submissively.

'All right, my dear, all right! There's no need to quarrel! Please let go my arm, you're hurting me!'

He stayed in the strip of shadow cast by the cross and watched her go up the three steps and into the main door; her rounded figure disappeared into the darkness of the nave. He waited, smoking cigarette after cigarette and pacing restlessly from shadow to sunlight and back again, his eyes on the door through which she had entered.

He had spent the night unsleeping; over and over again he examined the decision he had taken, approved it, summoned up all his strength to carry it out: he would kill Celita the next day. He felt no weariness now, but waited patiently in the heat and silence all about him, heat that beat down from a glaring sky and silence that seemed born of the heat itself. The afternoon sun dazzled the eyes and made the sandy soil glitter. From time to time a swallow's wings sliced through the burning blue.

Celita came quietly down the steps, her face once more alive with laughter.

'There, I've been to Confession, told every single sin, every single one, you hear, Severino? Are you pleased now? Isn't that what you wanted? Well, stop looking so grim and let's go for our walk!'

She gave him her hand, anxious to make up the quarrel which had come about for no reason that she could see. The sand creaked beneath their feet as they walked down the street, followed by their linked shadows. In the hard sunlight the first lines of age showed on Severino's weather-beaten face. Childbirth had filled out Celita's figure, rounding her hips, but her face seemed younger than ever, her skin soft, her eyes wide and clear, her walk elastic with vitality and contentment.

They left Cathedral Square behind, with its tall bare trees and stone cross rooted in sand. The street stretched ahead of them narrow and crooked, lined on either side by tumbledown huts thatched with palm-leaves and fenced in by bare wooden stakes; they passed a cluster of bamboos, crossed the planks that bridged an arm of the river, and came out on the beach that swept away apparently endless, fringing the green headland reaching into the sea.

They came to the end of a long stretch of damp sand from which the tide was receding; Celita stopped and leant forward, her hands on her knees.

'Aren't you tired, Severino? This is far enough for me; my legs are aching!'

The beach was empty; he pointed to a smooth rock, surrounded by foam, that rose from the water further ahead.

'Let's sit down over there', he said.

Celita took a step back.

'Over there? The water'll spoil my new dress, Severino! And it was you who made me wear it! No, I'm not going out to that rock, I'm staying right here!'

'I want you to come with me', he insisted, pulling her by the hand.

And when she tried to free herself, saying, no, no, she wouldn't, looking at him with the beginning of fear in her eyes and her voice, he took her by the shoulders and then by the thighs, lifting her from the ground, and walked straight into the water, as if it were the shortest way to reach the rock. Celita struggled in terror, writhing in his arms, tossing her head backwards and forwards, desperately fighting to get loose.

'Let me go! Let me go! For God's sake, let me go! I don't want to go there! I don't want to, I don't want to!'

Severino's arms were like bands of iron about her; he walked steadily on until the water reached first his knees and then his waist; it lapped around Celita's struggling body, soaked her feet and long hair; and he walked on into the sea that tossed and boomed around him, a long way from the rock.

Her eyes wide in panic she screamed.

'No! No! For God's sake, don't kill me!'

They were alone in the emptiness; nowhere was there a house, a wretched cabin — not a fishing boat to be seen, only a few lazily coasting gulls, no one to see or hear, Celita's last scream was lost in the cry of the wind.

Her face came up from the water, she tried to shake the wet from her hair.

'Don't kill me! Don't —'

Afraid of weakening, he flexed his knees and thrust her under. She fought between his hands, her face showed once more above the water, eyes distended and bright with horror. He took another step and pushed her down again, bracing his arms and legs, until he felt her struggles cease. He stood for a few minutes, holding the limp body beneath the surface of the sea. Then he drew her slowly up again; in the still face the beautiful eyes were wide and blank; the fixed pupils stared unflinching at the sun.

He laid her on the sand and with trembling hands pressed down her eyelids. Then he fell to his knees beside her, shaken by sobs.

'I had to do it! I had to do it before you left me, before you went to your ruin!'

Now, sitting on the steersman's bench, Severino directed Pedro:

265

'Shorten the mainsail and turn the tiller to port. That's it. Look! There's the town!'

Not only the town was directly ahead of them, but the pier also. And at the end of the pier, Antonia, who had not yet sighted the 'Fair Weather'.

Paris,　March 1969
Petropolis, February 1971